Upheavals

Upheavals
a memory

Robert Scholten

Copyright © 2013 by Robert Scholten.

Library of Congress Control Number:		2013912809
ISBN:	Hardcover	978-1-4836-6951-9
	Softcover	978-1-4836-6950-2
	Ebook	978-1-4836-6952-6

All rights reserved. No part of this book may be reproduced or transmitted in any form or by any means, electronic or mechanical, including photocopying, recording, or by any information storage and retrieval system, without permission in writing from the copyright owner.

This book was printed in the United States of America.

Rev. date: 10/22/2013

To order additional copies of this book, contact:
Xlibris LLC
1-888-795-4274
www.Xlibris.com
Orders@Xlibris.com
138274

to my father . . . .

PREFACE

UPHEAVALS—The title applies both to the events, momentous ones, that occurred in the first twenty-three years of my life before sailing to America in 1946, and to a physical uplift of the Earth's crust, the subject of my research in tectonics since then. Initially, the title was to be "Echo", which seemed right for a book about "Ego". The words spell nearly alike, but I am keenly aware of the difference: the sounds of the past reflected down the walls of memory arrive distorted. These memories are more than half a century old. How much has my mind subtly shifted, colored, embellished, magnified or suppressed events of the past?

Yet, there is a link. The past, says Hegel, can be approached by discovering the rational within the real, not by imposing it on the real. Remembrance of one's youth, undramatic daily life as well as upheavals, can stay surprisingly vivid. Now, when I am very still, I can feel close again to that young adult, that adolescent or ten-year old boy, and even to that infant that was I. Fleeting encounters . . . .

As echo differs from ego, so does memory from what was. But it can hover very near it.

State College, Pennsylvania
January 11, 1991

APPENDIX; These pages, written almost twenty-five years ago, are published now because a personal perspective on the traumatic years between 1923 and 1946 by a witness and participant may again be of general interest, and because not many are left to provide it.

For helping to make this publication come to fruition, I am grateful to Claudia Mauner (*cmauner@artboxstudios.com*) who read the manuscript, suggested I look for old photos and documents, designed the cover, wrote the book description, and made her enthusiasm contagious.

Boalsburg, Pennsylvania
July 22, 2013

PART I

HOLLAND: THE WAR AND BEFORE

1

Something woke me up very early on the tenth of May of 1940, that day when everything was going to change. I had been studying till late the night before, preparing for the finals of the Dutch State High School Examinations, which were to take place the last week of the month. To be awake at this early hour (how early?, I briefly wondered . . . five o'clock?) was exceptional, to say the least. I stayed quiet, letting awareness creep in, conscious now of the sun streaming in through the half-open window, and of a sparkling blue sky. I sensed my brother Jack was awake, too. What was it? "Do you hear them?" he whispered. Suddenly alert, I heard a deep growl fill the sky. "Planes," said Jack, "Germans on their way to bomb England." Holy smokes, there had to be zillions of them, I thought, and jumped out of bed.

Jack had already opened the window wide, and together we peered up at the unbelievable sight. The planes seemed everywhere. "Hundreds," Jack said, answering my unspoken question. "But how can they do that?" I exclaimed, we are a neutral country. They are not supposed to fly over us!" For that had been the myth all along . . . war could break out all over Europe, but Dutch neutrality would be respected, just as in the First World War. Actually, when I thought of kids my age in those other countries, I rather envied them their good fortune of being part of a war. Neutrality seemed pale by comparison.

By now the whole family was up, all of us watching that amazingly blue, innocent sky, so harmless-looking that the angry buzzing of the planes seemed uncalled for. What was going to happen? All outcomes were inconceivable.

And then the inconceivable did happen: anti-aircraft guns went into action. Sharp ak-ak explosions came from several directions, and little puffs of smoke appeared in the sky like so many tiny cotton balls, too delicate, it seemed, to do any harm.

Next, fighter planes rose up. "G-1's" someone said, and we all recognized the double-tailed profile invented at Holland's Fokker Aircraft (soon to be copied in both Germany and America). Gracefully they danced and darted around the heavy bombers, one of which started to spiral down to earth, trailing black smoke. Then a second, a third, and with it a fighter. It was all too unfamiliar and too far away to frighten, but the momentous thought did at last dawn on us that this was perhaps more than a violation of air space, but that we were being invaded.

I turned on the radio, and in silence we listened to a solemn voice repeating that the German army had crossed the border in several places, meeting with fierce resistance, and that German paratroopers had been dropped at the great Moerdijk bridge across the Waal River south of Rotterdam. Civilians were told to stay inside to avoid being hurt by shrapnel.

And suddenly I felt that things were not quite so cozy any more below the brick tile roof of our gracious house, nor quite so safe in our flat, defenseless country, which only a short time before had seemed far from the exciting threat of Europe at war.

2

One of the peculiar things I was going to find out about the war, now and in the next few days, was that life goes on. A momentous shift has occurred, but the sun does not stop in its track. What does one do at seven in the morning? We ate breakfast and talked—I'm not even sure we talked about the invasion.

Afterward, Jack and I walked over to the railroad yard, which was five minutes away from our house. The Dutch army had never had to deal with an invasion, but someone had decided that strewing the main railroad tracks into town with derailed wagons would be an efficient way of blocking a German assault by train. This was a boy's dream come true! A puffing locomotive hauled three or four wagons at a time over to the main track, where, uncoupled, it pushed them forward toward the place where a section of rail had been removed. A final shove, and then the engineer put on the brakes, letting the wagons roll on toward their doom—towards my joy. It was deeply satisfying to watch them bash against each other in an ear-splitting mayhem of destruction, wood cracking, steel crunching, wheels coming off, until all of it came to rest in a zig-zag of mutilated boxcars and coaches. My model train never gave me such pure pleasure. Not until now did I understand why the Hindus needed Shiva, god of destruction, and how he could be at once the god of ecstasy. Anyway, I felt the war had started out very well, and thought the enemy would have trouble advancing across this mess.

The following days were confusing. There were rumors of all sorts. The Dutch army, it seemed, had repulsed the enemy along the southern part of the front and was advancing triumphantly into German territory. Farther north, a single machine gunner was said to have held off an entire enemy battalion for most of the day and, when finally overrun, had been presented with the German commander's sword in admiration of his bravery. I was proud. But the unmistakable truth was told by the canons, for it could not be denied that they were getting close.

I roamed the city on my bike. At the outskirts convoys of people on foot and on bicycle were gathering to flee town, southward, toward Belgium and France—who knew? Briefly, I toyed with the idea of joining up to see the world, the great unknown, where anything at all might happen. For such was the promise of war: it seemed as if all bets were off, all rules were broken, all responsibilities gone, all things possible. School had already become unthinkable, and the State exams implausibly remote and unreal. Should I join them? But I was hungry and went home.

And then came the day the Germans took the town. There was no battle, the Dutch army just withdrew. It was late afternoon. I took my bike and went to watch the first enemy tanks roll through the main street in the downtown area, followed by a défilé of sidecar motorcycles. They pulled machine guns that were aimed upward at windows where snipers might be lurking. An order was barked out (five years of German shouting and yelling had begun) and a window slammed shut. People watched in silence. I felt the stirrings of hatred.

That evening we were all sitting on our back yard terrace, each of us telling what we had seen. "And now" I said, half enjoying the tremor of indignation in my voice, "now we are vassals of the rottenest people . . ." (I doubt I really said "vassals," but it was something like that.) My mother tried to calm me, but it was not she who had stopped me. What stopped me was that I had seen a shadow, the outline of a man, moving in the half-dark behind the hedge at the end of our yard. For the first time I experienced what was going to become second nature for the rest of the war: the knowledge that one had to be careful, that someone might be listening, that we were no longer a free people.

By the end of the week it was all over. Rotterdam, although declared by radio an open city from which all air defenses had been removed, was bombed for hours on end by German planes lazily flying at rooftop level, till nothing remained of the heart of the town. Thousands perished, it was said. Utrecht was threatened next. Holland capitulated, and the cabinet and queen went into exile in London. We had formally become occupied territory, with an Austrian Nazi called Seiss-Inquart as its civilian governor. Buttons of the Dutch Nazi party sprouted on the lapels of a new subspecies of man known as collaborators, feared by many, and detested by most for years to come.

We never saw a single Allied soldier in those days, except in defeat. For days on end long trains carried French and British prisoners eastward to camps in Germany. We went out to watch them in the same place where the wagons had been derailed earlier that week—those hadn't been much of an obstacle, after all. A hundred or more soldiers were crammed into cars built to hold half that many (the famous words of World War I, "40 hommes, 8 chevaux" still showed on some of them). Still more were hanging on to the sides. Someone told how cool the French *poilus* had been under fire—they'd be rolling their cigarettes behind a tree while watching enemy dive bombers screaming down on them. It sounded like a made-up story, but we needed to believe in heroes. In defeat, all those soldiers only looked exhausted, famished, and despondent, and that was hard to take. Still, some waved at us. We had been warned we would be shot at if we waved back, and machine guns were mounted on the trains to make us believe it. So we did not wave back. When the train was out of sight I felt ashamed at my lack of courage: all those prisoners had looked for was some sign of empathy, of common cause. But we had not given it, we had just stood there as if they were already passing through Nazi country. To this day I feel that I failed at something then.

3

Normalcy of a sort returned. The State Exams did, after all, take place: five days of tough written exams, followed a week or so later by several days of orals. On the first morning I was so nervous that I handed in almost blank pages, but after that I steadied and ended up flying all colors. There were parties, and we slid into the warm days of a lazy summer.

I was confronted with something I had never had to think about: what to do with my life. I had always accepted that I would carry on the family tradition and become a naval officer . . . not because I particularly liked the idea, but because it was expected of me. My father had tried hard to talk up the Navy, though it always puzzled me that the main argument seemed to be how well the Navy prepared you for other jobs once you were through with it. That had been his own career. To instill in me the love of the sea he twice arranged a summer voyage on a cargo ship, once for me alone when I was fifteen, to Trondhjeim in Norway (a trip that left me sick as a dog when we ran into one of the notorious North Sea storms), and the next year together with Jack, to Hamburg and on to Narvik, above the Arctic Circle. That time the sea was a mirror and, when the captain gave me a daily shift behind the steering wheel, came close to seducing me. But even closer came the prostitutes in Hamburg, seated behind their windows or standing by their doorways in the two narrow streets off the Reeperbahn, which you had to cross a gate to get into. They called me sweet names as if I were a grown man, and set me into such obvious confusion that the captain went into a belly laugh and warned me that a man had only a given reservoir—and once he had used it up, he was finished for life. I half believed him. In Narvik we climbed up a hill to a dancing hall under the midnight sun, and later took the train into Swedish Lapland, where people walked around with fencing masks to protect themselves against the fierce hordes of mosquitoes, and where we saw reindeer. The Navy just couldn't compete against so many impressions and desires—an adolescent's desires who, above all, wanted to know continents, rather than oceans and sea ports.

In fact, I disliked the idea of the Navy so much, that I secretly considered flunking the entrance examination on purpose and going, even if halfheartedly, for the fall-back option I had been given since boyhood: a government-paid program called "Colonial Administration" at the University of Leiden, which would at least have destined me for inland, rather than offshore, duty, most likely in the Dutch East Indies. It would be the nearest thing to becoming a regular university student at Leiden, Delft or Amsterdam, which was where the majority of my classmates were headed, but for which there was no money in our family.

Now the Navy was gone, the colonies were adrift, and I was free to start thinking about alternatives. Suddenly I became interested in my future. Could I become a university student, after all? I wanted to apply for a scholarship from the Philips Corporation. But a student, of what?

Over a period of weeks I came up with one thing after another and tried them out on my father. International Law—out of the question he said, you had to go to school in Geneva for that, which was impossible now, and, given the circumstances, what kind of a future was there in that, anyway? I had to acknowledge there was a good deal of truth in that. History, then, or Dutch literature—my father harrumphed, and I didn't want those enough to put up a fight. Economics? "Not bad," my dad said "but you had better find out more about it." He telephoned an economist acquaintance at Philips to set up an interview, and I had a half-hour discussion with the man in his office. While I was bicycling back home he phoned my father and was categorical: anything but Economics. To this day, I am grateful to him: all my life I have been frustrated by my inability, bordering on unwillingness to get the basics of money matters into my head, and for all I know it may have been an obstinate sense of contradiction that made me offer it as something I might study.

Well, how about Ethnology? I suggested next. What little I had read about that sounded great. It was easy to imagine the thrill of world travel, primitive places, friendly overtures to astounded natives and beautiful daughters of chiefs, with periodic returns to civilization, when I would listen to Schubert Quartets and weep. Also, Ethnology seemed closer to Colonial Administration, for which I had mentally prepared myself for some time. "You'll never get a scholarship for that," said my father, "at Philips they are interested in useful subjects—think about the hard sciences." I think he truly believed that; in any case, I accepted it.

It was true that science had been an early and steady love of mine. When I was seven years old my father told me about atoms and how they were the smallest things in the universe. That made no sense to me, and I set out to test the idea. I cut up a lot of paper into a bowl and for the next few weeks took the scissors and clipped away randomly inside the bowl, thinking that some day I would split an atom. The experiment failed, but that was the fault of our German governess, a stout and formidable woman with a moustache (Jack and I called her "Moustache" behind her back), who made us glue colored squares and triangle into a book on sunny afternoons, when we could hear our friends play soccer in the field across the street. She had discovered my experiment, and her orderly Germanic mind had decided it was trash and should be thrown out. Back from school I found my bowl empty and wept tears of rage. But Moustache got her comeuppance when the sultan of Jogjakarta gave her a holy scare.

To explain that I have to say first what my father's job was in the Philips Corporation. From boy-scouts to royalty, whenever there were visitors, it was he who had to steer them through that immense industrial complex. And this day it was the sultan. My stepmother went along because she spoke fluent Javanese (High and Low). The Sultan was invited to an Indonesian dinner at our house on the very day a forlorn, culture-shocked seventeen-year old arrived from the Ruhr area to be our kitchen maid (German household help was affordable in those days even to modest families such as ours.) It was she who was to serve coffee in the living room, and there she saw the sultan pass around his jewel-encrusted sword to my parents. In panic she fled back to the kitchen to tell Moustache that our house was a center for white slave trade, and the two, in full hysteria, decided to flee. For obscure reasons they did not take the kitchen door into the back yard, nor the hall door into the front yard, but went upstairs to the room where I was sleeping away soundly. They blocked the door with a heavy cupboard and tied bed sheets together to fasten them to the balcony, and slithered down that way. The new arrival, being seventeen, slithered without mishap, but Moustache's avoirdupois did her in: the sheets tore and she crash-landed into the front yard, badly hurting her leg. Hearing the crash, my parents opened the curtains and saw the torn sheets flapping away in the wind, plus a glimpse of the governess hobbling down the street. They raced upstairs, where it took a big shoulder shove from my father and the Sultan of Jokjakarta to make the cupboard topple over and me wake up. I have always been a heavy sleeper. The girl went back to Germany the next day, but our governess, incredibly now that I think of it, was rehired. It was, however, the end of Moustache's reign of terror and the end of the colored triangles.

I had other early scientific musings, world questions such as many kids have. "Why isn't there nothing?" I asked my mother, who was strong on mystic problems. She said: "Don't think about things like that, they drive people crazy". She was right: It did drive me crazy and still does. When I got older, my interest in science inevitably matured along lesser pathways, but it stayed real even if the questions didn't necessarily boggle the mind.

The hard sciences, then. For me, all forms of biology were out, mathematics too dry, physics acceptable but remote. I had liked our high school chemistry teacher and got a kick out of organic chemistry, as out of chess or crossword puzzles, but those didn't seem very strong reasons to hitch my star on chemistry. Still, I offered the thought. Fine idea, my father agreed, but as soon as we seemed to be settling on that I didn't want it any more, which brought us back to zero.

I remember that summer as being especially beautiful. The rumblings of war had receded, and so far the occupation wasn't much worse than the unwelcome reminder of an insult, the daily irritation at seeing enemy soldiers and hearing the enemy language. Naively, we thought it wouldn't last long, that the Allies would soon come back and make short shrift of the Germans. Stunned disbelief set in only gradually as, on English radio, we followed the battle of France, the debacle, the surrender, and the evacuation pulled off at Dunkerque. The Nazi-controlled Dutch radio played triumphant German martial music and boasted about the impending invasion of England. Yet, so little we knew that we actually wished it would happen soon—not so much because we hoped the war would be over soon (after all, we had barely had any), but because we wanted to see the Nazis get their noses bloodied on the beaches of Britain. For about that there could be no doubt: things would go bad for the Germans once the British got going.

My days were spent at the open-air swimming pool, a large lake at the edge of town, not far from our home. Here, occupation had already wrought a remarkable change. This being a highly conservative part of Holland, much influenced by a conservative Catholic church, the lake had always been strictly divided into a male and a female part, separated by a twenty meter strip where no one was allowed to bathe. Furious whistling was heard as soon as anyone entered that strip and the old, whiskered guard would come out in his rowboat to chase away offenders. The women, on their side, all wore bathing caps, and sometimes the young men would put on caps, too, take a deep breath, and swim under water to emerge where the girls were. There we would finally create so much ruckus together, so much male raucousness and female giggling, that the guard would catch on and the rowboat would come out.

But all of that had now changed. The German soldiers were not about to go out swimming without their girlfriends, and the barriers came down. Suddenly I had to get used to lying on the beach with girls in bathing suits stretched out next to me in the warm sand, close enough to make furtive glances so rewarding that I didn't dare turn over on my back, and burned it badly. It was hard to keep my thoughts on my future.

It was about then that the mail brought a booklet from the University of Amsterdam, with one-page descriptions of each discipline. I read it and came upon Geology. Whoever wrote that page certainly knew how to grab me. It had it all, or almost all: the look into the past of History, the exotic places promised by Ethnology, with enough scientific hardness, my father agreed, to satisfy Mr. Philips. He made me meet a geologist who happened to be in town to give a lecture, in which he spoke of the dark jungle of the Amazon, of snow-capped Andean peaks and smoking volcanoes, and of living in tents. A half-forgotten comment once made by my High school Geography teacher came back to mind, something about my having an affinity for things having to do with the Earth.

Sold: Geology it was! I applied for the scholarship and waited out the rest of the summer for word that I, too, would be among the privileged who would go to the university. Word came in late September, already several days into the academic year and well after the onset of anxiety on my part. Suddenly in a daze, I packed my bags and went around to bid farewell to friends. And there, at last, I was in the train that was to take me to far-off Amsterdam, scary Amsterdam, the unknown Amsterdam of my daydreams—off to life as a man and to a future I was ready to embrace.

4

The train passed by Rotterdam, I don't know why—normally that's not on the way to Amsterdam. Slowly it moved through the devastated center. It was a surrealistic scene. So inanimate and mute that I found it impossible to picture what had happened here: the menacing rumble of the approaching planes, the explosions of the first bombs, the panic, screaming, running for shelter, the fires out of control, the total terror. I could say those words, but not feel what they stood for. I couldn't even feel commensurate hatred. The carnage finished, it had all become too impersonal to comprehend. Impossible, also, to absorb the contrast with the peaceful countryside beyond, where the only reminders of the war were the German soldiers in the train.

Amsterdam at last! From the moment I stepped out of the Central Station the town swept me up, carried me along, somewhat out of control. I had been there before, but for a day at a time only. Once, in second grade, on a school trip guided by Miss Statema, our teacher. I loved Miss Statema and hated the fifth grade teacher, Mr. van Dam, with whom she was in love. I knew that, because I had found her sitting at her desk, weeping, when I returned after class one day to pick up the briefcase I had forgotten, and my seven-year old mind had guessed she wept over Mr. van Dam. Now, on the bus to Amsterdam, I swore to her I would never marry, never. She smiled and looked out the window.

The second time I saw Amsterdam was when my stepmother took me along to buy a new piano, and the third trip was because of a promise my father had made when I was fourteen. In April of that year I had been severely injured by a field hockey ball walloped towards the clubhouse by my friend Jan Boutkan at the end of our thrice-weekly sports hour. To this day I have no trouble reliving that moment when someone screamed "Watch out!, and the instantaneous explosion inside my head that made me fall over and lose consciousness for a few seconds. When I came to, I wanted to act tough and, with a major concussion, tunnel vision and a brain hemorrhage that gave me nausea and an enormous headache, I walked back to school with the others. Finally, when I couldn't go on, I got permission from the teacher and the High School Principal to walk home, where I fell on my bed and into a two-day coma. When I drifted back up, our doctor, a nurse, and a hand-wringing Principal were sitting by my bed, and I was instructed not to move a limb for a whole excruciating week. Recovery took a month-and-a-half, and then, for being so stoic a patient, my dad took me to Amsterdam by plane (by plane!, and with a stewardess to boot) to see an international soccer match—the kind that had always kept our family, along with the rest of the country, glued to the radio to follow the blow-by-blow account by the incomparable Jan Hollander. It was hard to get it into my head that I was now actually seeing one, cheering on our team against Scotland. I still cringe with despair when I think of the long shot by the Scottish left forward, which seemed to travel in slow motion towards the Dutch goalkeeper before it disappeared over his head into the net to give the enemy its only point—the winning one, unfortunately. But afterward my father took me to a restaurant.

Neither from that trip, nor from the previous ones, had I retained a great deal of knowledge about the city, but what stayed was the feeling that this was an altogether different world from the one I was acquainted with, and that I wanted to be part of it some day. And now I was! For weeks it remained a heady experience, a little overwhelming at times, but mostly one of intense pleasure. There were moments, during the first few weeks, when I was so conscious of my love affair with Amsterdam, that, while bicycling along one of the canals or weaving in and out of car traffic, I would draw myself up, look around, and say aloud to no one but myself: "This is my town, and I am part of it!" Sharing in the city's sophistication allowed me to do some fast growing up in a very short time. Not that that did away with the self-doubt I had been plagued with throughout High School. The two simply coexisted in implausible partnership.

I enjoyed my spirit of discovery, getting to know the layout of the town, the half-circles of its old canals, the patrician houses lining them, the connecting streets radiating away from the wide harbor to the north. There was a lot of hustling to be done in the first few days: pay puition, register for a curriculum, hunt for a room, go to my first class. The sweet old aunt who had offered me a place to sleep actually left town, leaving me her apartment, where I could live in splendid independence for two weeks. At the Geology Institute, there was a doorman who seemed to understand a freshman's pains of disorientation; he told me where I was supposed to go and steered me around the building until it felt less intimidating. And then there was Walter, himself a freshman, but one who held a great advantage over me in that he was from Amsterdam. He struck me as most debonair, which, indeed, he was. When I first walked into the main geology classroom, uncertainty in my heart and, no doubt, written all over my face, he actually got up and introduced himself. It was a gesture that meant a lot to me just then. Walter quickly became my best friend.

It seemed as if adulthood, or at least student-hood, was going to be a cinch. I didn't know there was going to be an earthquake, and very soon, at that.

5

It struck on a limpid day of fall at the end of my first week in the city, when I stopped my bike at a red light in front of the old Municipal Theater on Leiden Square, and looked around aimlessly. Suddenly I saw Sylvia. She was standing on a streetcar island, and at the moment I saw her she noticed me, too. She smiled and walked over. "Well, hello!" she said in the mellow voice I liked in her. "I bet you didn't expect to see me here."

Sylvia and her husband were friends of my parents, though she was much younger, in her thirties. They lived in a villa in the woods outside my home town. Sometimes, on summer Sundays, our whole family would go out there on our bikes, to sun ourselves in their backyard or play ping-pong, or walk in the woods. I liked them, but mostly her, and so it was a pleasant surprise to see her. Nevertheless, to run into someone from back home was unsettling. It yanked me out of the euphoria of my anonymity. No doubt aware of my confusion, she chatted. She was in town to do some shopping. Wasn't this a marvellous coincidence? How had things gone for me this first week of my new life? How about having dinner together? And, by the way, where did I suppose she was staying for the night? I said I couldn't guess. "I'll tell you," she said, looking straight into my eyes, a light smile in hers. "Did you know they rent out rooms by the night where your aunt has her apartment, where you are living right now?"

There have been seconds in my life, fractions of seconds, both before and after this day, when, in a flash, I was aware that something momentous had just occurred to me. When that hockey ball struck the back of my head two years earlier, I at once saw myself lying in bed, and knew this was going to affect me for the rest of my life. Now, what came to me suddenly on this warm afternoon was the knowledge that a door had been opened into the new world of manhood, and that I was meant to walk through that door.

It was not as if, back home, I had not been conscious of Sylvia's beauty, but it had been something that radiated out equally in all directions. Here it was different—it was as if that radiance was directed towards me alone, apparently meant for me, oh God, yes, clearly meant for me, focused on me, enveloping me in a way nothing ever had. The smile that had played around her lips and her eyes was gone now, replaced by something very serious and infinitely tender. I was conscious of her skin. It had a warm glow. I shivered uncontrollably. It was too hot, or too cold. Words had to be found somewhere.

At last I managed to say that it was certainly a nice idea to take a room close to where I lived. It sounded dumb. "Well" Sylvia said (her smile had come back, she was all business now), "I'll take the streetcar, and we'll see each other shortly." The streetcar arrived, and she was gone.

Riding home, I was in a daze. What would happen next? What could happen? What was expected of me? Call her by her first name? It seemed unthinkable. Had I, God forbid, perhaps misunderstood the whole thing? How could this beautiful, mature woman possibly be interested in me, inexperienced, half her age? But I remembered those serious, unsettling, eyes. I felt gauche. What did I have to offer her . . . and, most, of all, how?

An hour or so later Sylvia phoned. She had discovered one could order up food from the hotel kitchen. What if we ate dinner at my place, just the two of us, instead of going out to a restaurant? I heard myself say that was fine with me. Flashes of recklessness had begun to get hold of me. After the eternity of a minute Sylvia was at the apartment door. As she passed through the narrow corridor on her way to the living room she seemed (or was it my imagination?) to brush against me very lightly. I experienced the function of perfume.

For the first time in my life I was conscious of being alone with a woman between four walls, without anyone knowing about it. The secrecy enhanced her beauty. She talked about her childhood. She was half-French, and her cosmopolitan background dazzled me. Then she wanted to know about me. She was a good listener, and I was flattered, because I seemed to be important to her. But in the back of my mind there was apprehension. There was also a faint feeling of guilt about something, and when the doorbell rang it startled me out of my seat. But it was not the police, only someone from the kitchen with the dinner we had ordered.

We dined by candlelight, which gave the honey color of her hair an almost reddish tint. Each time I looked at her my heart sank. Would I be up to "it", whatever "it" turned out to be? But dinner passed so normally that the thought came back I must be mistaken about the whole thing. After all, why couldn't she just have tried to call me at the apartment to bring greetings from my family (though it struck me only now she hadn't yet mentioned my family), and then found out this place was a residence hotel? The rest was coincidence with a dose of my imagination. No doubt, that, must be it! My relief was a sharp disappointment.

Dishes done, we moved back into the living room, where Sylvia sat down on the couch, her legs crossed in unbelievable elegance. Without warning she asked me, turning her face up towards me: "Isn't this is a bit silly? Don't you feel you ought to call me Sylvia?" I was just bringing in the coffee, and the cups began to tinkle so loudly, they had to be put down in a hurry. I looked at her in despair, then, with a gesture of abandon, sat down awkwardly on the armrest of the couch. The die was cast now—all doors were locked, there was no escape from from her luminous blue eyes, her perfume.

The soft brush of her lips against mine surprised me. It seemed to draw me into an unimagined universe, where it would actually be possible to pronounce her name. "Sylvia", I managed to say, and saying it knocked me so thoroughly off my last moorings that her mouth now seemed to be the only reality left in the world, and I sank into the nameless delight of our first long kiss. A wetness on my cheek made me draw back to look at her eyes, and I was amazed to see they were filled with tears, and then the knowledge that she wept because of me filled me with a tenderness too great to contain, and tenderness turned into incoherent chaos in which I could only repeat her name over and over, and kiss her again, her eyes, her mouth, then her eyes again, to taste the saltiness of her tears.

When at last the wildness ebbed away, I became conscious of my failure. I did not dare speak, for now I fought back my own tears. It was Sylvia who spoke, caressing me, telling me it was often that way the first time. "Isn't it wonderful", she said, "we both cried this first time." But I knew there was a difference between her tears and mine.

Sylvia's intuition told her I needed to be alone that night. I spent it in fitful sleep, my face turned to the wall, my heart a tempest of guilt, shame and abject despair. When I woke up, the sun stood high in the sky. Then, only then, did I realize that Sylvia had said "this first time." So there would be other times, my love life would have a second chance, a better start! With her, with her, with no one else! I had fallen in love, or at least in lust, and believed myself ready to face the consequences.

But wise Sylvia knew something about the need for time to heal a lover's wounds, and of absence to restore his fragile confidence and sexual vigor. Under the front door was a note in the hand writing that was to become the dearest of sights to me, and in the only language love would allow.

"Mon trésor", I read, "J'ai un train tôt ce matin. Je ne veux pas te réveiller. Hier soir était doux. La prochaine fois il n'y aura plus de larmes, rien que la lumière de notre amour. Je t'écrirai bientôt Je t'aime! S."

The pang of the let-down was matched by my elation as I read and re-read those word of pure wonder: " . . . the light of our love." The door had been opened. My foot was in it, at last.

6

The following week I rented a room in the south-central part of the city, in a neighborhood I thought of as genteel, right behind the Concertgebouw, Amsterdam's famous concert hall. I couldn't have picked a worse location. Right below me was a pastry shop that stayed open long after dark for the express purpose of torturing me. Merciless baking aromas wafted up into my room, competing for my attention with differential equations, the laws of thermodynamics, and the evolution of ammonites. Should I spend a dime to stop my mouth from watering? Bakers, in those days, used to bake a cheap sort of cake from whatever they could sweep up off tables and floors towards evening. Those cakes were known for their surprises in taste and composition. One might easily come upon a baked-in bit of foreign matter, a stub of pencil, for example, or a piece of straw from the broom. A young uncle of mine swore he once bit into the tail of a mouse, but he was a notorious liar. In any case, the thing that mattered was not content, but size; a dime would buy you a chunk big enough to still, for a while at least, the howling of a cavernous stomach. But was it financially responsible to sacrifice, in the space of minutes, so much of the money I had for the entire year? More often than not, thermodynamics lost out to irresponsibility, ammonites to greed, and I rushed down just before closing, praying they would be sold out and hoping they wouldn't.

On weekends the baker stayed home, and it became the soul's turn for torment. From my window I watched limousines and taxis drive up to the side of the concert hall. Elegantly dressed women swept into the soft auras of street lanterns and disappeared inside the building. Their male consorts always carried the right amount of cash to tip the drivers, but didn't otherwise impress me. After the great doors closed, I tried to imagine the unattainable—the plush seats and cut glass chandeliers, the tuning of the instruments, then the hush, the applause for the conductor, and the familiar first chords of the symphony that had been announced all week on the billboards.

Elsewhere, civilization was falling to pieces, but here its forms were intact, fossilized, an insect caught in amber—all the more attractive for being so out of time. I felt as if excluded from a birthright.

I knew I had to move, but a decision became imperative only on the day I knocked over the inkwell and created a baby blue stain on the carpet. It was a reed sort of material, and furious scrubbing got most of the blue out. But I knew my landlady's eagle eye would spot the lasting damage if ever she came in, and I feared her wrath. What if she demanded financial compensation? Unable to pay even a token, I would have to go back to the provinces in disgrace, end the life onto which I had barely embarked. In growing panic, I put a chair over the spot and started planning for a dignified departure. No use: the landlady came in the very next day to ask me something or other, and the displaced chair waved its arms to attract her attention to the spot below. Because she said nothing then, hope stayed alive, but she cornered me in the hall the next day.

"Just a moment there, Mr. Scholten! would you please tell me how that blue spot got on the carpet?" My heart froze. Unmasked!

"I haven't seen any blue spot" was all I found to say. A shameless, useless feint, but I had not prepared for a better one, or for a clean confrontation.

"Mr. Scholten, you know what I am talking about." Her eyes narrowed as if sighting the stain through the door of my room. "It's that inkwell, isn't it . . . there's no ink left in it."

Rats, I had not thought of refilling it. Guilt colored my face, for the entire world to see. But there was no backing out now. I stumbled on.

"Well, eh, I . . . eh, I'm sure it was there when I moved in." I raged at myself for being such a yellow-livered and, above all, obvious liar.

"You know that's not true", she said, echoing my thoughts. "You hear me, Mr. Scholten. Either you pay me for a new carpet, or you move out! I mean, move out by the end of the month."

What was that? I couldn't believe my good luck at getting off with no more than the loss of my self-respect. Wrapping myself in the few shreds that remained of it, I drew myself up and announced I was giving notice. And so, before Christmas of that first academic year, I stole out on a moonless night and resettled in a small, high attic room in the de Lairesse Street, a few blocks away.

My new room had an unpretentious charm, a foldout bed, a small desk, and a splendid view of part of the city. It couldn't have been a very healthy place in winter, for it was heated by a small stove with an open gas flame, which must have blotted a good deal of oxygen out of the air. But I could boil water on it for coffee or oatmeal. On blue days of spring or fall the sun streamed in through the dormer window, and it was a joy to lean out over the gutter to watch life in the street below or look out across the roofs of Amsterdam.

That window also jarred the war back into focus. The wail of sirens, the drone of allied bombers, and the sharp bark of anti-aircraft guns had become familiar aspects of night life. We knew the bombers weren't out after us, and so we silently cheered them on without being very conscious of the drama in the sky. But now I had a front seat to the air war, and night after night I watched with suspense the play of the powerful search lights above the blacked-out city. Now and then a plane was caught in one of the beams, and immediately other beams pinned it against the starry sky. The guns zeroed in and shrapnel began to clatter on surrounding roofs. Swerving and diving, the plane tried to get back into the protective darkness. I imagined what was going on inside it, the shouting and the fear, the tense competence of the pilot, and I willed the plane to escape. I never failed.

The faces of the good guys in those shadow fights had to be invented. Those of the bad ones were all over—in the streets, trolley cars, shops, movie theaters, restaurants. Dislike of their uniforms, dislike for them in groups, especially singing, marching groups ("Eins-zwei-drei SINGEN!") came as readily as a knee-jerk, but it could be very disconcerting to discover, on occasion, a pleasant individual inside that rejected uniform. It could leave you rudderless, for there was no blueprint telling you how to feel or act in such cases.

It happened one day in the restaurant that had become my favorite place to eat because of its vaguely eastern European atmosphere and food. Hungarian goulash was only 60 cents and two food coupons. I looked forward all week to that Saturday night outing. One especially crowded night the waiter directed a handsome young Army lieutenant toward the empty seat opposite my side of the table for two. More than handsome, he was positively engaging, and soon broke down the bristling communications barrier I had hastily thrown up.

"Pleasant place, isn't it?", Enemy smiled at me. "Do you often eat here?" I considered not answering, but showing the Enemy I could speak his language made me feel superior to him.

"Not that often," I said stiffly. "They ask for too many ration tickets." That wasn't really true, but never mind.

"Ah yes, this damned war!", Enemy said, his voice expressing sympathy. "What a marvelous city this must have been before! Even now it has such warmth, you feel at home right away. And all those splendid museums, the concerts!" The enemy soldier was beginning to take on human qualities. He liked my city for the same reasons I did, and seemed almost apologetic about the invasion. And he liked music! (The world had yet to find out what some lovers of Mozart were capable of doing to others.)

"Are you a student at the university?" The officer leaned back, and I said I was.

"So am I—physics in Heidelberg. Those were the good days." I ached to accept the cigarette he offered me, but, summoning all my will power, I said no.

"You're lucky", he added, "I'd give anything to be back in the lab." That briefly changed my perspective. I had never thought of myself, citizen of an occupied country, as privileged compared to the aggressor. And here the aggressor was, like me, a scientist!

"Well, I'm just here for the day", he said, "but tell me if you will, do you often get air raid alarms here?"

"Almost every night, usually several times", I lied proudly. Just then the sirens began to wail.

"Terrific!" exclaimed my table companion. "That'll give me an excuse to miss my trip back to my unit—a chance for a night on the town!" He stretched, blew out smoke, smiled at my agony, and asked: "Are you sure you don't want a smoke?"

I caved in. Why refuse a cigarette from a fellow student? Together we smoked, then he got up.

"I think I'll take a walk", he said, "but it was nice to talk with you." I smoked the stub till my fingers burned.

7

The ambiguity of that experience bothered me all the more in that it undercut my position in the silent dispute I had with my father. It revolved around Herr Liese, a German civil engineer whom the Nazi regime had appointed to be overlord of the Philips factories in my home town of Eindhoven. Herr Liese presumably was a Nazi himself, though he never showed it in word or act. He was a cultured man, and, above all, courteous—and courtesy was high on my father's list of values. I had seen my dad discourteous only on rare occasions, as when he dismissed the enraged father of an urchin who had tried to sneak some walnuts from our yard and had received a solid slap on his behind from the rolled-up newspaper wielded by my dad. But Herr Liese was class, and my father not only reciprocated his courtesy, but quickly got to liking him, and in his world of honorable men there was no room for built-in animosity. It was true that the two were made to like each other—they even looked alike. War or no war, Herr Liese was soon invited to our house. I was angry with my father. But now the purity of my anger had been corrupted, for I had myself taken to a German officer.

But I was soon to be initiated into a quite unambiguous feeling, the new one of white-hot hatred. It happened on a sunny day of spring in the year 1941. I was passing by a large building occupied by the German Navy. There was still a romantic notion around at the time that pictured German Navy men as less Nazi, less violent—just professional soldiers doing their duty, perhaps somehow washed clean by the sea.

But not here. Young, blond sailors were leaning from the windows, laughing uproariously at something up the street. I looked, too, suddenly afraid there was horror there. A staggering group of men and women was hounded along the street by shouting SS-men. Rifle butts were slamming into heads and bodies, people fell and were kicked senseless by heavy black boots. The sailors jeered at the terrorized Jews. "Stick it to the pigs!" one of them yelled. Looking up, I saw his face flushed with excitement.

If pain and panic made the Jews scream or whimper, as they must have, I do not remember it. Through the filter of the years I see them now as if in silent pantomime, slow and ghost-like, yet no less real for all that. With the rest of the bystanders I howled in silent rage, incapable of comprehending their physical pain, the heat of their fear, the depth of their shame.

That scene changed forever any remaining notions I may have had of war as high adventure. And it comes back to hound me now, as I watch Israeli soldiers on television club Arabs into submission with the butts of their rifles.

I talked about it with Kees, one of my fellow freshmen. Kees was a reticent fellow, but his face could light up like a candle when he smiled. We were in the process of becoming friends.

That day we were sitting in the small reading room of the Geology Institute library, unaware of the presence around the corner of one of the junior professors, a known collaborator who walked around with the insignia of the Dutch Nazi party in his lapel. Enraged, he stormed in, yelling: "I heard that! I'll get you for that!" Coming from someone like him, such words could not be dismissed lightly. I willed that man's death, as I had willed the Allied bombers' escape. Again it worked. The rumor that he was to undergo an operation for cancer that week turned out to be true. Somewhat to my surprise, he died on the operating table.

He had scared me, that man. But his death was more than a personal relief at danger averted. It seemed, above all, a proper revenge for the agony of those Jews.

8

I looked forward to Sylvia's return, to take up where we had left off. Her letters, always in French, spoke of love and, beyond that, hinted at delights I could only imagine. Skillfully, she orchestrated the growth of my desire and my need of her. Once, she sent me an erotic French novel, which I devoured. A phrase from it: "L'enlèvement de la jupe prit un temps infini..." stayed stuck in my fevered fantasy and came to plague me at unexpected moments, as during lectures in physical chemistry, or while crossing the city on my bike on the way to my ping-pong club (I had joined the club of which Holland's champion was a member and once a week could play against the best in the country.)

"The removal of her skirt took an infinite time..." That sentence became a metaphor of my long wait for Sylvia. A hundred different times I removed her skirt, in a hundred different ways. It all confirmed what I had learned at the age of eight from my readings of Winnie-the-Pooh, that pleasure is enhanced by anticipation. Winnie, in fact, never could figure out whether the best moment came with the first spoonful of honey, or at the moment just before. Delayed gratification—a most Christian dilemma, as I would learn later.

And still Sylvia held back. She might come in the spring, she suggested. The spring?! That was eons away! "Perhaps we could have dinner and go to the Opera," she wrote. Yes, yes, but then what? How about that skirt? And also, then where? My room? That might be difficult to maneuver without being seen. A hotel?

Then, at last, she did come. I met her at the Central Station, and she seemed more lovely even than I had remembered. For the first time I experienced really *seeing* her: what she was wearing (green, her favorite color, matching the green in her eyes), the exact shade of her blond hair (close to fool's gold, said my geologist's eyes, but much warmer, glowing), and her way of walking, which spoke of grace and, to me, of Paris. It still seemed hard to believe that her woman's gift was for me, but how could I not be immensely proud that it was? I carried her bag.

Sylvia had reserved a room in a first-class hotel in the center of town. In the elegant lobby it suddenly struck me that there was such a thing as a hotel register. My confused heart pounded so hard that I feared the clerk would hear it. Was I, too, supposed to sign before they would let me in? By what name?

The clerk handed me an implacable pen. "Sir?" he asked, but it was a polite order, not a question. I wanted to give a false name and address, but against my will, the moving finger wrote my own name and that of the street where I lived, right here in Amsterdam! Mortified, I looked at what could not be undone, and steeled myself to meet the clerk's cheap smirk above my head. Would he point at the entrance and extradite me from paradise because I had fallen into temptation? The clerk, however, did not show the slightest interest, but called the general nearby, who gave out orders to have our baggage (Sylvia's, really) taken up.

When the porter had at last finished all of his fussing in our room, and all of his explanations, and had finally closed the door behind him, Sylvia did something unexpected, at once gentle and terribly exciting: she walked up to me and undid my tie. Dinner and opera would wait. Did she or I remove her skirt? I do not remember, for, unlike in the scene so often imagined from the novel, it took less than a second. Then came the moment of great wonder: for the first time I looked at the nude body of a woman, and it took away my breath. We made love beautifully, I thought later. It was only much later yet that I learned I was expected to give her as much pleasure as she gave me. For me, it was exquisite. The glowing intimacy I nurtured in the fullness of my heart continued during dinner in a restaurant near the opera. And then, at last, I was admitted into the world of red plush, crystal chandeliers, and music. I have seen many operas since that day, but never that first one, nor even heard it. It was "Tiefland" by d'Albert. I knew nothing about opera then, but felt certain I was listening to one of the great masterpieces of all time.

During intermission I mingled in easy grace with the crowd in the lobby. A German officer asked me for a light at a moment when Sylvia was not at my side. I was smoking myself (tobacco was severely rationed, but this occasion had called for it), and could not very well pretend I was not carrying matches, so I lit the officer's cigarette. Sylvia turned and saw. She pounced on me, dragged me away. To my surprise, she appeared to be angry.

"Didn't you realize what he wanted?", she asked. I was puzzled, and showed it.

"He wanted a light for his cigarette", I said.

"That's not all he wanted" said Sylvia, still showing anger. "Don't you know German officers like handsome young men?" (I still had to get used to being called handsome by Sylvia). The subject of homosexuality was not parlor talk in those days. In fact, I don't think I had ever heard it mentioned explicitly. But I understood what Sylvia meant. It amazed me that I could be sexually attractive to men; it was not something I could grasp.

For years afterwards I kept running into such situations. During a sailing vacation in Friesland the following year, a thirtyish-looking Dutch industrialist invited my friends and me to a fancy bar. Over cocktails he said he could read palms and, reading mine, asked me if I knew there was something about me that made me different from other men my age. Thinking that the lines in my hand showed I was the lover of a married woman, I said "Yes", which seemed to please him. He was discreet and did not press, but showed up later that month in our home in Eindhoven, where he delighted my parents by his superb rendition of a Bach fugue on our grand piano. I did not follow up, then or later, on his invitation to stop off for the night at his place in Utrecht, on my way to Amsterdam. It was not until I saw him again in the Amsterdam train station, a year later, that, during dinner together in a Chinese restaurant, it dawned on me what he had wanted me to understand from the start. He called my attention to someone two tables away, whom he knew to be a homosexual, and watched my reaction. After that, he never mentioned the subject again. I liked him: he was intelligent and tactful, a cultured and interesting man guided by respect for others. And it was only now, in my rejection of him, that I was aware of his discretion. I hoped I had not hurt him. Later run-ins with other men (an American G.I. in Germany after the war, a former monk at the University of Michigan) were less discreet, far more awkward.

During the months to come, Sylvia returned several times to Amsterdam. She showed great patience with me, guiding me forward to become a better lover. She bought me an illustrated translation of Ovid's Ars Amandi to help me along. We did away with the hotel routine and, heedless of danger, climbed the four staircases to my attic room to sleep together in my narrow bed. One morning the landlady saw us, but said nothing.

During summer vacations, which I spent back home, I biked out to Sylvia's villa in the woods whenever her husband was out of town, which, fortunately, was often. She kept me informed. In the week leading up to a visit I could think of little else, though I had to pretend I did. "What will we do?" I asked of my fevered brain. "You will take a shower together, first," it replied, "and then you will towel her dry, slowly." I reran that film over and over, and it always got stuck at that frame; My obsession with Sylvia nude was turning into a form of clinical madness, and the madder I became, the madder I wanted to be.

At last came the promised day. Alas, no! A voice intervened, my mother's, at breakfast. "This would be a wonderful time to be out in the woods. I think I'll give Sylvia a call and see if she's going to be in today." It was Gabriel's trumpet, announcing the collapse of my world. In my panic I almost said: "I know she'll be there today, mother", but held back in time. What to do? I had to act fast, for my mother was already on the way to the phone.

"Come to think of it, that sounds like a great idea," I lied. "Why don't you ask her if I can come along. I like it out there."

And so it was that I rode out to my love nest in the company of my mother. Sylvia was so beautiful that it hurt, but she was not for touching. She largely ignored me, but engaged my mother in lively conversation. In the afternoon we drank tea in the garden. I thought she winked at me while pouring the tea, but wasn't sure. A little later, my mother, stretched out on a lounge chair in the sun, fell asleep.

We tip-toed out of the garden and ran into the surrounding woods. "Did you really . . . ?" I started to ask when we halted. But she put a finger on my lips and did not answer. We laughed, not because we had put one over on my mother, but because we were alone in the world. We left the footpath and walked among the trees until we found a sun-dappled bed of soft pine needles.

When we got back to the house, my mother was just beginning to wake up. How well we had timed it! Briefly, I wondered if it was perhaps my mother who had timed us. If so, she never let on.

In the cold light of the day after I was, as always, beset with confused doubts. Was our secret a secret? I thought so, but couldn't be sure. Did Sylvia's husband suspect anything? If he did, he certainly seemed indifferent (how a man could be indifferent about a woman like Sylvia surpassed my comprehension.) Aside from that, was it morally right of me to make love to his wife? From somewhere in my make-up I received a stern "NO!" in reply whenever I asked myself that question. So in the end I learned not to ask it.

9

My course work at the university was going well, although my first oral exam almost turned into disaster. It was in crystallography, not my favorite subject to begin with. The professor was a woman we had always tormented with noise during lectures, but now it was she who was in charge and I who lost my head. Crystallographic systems swirled through my head without connecting to anything, least of all her questions. I felt on the road to failure. Then something terribly embarrassing occurred, something that had first happened to me when I was fifteen years old and climbing a rope during gymnastics: unable to go on to the top, in utter exhaustion and frustration, I hung there and ejaculated. At that time I had no idea what was going on between my legs. Did this happen to others? Now, in front of the professor, I turned scarlet, trying to wipe myself inside my pocket and hoping she hadn't noticed. But it calmed me down enough to begin answering her questions and she soon dismissed me saying I had squeaked by. Perhaps she had noticed. I limped out of the room and fled for the toilets. It took me a year before I learned to steel my nerves at times like that.

Periodically, doubts still assailed me about my career choice. My fantasies of Life-as-a-Geologist began to wilt in the arid atmosphere of facts and figures. Mountains, jungles, volcanoes receded into a future too far to imagine. Was I made for science? Or science for me? Off and on, for months, I worked on a letter to a well-known Dutch poet, a professor of Dutch literature at the University of Amsterdam, begging him to rescue me from the dungeons of science to which a cruel parent had condemned me—to fly to my aid, for I was the secret keeper of a poet's soul. I didn't know how to finish the letter, for it seemed to call for some sort of proof of my genius, whereas the uncomfortable truth was that, poetic as my soul might be, it had written no more than a single poem in its life, a bad one. I didn't even read much poetry. The letter was never sent: way down I knew it was dumb and dishonest.

Still in search of things less than rational, I sat in on a course on Ethnology by a famous anthropologist. Three times a week I pedalled through rain, sleet, or sunshine to the old, picturesque part of town, where the central University building was housed in the seventeenth Century's Old Men's Home. The professor was unlike any I had seen. Sitting cross-legged on a table in front of the class, he spun tales of jungle rites and tribal gods, and held me in the palm of his hand. Then, one day, the professor didn't show up, nor the next time around. He had simply vanished. Much later, we heard he had escaped by boat to England, where he became Minister for Colonial Affairs in the Dutch government-in-exile. With his departure, the spell was lifted.

In time, I started to realize that the field into which I had blundered was probably a good one for me—that, in it, my somewhat dreamy nature, opposed as it was by a capacity for stubborn discipline, might at least be tolerated, and perhaps even prove fruitful. Unknowingly, the principal Professor of Geology, whose name was Brouwer, helped in no small degree to convince me. A lean, sardonic man capable of much scorn and minor cruelty, who ruled the Geology Institute with a grip of iron, he could change personality in front of a classroom, now burning with the cold flame of logic, then soaring to the limits of the imagination. He was a magician, who, himself already under a charm, would rush into the lecture hall and start casting his net before he even got to the podium. So great was his teaching ability, that he could make the story of stones as impelling as that of man, and, to me, that was the key. On our first field trip, in the spring of 1941, he took us to the southernmost part of the country and we hiked to the place where one can see the oldest rocks exposed in Holland. It was a sandstone, which, he said, was formed as a beach close to four hundred million years ago. He asked us to listen to the thundering surf of the Devonian sea and (sacrificing scientific to poetic truth) watch the waving branches of the ancient palm trees.

When the group turned back to the bus, I stayed behind for a while, alone with that rock. Slowly, I passed my fingers across it. I held my breath. And suddenly I felt within a wing's beat of eternity. Those mute grains had never been touched before. Between them they had kept their mystic secret, that of pounding waves on a distant beach, waves that had rolled them over and over for countless days, until a last ripple of water had forever joined them together and buried them beneath other grains. If they spoke to me now of that remote swirl of time, would it forever change my arrow's flight? There was no sound.

Then it was over. I was sitting on a moss-covered outcrop of weathered rock. For a moment I had touched, or almost touched, what was beyond me, and more grand.

A year later I did my field work for a Bachelor's thesis in that same area and came upon that same outcrop. The pounding now was not of waves, but of my hammer, as I took a sample of that old rock. In my notebook I wrote: "Quartzose sandstone, Upper Devonian, N2OE, 35W.

10

My second year as a university student was a good one, on the whole. At times I felt lonely, but the ping-pong club, and the field hockey club I also joined, helped me cross some low points. Slowly, I was developing friendships, a few of them close. Besides Walter, there was Kees—Kees of the timid smile. I had a warm spot for him, an empathy for his reticence, which, though deeper than mine (he could be positively taciturn), in no way diminished the resolve in his character. On occasion I spent the weekend with him at his family home in Bloemendaal, a sleepy little town near Haarlem. We took long Sunday walks in the nearby dunes, and sometimes he talked.

During other weekends I bicycled out to the nearby row house village of Amstelveen (now a major suburb of Amsterdam). Walter lived there with his mother, a gray-haired little woman originally from Germany, but fiercely loyal to the Dutch cause now.

My friendship with Walter was genuine and strong, though for a long time there was an imbalance about it. I wanted to be in some ways like him—more distantly amused by life, more pipe-smoking self-assured, less plagued by ambiguity. In spite, or because, of our differences, we got along better all the time.

Walter's mother thought I was undernourished, which I probably was, and determined that I should eat well in her house. We were having breakfast one Sunday morning, when we heard a plane overhead, then the sputtering of an engine and a loud explosion not far away. Walter and I jumped on our bikes and raced out to the place where a German fighter plane had crashed into a meadow and burned. An army ambulance had already arrived, and medics were extricating the pilot, a young man. He was burned black from head to toe, but he was still alive and talking. He seemed to feel no pain, and spoke in an almost casual way, as if he took it all lightly. Yet, it was clear that he would soon be dead, and he must have known it. Already, he was no longer a German, that young man, no longer an enemy: dying had made him human.

It was Walter who introduced me to another Kees, who was soon going to play an important role in my life. Kees number two was an old High School friend of Walter's and was now a medical student. He was an ebullient person, full of irrepressible humor. His father was a respected Amsterdam physician, but the son seemed unaware that such a pedigree, in my eyes at least, also entitled him to a measure of prestige.

Moreover, Kees owned a sailboat. An invitation for a day on the lake was for me a heady experience, for I felt as if on the edge of the sailing crowd, which, in Holland, carried the same status as the skiing crowd of winter resorts elsewhere. Not that Kees' boat was anything fancy. It was only a sixteen-foot sloop, kept in a ramshackle harbor on a large but unpretentious lake southwest of Amsterdam. Never mind, it was enough that it sailed. The boat was called Schimmelpenninck, which was the name of a Dutch equivalent of Talleyrand—why it had that name I never knew. (At the end of the war, when he recovered his boat after three years of war-enforced neglect, quick-witted Kees rebaptized its half-rotted hulk Schimmel-ben-ik: "Mildew-I-am.")

Now and then, when a spring or autumn wind was changing from southwest to northwest, promising blue sky for the next day, I received a phone call from Walter or Kees, and the next morning four or five of us would bike out to Schimmelpenninck's berth. To learn how to handle the boat myself, feeling the stem's and mainsail's best angle to the breeze for greatest speed, knowing the precise moment to tack, developing the cool competence to skirt the danger of keeling over without keeling over—it all gave me a new and intense pleasure.

One time a girl called Nellie joined us, a maid whose robust sexiness blended delightfully with a tendency to fall into helpless laughter. Unfortunately, she was more or less Kees' girl for the occasion; at least, I assumed she was. By a steady wind we crossed and recrossed the lake, and at noon picnicked under a huge billboard with the name of the nearby village: Kudelstaart. That word, derived from the Dutch for "cow tail", has a more comical sound to a Dutch ear than its English equivalent, and had an immediate effect on Nellie's funny bone.

In the afternoon we were suddenly becalmed. Barely a breath stirred the fog that had settled down on us, and soon we had no idea where we were or were going. "What do I do now?" I asked, because I was at the helm, steering not so much to go anywhere in particular as to take advantage of the slightest puff of wind that came along. Divergent opinions were advanced, but Kees, being the owner of the boat, had to decide. He figured we must be about opposite the little harbor along the shorter axis of the oblong lake. "Watch the ripples," he counselled. "Steer a forty-five degree course to the wave crests.

It will take a while, but with luck it should get us back somewhere near the harbor." In later years I learned enough about wave patterns to know that Kees' advice, even if I had been able to follow it in the fog, would not necessarily have yielded the desired result. However, it seemed sensible at the time, and there was no better idea around.

On we bobbed, and rowed at times, immersed in the silent world of the dense fog. Our progress, I feared, came at the speed of a snail. Towards the end of the second hour Walter shouted: "Land in sight!" A dark rectangle loomed immensely out of the gray. When we finally came close enough, we could read the sign painted on it: Kudelstaart. "Good grief," said Kees, "we're still as far from the harbor as before." From the harbor, and from our bicycles, of course. Nellie collapsed in laughter, while I concentrated on the geometry of intersecting lines: the shore, the wave crests, and the course we should follow.

"I think I figured it out," I said. "We had set course at right angles to the shore, thinking we'd be going northwest. But if I remember well, much of the shore opposite the harbor actually runs north-south, so to go northwest you have to go at forty-five degrees to the shore. Since the ripples come in at about that angle, we should be steering about parallel to the waves." My reasoning was tortuous, at best highly approximative, at worst completely erroneous. It also failed to explain how we could have come back to the same point, but that thought did not strike me until later. For now, my dubious proposal carried the day.

We set out again. At times the gluck-gluck of the water against the hull told us we were moving, even though the sail stayed pretty much slack; much more of the time there was no gluck-gluck at all, and we went back to rowing, hopeful of our course. It was starting to get dark. After a long time there was another shout: "Shore!"—and we all strained our eyes to make out the shape of our salvation. It was a large sign carrying the name of Kudelstaart. "Damn," said Kees. Nellie now had a serious attack of the whoops; her gorgeous body was shaken by hysterical hiccups. We all pounded her on the back until she regained enough breath to vote, with the rest of us, in favor of one last try.

Night was falling. Our journey began to feel like a descent into Hades. But near midnight we did at last come to a different shore, where we decided to throw in the towel and pull up the boat. A footpath followed the shore. Kees suggested I stay with the boat while the rest went to look for our bicycles or, failing that, find some other solution to our various needs, one of which was sleep, and the other food, much of it. But Nellie said she was too tired to walk and preferred to stay behind with me. At that, my heart leapt into my throat. Alone with Nellie!

When my companions' voices had dwindled into the stillness of the night, I sensed that the situation probably called for action on my part. Nellie might start laughing. But would it be to ward me off, as I feared, or be a giggle of delight, as I also feared? An ocean of agony separated lust for Nellie from loyalty to Kees. And what of Sylvia? She was there, too, though more sketchy in outline (with hindsight I realized later it would probably have amused her to know I had jumped Nellie.)

Time passed. The fog started to lift a little, filtering the pale blur of a half-moon. Nellie shivered, and I, too, became aware of the cold. I reached for the two blankets behind the helm and we covered ourselves, leaning back uncomfortably in Schimmelpenninck's hold. When we had warmed up, we talked. Something I said made both of us laugh. Laughter and speech dissipated the unspoken desire that had hung between us. Had I disappointed her? Had I disappointed myself? Yes, I had. No, I hadn't.

The others returned with the news that they had come upon a farm, had awakened the farmer, who had awakened his wife, who had pulled out blankets for us to sleep under and was right now baking us a pile of bacon pancakes. It was too good to be true, but true it was, and a little later we were eating like ravenous wolves beneath a bright kitchen lamp, pouring beet-sugar syrup over pancakes the likes of which we hadn't seen for a year or more. All that without food coupons! The farmer and his wife sat down at the table with us, and Nellie told our story. Toward the end of each of our trips around the lake she began to accelerate and raise the pitch of her voice, until, when she came to the word Kudelstaart, she was unable to pronounce it, but crumpled instead into weeping laughter. Later, we slept soundly in the hayloft, and did not wake up before the sun stood two hand's widths above the horizon. I may never have felt better in my life

But when we bicycled back to Amsterdam and I looked again at Nellie's splendid body, I thought that, between loyalty and lust, the greater good perhaps was lust.

11

The year 1942 was the last one of relative unconcern under occupation—the last year when it was still possible to go about one's business, even enjoy life, without being haunted by the knowledge that something monstrous was loose in Europe, far beyond the normal madness of war. By now, everyone had heard about Gestapo torture, reprisal killings, about the concentration camps near Amersfoort and Vught and a vaguely understood horror in eastern Europe called Buchenwald. Many of us knew, or knew of, someone who had been arrested and had disappeared, and we became the guilty spectators of the deportation of Jews . . . involved in it because of our knowledge and our silence. For centuries the Jews had been a rich and intimate part of Dutch culture. Now, the yellow stars of David on their clothes, the offensive radio broadcast dictating another restriction to their freedom, another insult, another threat, together accomplished their insidious purpose on the rest of us: to set us apart from them. Alone, they went towards darkness and death. We tried to look past it, to go on with our lives, and kept convincing ourselves that the war would soon be over. For sure, the Allies would invade the continent in a few months, or by the end of the year, at the latest. Through the jamming of BBC radio came Churchill's gravelly voice, infinitely stronger than the shrill rantings of Adolf Hitler. He made us feel confident that the Allies were straining at the bit to come back and chase the Germans out. And in a battle between Good and Evil, was there any doubt which would win?

On my Short Wave I could also hear Radio Schenectady. Why Schenectady I had no idea; I doubt that I knew where Schenectady was in that immense far-off continent, but the name has stuck in my mind ever since. It was on that station that, very late one night, I heard Roosevelt declare war in a speech before Congress and, as if in the List of Ships in the Iliad, tally the endless numbers of planes, tanks and boats that America would produce within the year. I was elated. It was all over for Hitler now, I thought; nothing could hold out for long against that much hardware! We still didn't understand much about Nazi megalomania and the contagious irrationality of a whole people gone insane.

We also knew vaguely about something brave called "The Resistance." I was personally acquainted with someone who was in it, a swarthy man called Joe Snoek, who had been in High School with me, though he was much older than the rest of us (his High School career had been interrupted when he ran away to France, where he worked, so he told us, as an assistant camera man in the French film industry, and personally knew Danielle Darrieux). One day in 1942 I ran into him in Eindhoven, and we had coffee together in a restaurant near the railway station. I was envious, but also uncomfortable, when he told me about the dangerous role he was playing in the resistance. At one point he showed me a sheaf of papers with drawings of a system for guiding bombs to their targets, developed in secret by Philips electronics engineers. It was his job, he said, to get those plans to London. Not much later, Joe disappeared, not to London, as it turned out, but into the uranium mines of Czechoslovakia. Though weak and ill, Joe had great willpower and survived the war. But in the U.S., some ten years later, the mail brought me an envelope bordered in black and carrying the announcement that the mines had gotten to Joe at last. He had been a courageous man, but recklessly talkative, perhaps out of pride.

It was through Joe that I learned how documents and people were smuggled into Holland and out to England, about nocturnal parachute landings in the moors of Brabant, right where we lived, and amphibious plane landings on the lakes of Friesland. I knew, therefore, with a sudden start, what was happening in the middle of one night, as I was pedalling back from Sylvia's home in the woods. Through the pitch dark and windy night came the rapid burst of machine gun fire; search lights criss-crossed the sky, and in my excited imagination I felt sure that spies from England had been dropped off not far away. Secretly, I hoped I would come upon those parachutists along my bicycle road, that they would ask me for help and I would find a hide-out for them (but where? I had no idea ... maybe at Sylvia's).

Much of the summer of that year I spent in the company of Walter. For our Bachelor's thesis we had been assigned adjacent areas to study in the south of Holland, near Maastricht, and we decided to share lodgings. On our bikes we went from one little country hotel to another, but all were too expensive and cost us too many ration tickets for meals. The prof came out to see us and, on his most charming behavior, disappeared behind the scenes with the proprietress of the place where we were staying just then. How he did it, we never found out, but when they emerged the price had been lowered. But mostly we needed food, much of it, to sustain us during our days of hard work in hilly country, where we covered many miles on bicycle each day. At night, we returned exhausted and ravenously hungry—a hunger too great for our food stamps. Hungrily, on our first Sunday off, we passed through the village of Margraten, which was then off the main road (it now houses one of the largest military cemeteries in Europe). Hungrily, we drank coffee in a little cafe on the village square, and spoke of our problem with the owner, a stout, pleasant woman full of sympathy.

"I'll tell you what," she said, "if you give me your food coupons for the week and take your meals here, I guarantee you you won't be hungry, and it won't cost you much, either. But you'll have to find lodgings somewhere else."

She was true to her word—more than true. For the next three weeks we breakfasted on bacon and eggs, unthinkable delights by then. Our cheerful hostess made us sandwiches for lunch with heavy country bread, the existence of which we had forgotten. Dinners left us gasping. We had talked a farmer into letting us sleep in his hayloft for next to nothing, and, on the grass in front of the barn we had long evening conversations lying on our backs, arms folded behind our heads, looking up at the starry skies. We slept lightly and woke up early, full of energy. It was life lived unaware of itself because it was fresh and complete. So unaware we were how good it was, that we left without regret, Walter by train to Amsterdam, I on my bike to Eindhoven, holding on to the back of a truck for most of the way.

In July we took our great exam in mineralogy. The professor shared his duties between the universities of Amsterdam and Groningen, in the north of Holland, where he lived. Because summer vacations had started, we had to go out to his place for the exam, and in a letter he suggested we take the boat across the Ysselmeer (the Zuiderzee before a great dike cut it off from the North Sea) to Friesland, and from there by tramway to Groningen, rather than by train. We made the crossing in the morning.

The tram, in the afternoon, took us at a snail's pace through the incredibly peaceful, lake-studded grasslands and farm country of Friesland, by sleepy villages and along the dikes of long canals. It was that tramway's last year of existence. The exam the next morning was like cake. I have never known my minerals better than on that day. In the afternoon, Walter took the train back home, while I went on to the village of Grouw, the main sailing center in Friesland, where I had by mail reserved a boat for a week, and a place to sleep in a waterfront farm. Jack was supposed to have joined me from Eindhoven with two friends from our high school days, but then Jack decided to get married, and only the friends, John and Oscar, showed up.

When I had first proposed a sailing vacation, I had done so with much overconfidence in my abilities as a sailor . . . and I was to be the sailor, for the others had never been in a sailboat before. But I liked risks, and counted on safe weather conditions. The night of my arrival the sun set in a crimson sky as we took proud possession of our rental boat. She was not a thing of beauty, but I saw with relief that she looked sturdy and reliable. Still, as I fell asleep that night, I was apprehensive of being exposed the next day for the incompetent fake and braggart I was. Would I sink the boat?

During the night I was vaguely aware of sloshing waves, the rustling of trees, the creaking of hulls. We woke up to a lead gray sky and a full-blown "northwestern" in gale force. With baleful eye I looked out over the lake. Not a boat was on it. Damn, I thought, a whole day down the drain—our first day! An old salt leaning against the fence next to me asked why I looked so upset. I told him.

"Bah," he said, "it doesn't look that bad." At that moment a single boat ventured out into the open. "Look," he added, "that one doesn't have any problem, does it?" Yes, I thought, but whoever was steering "that one" probably was an experienced sailor. "Ah, go on, you can do it," my neighbor egged me on, within earshot of my friends. There was no drawing back: out we must go.

Before the wind, the main sail out in full, we shot across the lake like an arrow. I felt proud, but only until we got to the end of the lake, where I suddenly realized I had to perform some sort of drastic maneuver. In panic, at the very last moment, I pushed the rudder way over to the side, forgetting I was supposed to haul in the main beam first. At terrible speed it swept over us, miraculously missing our heads by inches. The mast creaked in agony but didn't break, the boat shuddered, leaned over dangerously, then righted itself and triumphantly galloped across the waves, against the gale and back to port. No one but I knew how closely we had skirted disaster, and I wasn't about to let on. But that one crossing was enough for the day. In the afternoon we strolled into town, casually and confident, as if we belonged by rights to the exclusive club of the beautiful people with their sweaters slung over their shoulders, who looked as if they had sailed since birth. We had drinks in the fancy bar by the port, and it was there that I met my charming palm-reading, Bach-playing homosexual friend from Utrecht.

The rest of the week was glorious. From one sun-dappled lake to another, we tacked against steady winds through the connecting canals, between emerald meadows filled with fat cows, past brick-tiled farms. Holland never seemed more beautiful, more at peace. On the third day, going at top speed, I held my breath and made a risky turn against a strong wind to stop off at an expensive looking waterfront restaurant. Behind the plate-glass window a man holding a glass of gin jumped up in disbelief, sure we were duffers and would crash into one of the many boats already docked there. But I managed to slip ours into an empty slot and make it stop dead inches away from the pier. "Bravo!", I said to myself.

Why did I then have to turn into an insufferable ass and spoil the memory of the last two days? Oscar and I had begun to gang up on John, who really was a decent fellow, but somewhat prissy—the kind of person others smell out as defenseless. For no better reason than that John became the butt of our grimaces and secret jokes, until one day he left by the next train without saying a word. Slightly embarrassed, the two of us laughed away our little guilt and stayed out the week. Oh, but how that little guilt turned into lasting regret later on, when I heard that John had been arrested along with other young men in a sweep of our hometown swimming pool—arrested for no reason at all, and sent away in a convoy to that dreaded place Buchenwald, that black hole where all memory was lost, and from which John never came back.

12

Walter and I both decided we had better accelerate our studies, get all course work behind us, write our theses, and take the final comprehensive exam for the Bachelor's degree by February of 1943. The rumblings of trouble between Dutch university students and the collaborationist government in The Hague were getting louder, and we thought the doors might slam shut soon until the time the war would be over. So, for the next six months life pretty much revolved around books. And food!

Food! The mere thought of it could make me salivate. I was hungry much of the time, like any young man who depended on restaurants and didn't have the money to buy on the black market, or the time, for that matter. The university had started a lunch time soup kitchen, which went by the pretentious name of Mensa Academica. It was located in the center of town, not exactly close to the Geology Institute, but close enough to make me fight rain, sleet, and wind once a day throughout the winter. I also stayed on the look-out for leads about restaurants that provided the most bulk per coupon, if not necessarily the daily minimum of vitamins and minerals. Someone told me about an eatery in the Spuistraat, near the Central Railroad Station, where great quantities of soup were said to be served up for little money. I checked it out, and it was true, but the soup wasn't very good, and the place was so far from mine that I burned up more calories on my bike than were ladled into my bowl. After a week I gave up on it. Then I heard about a pretty good restaurant right next to one of the city's landmarks, the Lean Bridge across the River Amstel. It was called, inevitably, "The Greasy Spoon by the Lean Bridge", and it lived up to its name—almost too much so.

Then I made a grand discovery of my own: a tiny restaurant in the cellar of a house along the Prinsengracht, one of the city's old canals. You had to go down several steps to the door. A bell tinkled when you opened it. Inside were five or six tables. Behind was the cook, in command of a miniature kitchen. As soon as he heard the bell ring, he would call out: "Red soup or yellow soup?" They tasted pretty much the same, and I never found out what gave them their color. The most important thing was that they had a taste, that there was lots of it, and that the price was minimal. There were even desserts, mostly puddings, all fillers. It must have been there I picked up my life-long affair with tapioca pudding.

When it wasn't food I was devouring, it was class notes or books in the library. The librarian was Tjong, brought back from the East Indies by Professor Brouwer because of his astounding memory. Was I looking for an article by Harker on high-pressure minerals in Scotland? Volume eighty-seven, he said, number six, British Geological Society, 1937, second row, top shelf, near the middle. He paged through every new volume that came in and had total recall. To study class notes I stayed home, pacing back and forth and, geology being what it was then, memorizing interminable tables of rock and time units and fossil species from all over Europe, China, and the two Americas—one of the least useful things I have done in my life.

At last, in February of 1943, the final Bachelor's exam. It was a formal and formidable occasion, presided over by the much-feared Professor Brouwer. You were expected to wear tails and striped pants for his exams; without those you might as well not show up at all. God himself could be less forbidding than Brouwer. I can still perspire spontaneously when I think of the first time I had an oral exam with him, at the end of my first year. To schedule it, you had to go to a secretary to request a summons from the chief secretary, who would write your time of doom down in a leather-covered appointment book. To cut corners financially, I had borrowed a friend's tails and pants rather than renting them. It was a mistake: my friend was a bigger man than I had realized. I felt like a clown. At the dreaded hour my knock on the professor's door was more faint than my heart's thump. Half dark, the room seemed immense, and it took a while to make out a couch in the corner, with God on it, eyes closed. A hand waved me over, and, my knees turning to water, I embarked on the infinite space between the door and a chair next to the couch, stumbling across the excess inch of striped pant leg. And sat down. Silence. A clock ticked. Then God opened one eye and spoke a terrifying sentence:

"What is the volume of the Deccan Traps?" The eye closed.

The Deccan Traps? Good grief, I had no idea. I could have told him all there was to know about that gigantic outpouring of basalt in India—when it had occurred in the geologic past, under what circumstances, what the composition was, and why. But their volume? Five hundred cubic kilometers, or five hundred thousand, or a million cubic meters—it all seemed equally plausible. I couldn't come up with the simple procedure of multiplying a reasonably guessed-at surface area with a reasonably guessed-at thickness. Wiping my forehead, feeling small, sweaty, and ridiculous in my oversized tails, I closed my eyes and took a desperate jump into nothingness with a figure mumbled as a question more than an answer, and waited for scorn to come raining down. But there was no scorn, only that heavy silence again. At last came a deep sigh out of God's mouth, signifying he had expected nothing less dumb than that. Then he opened both eyes at last, to stare at the ceiling above, and, listlessly, said:

"That, of course, was wrong."

But somehow I knew that that sigh was also the breath of life, bringing forgiveness for all weakness, and with it another chance, with less obvious, more difficult questions to which I had no trouble finding the answer. With the barest hint at satisfaction, the great man declared I had passed . . . but what a lesson he had given me!

Since then I had become fairly seasoned at oral exams, adept at steering professors towards questions I could answer and away from those I couldn't. So it went with the Bachelor's exam.

In the evening there was a big celebration party for Walter and me in the apartment of one of our fellow students, Ed, an immensely likable, immensely lazy, good-looking man, who had girls at his fingertips and money to burn. After the war, when I was going to leave for America, I came to say goodbye to Ed in the Institute's chemical lab known as "the kitchen", where he was cooking up rocks as one of the requirements for the Master's degree. When, four years later, I returned with my doctorate from the University of Michigan in my pocket, I looked again for Ed, high and low through the halls of the Institute, and finally found him where I least expected him, in the kitchen, wearing the same white coat and cooking up what, for all I knew, might have been the same set of rocks. As soon as he saw me, he, too, remembered, and we both broke out in laughter. "No progress," he grinned. Nevertheless, a few years later Ed had it in him to become for a while famous as a geologist. He married a happy, wealthy girl, boasted of the fact that their bathroom had heated tiles you could sit on to warm your bottom, and joined the faculty of one of Holland's universities.

Ed's wartime apartment was two flights up near the center of town. All there was to help us celebrate our rites of passage was a large keg of beer and a small one of dill pickles. How Ed had managed to get even that much was a mystery I was not going to ponder that night. I was too excited, and soon too happily drunk, to notice much detail, including the fact that Victor, a bearded friend of ours, was filling the pockets of my jacket with pickles. At midnight Ed shouted we needed girls and left on a tandem bicycle that belonged to two classmates who had arrived from the suburbs. After an hour he returned with three girls, but without the tandem, which had collapsed under the weight of four. They had hidden it behind some bushes in a large park and walked the rest of the way. In panic, the two suburbanites stormed out to look for it. They found it, but contorted beyond use, so they hid it again and walked their very long way home.

The newly arrived girls were in high spirits when they walked in. Ed had roused them from their sleep and egged them on with promises of food, wine, and fellows. The scene they came upon was of an empty keg of beer, a handful of left-over pickles salvaged from my coat pockets, and a much becalmed party, half asleep, half too drunk to be much good to anyone, including themselves. Walter and I left. The cold air stung us back to life. The last I remember is the two of us walking under the clean light of moon, full of beer and full of the knowledge that we now possessed the official title of "Candidate"—meaning for the doctor's degree. "Robert Scholten, cand. geol." was what I was now entitled to put on my name card if I chose to have one made.

13

Soon after that, Walter said that Kees (the one of the sailboat) wanted to talk with me. Kees explained that he needed a front man for the student underground, of which, it turned out, he was one of the leaders—someone who would quite legally rent a large apartment, half of which would be used as a base of operations for Kees and another one of the leaders. He introduced me to Boetie, a congenial student of medicine, whose father for one year was known by the glorious title of Rector Magnificus, meaning, prosaically, that he was President of the University. Kees was too honest and too smart to tell me I would run no risk, but the risk didn't seem great and, in any case, was not much of a factor to me—flattery was, that I was asked to be a hero, and money was, with this sudden prospect of living for free in a place larger than the one I had. Where the money came from I didn't ask; vaguely, I figured it must have been smuggled in from England or printed illegally by the resistance movement. I accepted on the spot.

We found a perfect place in the newish southern part of of city: two rooms and a connecting hallway, under the roof, with direct access from the street by a steep staircase. The owner, a former Indonesia hand who had lost his wife, occupied the floors below with, oh joy, his daughter, a luscious seventeen year old with pouting lips. Our new landlord was a very polite and precise man who loved inventories and, at the oddest hours, would knock for permission to enter in order to check on items. At nine one morning, with all three of us still down recovering from the preceding Saturday night, he came in to count the blankets on our beds and take us to witness: three cotton, rosa (he actually said rosa not pink); one yellow, wool; two white, wool. And disappeared.

We might have become suspicious, but we assumed that anyone who could say "rosa" was unlikely to be a fink. After the war we wondered if he had known all along what was going on, without letting on to anyone; we found out he had shown steel in his character when things went awry, and the Gestapo came and threatened that his daughter might have to learn to live alone. Our methodical landlord had drawn himself up and declared his daughter was now of age and perfectly able to do so.

Before all this, however, before I could even occupy my new digs, a series of events arrived at a gallop postponing my move for several months. In reprisal for assaults on German officers and military installations, arbitrarily selected men were arrested and sent east to prison camps, and a "loyalty oath" was drawn up in February, to be signed by all university students, who would thereby declare their fidelity to the Nazi government and forswear any and all acts against the occupying forces. Those who signed would be allowed to continue their studies and receive a card signed by the rector of the university, another document issued by the Dutch collaborationist government, and still another signed by the German military commander in Holland, SS-general Rauter. More papers were added later, and all had to be carried at all times for the bearer to be "legally" in Holland. All students who refused to sign were to report for work in German factories.

For the next few weeks there were furious debates within the student body. Many argued that an oath of that kind was meaningless, committed you to nothing. It would be better, they said, to sign and stay here, go on with our studies, join the student resistance if we wished, rather than trying to hide out for the rest of the war and not be good for anything, or, worse, be sent off to Germany and actually support the German war effort by working for German industry. It seemed like good reasoning; it almost swayed me, and I advanced it in a discussion with Boetie. "Come with me tonight" he said immediately. He wouldn't tell me where, but intimated I'd be hearing the other side of the argument. In the evening he took me to an apartment along one of the canals, where ten or fifteen were gathered already, apparently waiting for someone. The door opened, a slightly built man walked in quickly—red-haired, alert, with eyes that flashed will and concentration. He spoke rapidly, intensely, for half an hour—perhaps the most intense half hour of my young life. He was eloquent, direct, convincing, and held his small audience captive.

He spoke of the need to think things through clearly and to the end, wherever it might lead us, and then act courageously—no false excuses, no wishy washy compromises. When he was young, he said, a man was blackmailing his brother to near-suicide, and he reflected it might be better the blackmailer die than his brother or some other victim. Once he reached that conclusion, he waited for the blackmailer to show up and shot him dead. He said he felt no pride at that act, nor did he regret it. He did years of prison for it. When he came out, he went to Spain to fight in the civil war against Franco, and lost his Dutch citizenship for some time after. Then he said how imperative it was to think about your thoughts, too, whether they were truthful or tarnished by a drive for power, by arrogance and corruption—to look into the mirror and not ever fool yourself. Lastly, he imprecated his listeners to be not only mentally strong, but feel deep concern for their fellow men.

I felt tears of deep emotion. The speaker now changed to the state of affairs in the Dutch universities, to the burning issue of the loyalty oath. Certainly, he said, there was superficial merit in the arguments of those who advocated playing along, but their thoughts had not been tough enough and hadn't gone the distance. Our privilege to be at the university carried with it a responsibility, that of drawing a line when the time came, of setting the example, of leading. If we didn't, who would? If we could not show how to resist, resist coercion, resist true evil, resist the oppressor, how could others take courage and resist, too? Some time we must act, some time our colors must be be shown. That time had come, the choice was now—to be wishy-washy and sign, or strong and refuse, whatever the consequences.

The speaker had finished. Someone opened a door, and he got out as quickly as he had entered. An electric silence hung in the room. We left without speaking. Night after night this man gave his unflinching message to small groups of students, and soon we were many, carrying his flame to still others. In the end, eighty-five per cent of the student population at the University of Amsterdam refused to sign.

I never saw that red-headed man again. Months later he was arrested for having led a resistance commando dressed in SS uniforms to the building alongside "Artis", Amsterdam's zoological gardens. That building housed the labor register for all of Holland, which the Germans used to decide who could be spared to work for the war industry in Germany. The commando had disarmed the SS-men who were guarding it, and tied them up in the zoo behind, and then they had set fire to the files. It effectively destroyed the register's usefulness, and kept many young men in Holland. But the tailor who had made the uniforms was careless and talked, and after he was arrested, they beat him to pulp until he gave away the names of the participants in that daring raid. Several of them were caught. They were tried in the same court where I later had my own trial. My lawyer told me that, when the death sentence had been pronounced, the orator of that evening I shall not forget made a brief, eloquent statement, saying no victory could ever be won over people willing to die. The judges, my lawyer said, listened to it in silence, and got up to leave in silence. I had no trouble believing that report. That man's death was the predictable end of a purposed trajectory.

But then, how bitter, how galling it was to be presented, less than ten years later, with a loyalty oath to sign in an America I so believed in, but an America hypnotized by McCarthy—to be told only I, among the entire Penn State faculty, objected to it, and find out that even the few who had been with me had signed within twelve hours of swearing they would rather suffer fire and brimstone (meaning possible dismissal.) Caving in myself after two more months of internal struggle was one of the worst acts of my life, one I have regretted ever since, for in doing so I betrayed not only myself, but that doomed red-haired speaker in an attic room along a canal in Amsterdam.

14

Too few had sworn the loyalty oath to keep the Dutch universities open, and within a short time the doors were closed for the rest of the war. Those who had signed received their documents to stay in Holland, those who hadn't were supposed to show up at one of several induction centers to follow the many young men who had already been listed as "non-essential" in Holland and drafted to work in Germany. My brother Jack was one of those. Soon after the birth of his son he was sent to Friedrichshafen, along Lake Constance, where the famous Zeppelin dirigibles had been built in the thirties.

Among the university students, some saw no alternative to reporting at an induction center. But the great majority became part of a new category, called "onderduikers", plunging out of sight and into hiding in the cities or in the countryside, wherever someone was willing to take the not inconsiderable risk and, furthermore, agree to feed them without ration coupons, for which they had become ineligible. I didn't quite know what to do at first; I had never really concerned myself with the consequences of what I'd argued others into doing. I had talked with a farmer near my home town of Eindhoven, who was not terribly enthusiastic about having me hide out in his barn, but would probably have let me if I had persisted. No doubt I would have eaten well, but I didn't persist. The idea of cooping myself up for who knows how long didn't much appeal to me.

For the moment I stayed above ground, took my chances, and traveled without the necessary papers, and with an ID-card that carried the incriminating year of my birth, 1923. Very soon, however, the student resistance developed ways to make "onderduikers" illegally "legal" again, if they wanted to come out of hiding. The first way, still rather crude, was to forge the year of birth on ID cards. On mine, the figure 3 was changed into 5 to read 1925, making me conceivably still of High School age and too young to be automatically arrested. But I was far from happy with the job that had been done. The change was so obvious that I would have been caught at the very first control, and I started to make detours around likely checkpoints. Trains were a great risk.

May of 1943 was to be the last month in my old apartment. I went to spend a weekend in The Hague at my aunt Clara's place. She was my father's much younger sister, a left-over from the flapper era, divorced from a man who, in peace-time, had been Director of the Holland-to-Harwich Steamboat Company. When I was very small, we had sometimes spent a week at their house near Vlissingen, in the Province of Zeeland, a big house on a wide beach, on which we would fly kites. Those days now seemed like a dream. Because she and my stepmother disliked each other, she seldom came to our house, and it had been years since I had last seen her. It was a pleasure to rediscover my father's family—not only my aunt Clara, but her four beautiful daughters. I would have been hard put to say whom I preferred: Prul, the oldest, funniest, and sexiest, married and divorced by the age of twenty-three, or Sonja, the sweetest, Annie, the deepest, most secret, or Liselot, a blithesome spirit and talented artist, who was just finishing High School—or, for that matter, aunt Clara herself, who was so good-looking (in spite, or because, of her large Scholten nose), so young-looking and young-acting, that outsiders found it difficult to decide which of the five was the mother.

That Sunday night in early May a hard wind flew in from the sea. We thought we heard something like a shot, but dismissed it and passed on to other things. The next morning, looking out the window, the street scene made me catch my breath. The neighborhood was swarming with police, SS-men, and Gestapo. On the radio we heard that the top general of the Dutch SS contingent, the detested organizer of a detested Nazi combat unit, had been assassinated. We expected a house-to-house search. With Prul, I investigated a narrow space above the ceiling between two rooms, the kind of space that house searchers love to poke their bayonets into, though that didn't occur to me just then. Being that close to Prul aroused me even in the face of danger. She had that effect on men without even trying. Years later, the memory of it came back to me in Toronto, where she was then living for a while with a brand-new husband, and where I was cordially invited to share their one bed, causing me a sleepless night of hopeless agony. On that perilous day in The Hague, no search materialized, and I left by train in the afternoon.

In Amsterdam, young men, university students especially, were being arrested everywhere in reprisal for the murder. At the house where I lived, the maid was shaking with fear, and in tears. The police, she said between sobs, had come just before, asking for me. I must have been on some arbitrary list. Knowing I had to move fast, I stuffed a few clothes and books into a briefcase (above all, not a suitcase, which would make me look like the fugitive I was), and went for food to the milkshop nearby, whose young owners had come to recognize me—they had sometimes given me a bottle of barley gruel without ration tickets because they thought I was too thin and looked hungry (which I was). They looked worried, refused payment for my bottle of gruel, and told me to avoid the Central Railway Station, where the Germans were waiting for fleeing victims like spiders in their web.

An idea struck me: the trolley car to Haarlem (a means of conveyance long since gone). It was unlikely the police would be watching it. From Haarlem I could take the train, though that had to be a fast, hold-your-breath dash to some place nearby. Home I ruled out as too far; moreover, the police might come for me there. But The Hague was close to Haarlem, and so were my cousins. Perfect! A triumph of smart thinking leading directly to pleasure.

Through back streets I quickly headed for the outskirts, and found the trolley car waiting. Everything seemed quiet, as if this were any ordinary soft day of spring. Soon we left and chugged peacefully through the sunny countryside. I began to let go of tension. So far, I had outsmarted them, I thought with some satisfaction, though, admittedly, luck had been with me. If only my altered ID card would stop burning a hole through my pocket! At the train station in Haarlem there was an hour's wait. From the deserted platform I looked out upon a nearly deserted street.

Suddenly there was a loud yelling and cursing in German. A group of young men with their hands on their heads were being marched to the station by soldiers. I had to get out of the way! Haven was the man's toilet, a short sprint away. Someone about my age was already hiding there. We looked at each other. He seemed fairly calm. As for me, I was afraid my heart was pounding loud enough to be heard across the platform.

"Where are you going?" he asked in a whisper. "The Hague," I whispered back. "You, too?"

"Not on your life," he replied. "The Hague's too dangerous—they are arresting people everywhere, and hauling them off. I'm waiting for the train to Amsterdam, to see if some friends of mine can put me up for a while."

It was ridiculous: we were each going to the place from which the other was fleeing. My raised apprehension at danger ahead put a quick end to the self-congratulatory mood I'd been in. Still, there wasn't much I could do but continue with my plan. I told my fellow fugitive about the trolley car, and to be careful in the streets of Amsterdam. Then we fell silent, for the soldiers and their quarry had entered the platform. I prayed that none of the soldiers would need to pee. After a while a train arrived, and they disappeared.

A couple of hours later I was in The Hague, where, by chance, I spotted my aunt in the streetcar to her apartment. I thought she winced slightly when I told her, sotto voce, that I meant to hide out for a while in her place. But, spontaneous as always, she quickly agreed it was a good idea. My aunt was not the sort to turn you down and avoid risk, and a year later that quality got her into serious trouble. Someone reported to the authorities that my aunt was hiding property of Jewish acquaintances who had been deported, and for her pains she was locked up in the notorious "Oranje Hotel," a temporary prison in Scheveningen, sea-side suburb of The Hague. It was months before Prul got out by charming the life out of the prison chief.

I let my aunt walk ahead of me, so as not to draw the attention of the neighbors by arriving together at her place. For the next couple of days I didn't get out. Surrounded by so much gorgeous and solicitous womanhood, I felt like the cock in the barn. But after I had had time to reflect I decided it was irresponsible of me to stay under my aunt's roof. With regret I left to brave the outside world. Things had calmed somewhat, and the train trip to Eindhoven was uneventful. From the station I gave Sylvia a call to let her know where I was.

"What are you going to do?" she asked, concern in her voice.

"I think I'll see about that farm again," I told her.

"Don't move," she said immediately, "I'll be right over," and hung up. I waited in a nearby cafe looking out on the triangular station square. Dreary under a constant drizzle, it looked more provincial than ever. Within the hour Sylvia arrived on her bicycle. I helped her out of her drenched raincoat and she shook the rain out of her hair. Her lips were cold but steady, and my heart jumped for joy and love. We sat down and ordered coffee. Sylvia was all business.

"You should hide upstairs in my house," she said. "It's out in the forest, no one will know, and no one will think of looking for you there." Right then I had a flash of heaven. Doing my duty to resist a mortal enemy by locking myself up at Sylvia's—was there a better way to satisfy soul and body in one single act?

A cloud moved across Paradise: Sylvia had a husband!

"Yes, but what about Ed?" I asked. With an impatient gesture she dismissed the problem. "I'll take care of that," she said, "He may not be too happy about it, but he'll go along, don't worry." She saw I was still hesitating. "He is gone much of the time, anyway," she added, misreading the reason for my reticence. But my fast-racing heart was miles ahead of my scruples. I concurred.

"Okay," she said, "that's decided. Now you take my bike and go out there by the back road. I'll take the bus to tell your parents—it's too dangerous to phone them. Then I'll take your bike to go back home." She had thought it all out . . . nothing was going to stand in her way. All I could do was enjoy being swept up in her energy.

And so I came to spend six weeks in heaven. Sylvia's husband, as she had said, went along, and with more generosity than I had the right to expect. The one condition was that I must never, but never, come down to the ground floor of the house, where I might be seen by neighbors or passers-by. What did I care, as long as Sylvia could come up?

I settled down in their small guest room beneath the slanting roof (living under a roof was something I was beginning to get used to). My days started when her husband left for the office and she entered the room dressed in her bathrobe, carrying my breakfast on a tray. We drank our morning coffee together and made voracious love. Each day I marveled when her robe came off. I also read a lot, borrowing from their excellent library, but often I put the book down just to listen to Sylvia busying herself downstairs, while the sun streamed in through the windows and Mozart streamed in from the radio. I would close my eyes and wonder what had made me deserve such delights. Inevitably, we had some close calls. Once, her husband had forgotten something in the morning and we heard him enter the garage shortly after he had left. Alert as a cat, Sylvia moved quickly, efficiently, while arranging her hair, to meet him smilingly at the foot of the stairs by the time he opened the kitchen door. I was full of admiration. And, each day, full of guilt, too, for accepting her husband's hospitality in the guest room and his wife in bed. But Sylvia brushed aside such thoughts, saying she was as free as she let him be. Yet, she would have had little in common with the latter-day women's libbers, not even her sense of freedom, for hers was not claimed in rebellion, but assumed to be hers as a birthright.

Step by step Sylvia introduced me into the art of making love. It took great patience on her part. For a long time my participation did not rise much above the level of greed, without much awareness of a male's role in the sexual play. But she made me discover what it was to feel joy in the other's joy. For both of us my days of hiding were a time of immersion in the unhurried happiness of unconditional love.

As the old Norse gods knew, heaven carries the seeds of its own end. I began to think of life outside again, which was passing me by. I should get out and do something—perhaps contact my father's old Navy friend, who, at our house one evening, had given me to understand I could "do things" for him sometime, if I wanted to. The word "resistance" was never spoken, but I supposed that was what he meant. I remembered that intense man in Amsterdam one night, and felt somewhat ashamed of my soft living. Slowly, the decision grew until it forced itself upon me: I would re-enter the world.

15

Re-entering the world was one thing, but to move around in it with none of the papers bona-fide students were required to carry at that time, except an ID-card that clearly showed tampering, was quite another. Somehow, I must at least get a new card. True, I had used the altered one successfully once, but that was just to get food ration tickets, which didn't involve the police or the SS. If I was going to get caught for not carrying any other documents, better with an unaltered ID, which would probably cause me to be sent to a German factory, than with the one I had, which could earn me a trip to concentration camp—Vught or Amersfoort in Holland, or worse, Buchenwald in Germany. I resolved on a plan: to take a deep breath and take the train to Amsterdam without coat or jacket, and there go directly to the police to claim my jacket had been stolen with my card in it, in the hope they would give me a new one without asking too many questions. From there, I would see if Kees, or those who were working with him, had perfected their forgery technique.

I told Sylvia of my decision. Did a momentary cloud move across her face? Was she disappointed in me, or afraid for me, or did she think my plans were hare-brained? But she was not one to stand in the way, and told me only to be careful. Two days later I was back in Amsterdam, where my scheme worked like a charm. At the police station in the Warmoesstraat near the Central Station, I filled in an application and was sent to a nearby photographer to have passport pictures taken. I felt relief when they handed me my new card, even if it did show 1923 as my year of birth, and pretty clever, too, now that all had gone well. I phoned Kees, and we got together later in the day.

"That was not such a smart move," he said. "It draws attention to you at the police." A little crestfallen I told him I had been edgy about walking around with my altered ID. Kees nodded in apparent sympathy with my worry.

"Anyway," he went on, "it's a good thing you went to that particular precinct. The sergeant in charge there is working for us. He has probably torn up your application by now."

"So where do I go from here?" I asked. "Should I have my new one altered, too, and hope for a better job this time around?" Kees grinned. "Ah," he said, "we've improved things a lot since then. We now have our own cards printed, and we fill them in and sign them ourselves."

He took one from a stack of brand-new blanks. With astonishing flourish he wrote several times a convincing facsimile of the police chief's signature on a scrap of paper, and then, without hesitation, at the bottom of the card. He certified it with a rubber stamp. In full admiration I compared it with my own card. They seemed identical.

"And that's not all," said Kees. "we've faked them all—all the papers you need. So we don't even have to change the year on your new ID-card." He took two other forged documents and signed General Rauter's name on one, and that of Professor Deelman, that year's Rector Magnificus, on another. Soon I had the whole panoply of papers a twenty year-old student was required to carry to be "legal." They all looked perfect to me. Free again!

With that, I finally made the delayed move to my new apartment. It was not without nostalgia that I said goodbye to the old one. I had felt content there, high up, it had felt like home. I imagined the last wisp of Sylvia's perfume on the pillow and remembered the nights she had slept there, pressed against me on the narrow fold-out bed.

There was no immediate need for my presence in Amsterdam, so I returned to Eindhoven to carry out the second part of my plan, to offer my services to Mr. Elkerbout, my father's old Navy friend. I also wanted to spend a little time with my family, of which I had not seen much lately. My father's health worried me. Our family doctor's lightning visits to minister to his grand mal seizures were becoming more frequent, and those attacks were beginning to affect his memory. During evening walks around the block he would sometimes tell me the same story three times over. Vaguely, he seemed to sense something was wrong and felt embarrassed by it. I wanted to protect him somehow. He was such a fine man, as straight in character as he was in posture, and he had been such a good father—a model for us in his integrity, stern at times (too much so on a few occasions), but not distant from his children, for whom he carried a deep affection.

In the train home I thought of the full-sized children's house he had built with his own hands in the back yard of our house when Jack and I were still very little and our mother was still alive. I thought of the many kites we had made together later on, and of the times he had dressed up as Saint Nicholas on the fifth of December, totally convincing us (or at least me) that we were really face to face with the holy man who, in the Dutch tradition, arrives from Spain once a year on his white horse, accompanied by his Moorish servant "Black Peter", to distribute presents to the good children and (oh horror!) take the bad ones back to Spain with him for a year in a burlap sack. And Dutch kids knew all about Spain, the country of the bad Duke of Alva against whom the good Prince of Orange had taken up arms in defense of his poor people! I have no trouble at all recalling my feelings when, six years old, I was seated on the saint's lap and, in response to his inquiry, heard my mother say I had not been a good boy that year. Black Peter bent over to pick up his sack and opened it up. I recoiled—and then a miracle occurred. As Francis of Assissi could suddenly understand the language of the birds, I discovered to my amazement that I could understand Spanish. For Black Peter, dropping the sack and holding on to his pants, spoke the following words in his native language, as clear as a bell: "O Jesos, my suspendros are loosos!" In the adult commotion and stifled laughter that followed, the bad kid was forgotten and slipped off the saint's knees to make himself scarce. Today, we would think of that as a cruel joke, but we felt safe enough with our parents for the terror to be no more than a passing thing, and in later years, when we could laugh about it ourselves, we were glad they had had more time for us than was perhaps customary in those years.

What would happen to him now? Would his health, his mind, continue to deteriorate? He was grateful for the competent and ceaseless care my stepmother provided for him and his family. There was no question of their mutual loyalty and affection, but I rebelled for him at his too great a dependence on her, and sensed he felt at times diminished by the brusque streak in her character, which he did not know how to oppose or deflect.

"I know sex can be a problem for a young man your age," my father had said once when he visited me during my first year in Amsterdam. It was his only reference ever to that subject. "I want you to know you can confide in me whenever you feel the need." I should have hugged him then, since there wasn't much I could say. Why hadn't I? Why had we hugged so little? Victorian mores did not leave room for much of that, and if anyone was Victorian in mind and habit, it was my father. What would he have thought if I had told him that my sexual needs were fulfilled by the wife of one of his friends?

16

Mr. Elkerbout was a square-set man with a determined jaw, which made him look much more believable as a former military man than my father, whose only vestige of that part of his life was a ram-rod back. It was he and another ex-naval officer, Mr. van den Bosch, my father had always held up as examples of the benefit of a Navy career for a young man—although the benefit seemed to lie not so much in the career itself (which, after all, the three of them had quit), as in the preparation for it and in the fact that you belonged forever after to a sort of national network of ex-naval officers who helped each other find employment elsewhere. Mr. van den Bosch had been instrumental in getting my father his job at Philips as Assistant Director, later Director, of what was then known as the "Visitor's Bureau", and would now be part of the company's PR branch. And I believe Mr. Elkerbout came later because of the two of them.

I called him in the evening of my return home, and he told me to come right over. Over a glass of aged Dutch gin, the drink only Dutchmen, and specifically Dutch men, claim to like, he told me enough to make me understand he must be one of the leaders of the resistance in the town of Eindhoven and its gigantic employer, Philips inc. Later I found out he was, in fact, the leader.

I suppose his confidence in me was founded on the fact that I was my father's son—other than that we didn't know each other all that well. If he had gone by the reputation my brother Jack and I had acquired in our mid-teens, he might not have told me anything, for both of us were then infatuated with the Dutch Nazi party. The party, in those days, held its mammoth annual reunion in a field near the farm where Jack and I spent part of our summers. The simple-minded conviviality of the crowds had taken us in, and we had been terribly excited by the blaring martial music that came in over the loudspeakers, by the over-towering swastika banners and the pompous speeches (the anti-semitic tone of those speeches apparently passed by me completely—at least, they never struck me as incongruous with my friendship for several Jewish classmates). The legacy of those earlier pro-Nazi years still clung to me in the first years under occupation—enough, at least, for one former classmate to eye me suspiciously and ask me if I could now be trusted as a "good Dutchman."

Elkerbout, in any case, trusted me. He explained that Allied intelligence needed a map of the city of Eindhoven and its surroundings, showing all German military installations. If a decision were made in London to bomb Eindhoven, specifically the Philips factories (which, inevitably, were now working for the Reich), or when an Allied invasion was in progress, such a map would be vital in the planning and execution of the operation. It was the Dutch Navy, or perhaps the Queen in exile, that spoke to me when Mr. Elkerbout looked me square in the eye.

"Are you willing to do it? I don't need to tell you it's dangerous business."

Dimly, I must have understood that getting caught would mean the firing squad, but that never surfaced as a concrete thought. It was not with courage, therefore, that I agreed to take on the job. The notion of hearing a shouted "Halt!" and looking down a gun barrel, simply lay outside the realm not only of my experience, but my imagination. I can only recall a feeling of excitement, as if I were on the front line of the war, and of wonder that my map would end up, by some circuitous route involving real spies, on the desk of the pipe-smoking chief of British military intelligence in London.

Mr. Elkerbout handed me a large folded plan of Eindhoven and its outskirts, told me to keep my eyes open, and wished me Godspeed. For the next two weeks or so I bicycled up and down the streets of the city. I had made a Legend in one corner of the map for all the various types of military installations: ammunitions dumps, truck garages, soldiers' barracks, concrete bunkers, anti-aircraft guns. Whenever I came upon one of those, I stopped, took the map out of my briefcase, unfolded it, spotted the location, and placed the appropriate symbol on it—not infrequently in direct view of a German guard. I was simply too dumb to be scared. Had I looked afraid, I would no doubt have been arrested on the first day.

When I felt fairly sure I had plotted most of what might interest an intelligence officer, I took the map back to Mr. Elkerbout. He looked satisfied and thanked me, but otherwise wasted no time on compliments. It was the last time I would see him. One morning, the Gestapo came for him at his house, unfortunately while his wife was absent. The maid said he had just left and where he could be found at work. In her terror she did not think of phoning his office, and by the time he arrived there they were waiting for him. It was he, not I, who got the firing squad.

One Sunday morning Eindhoven was bombed. I was back in Amsterdam, where Jack reached me by phone, his voice still shaking with agitation. He had seen the British bombers fly in almost at ground level, skirting trees and rooftops. One of them had plunged headlong into the main Philips building in the center of town. The bombs fell mostly on a city block, and none on German military installations. I thought that, perhaps, my map had not been consulted. I hoped not, in any case, for I would have hated to be even in a small way responsible for that ineffectual attack, in which the only building totally destroyed was the one that housed a splendid series of showrooms demonstrating Philips's manifold manufacturing processes—rooms, to the design and construction of which my father had devoted much of his energy and pride over ten years of his life. Because the building was closed on Sundays, no one was hurt, but my father suffered a shock from which he never quite recovered. It seemed to diminish his life in his own eyes.

17

Compiling that map had given me a taste for resistance work, and now I wanted to do something useful in Amsterdam, too, that fall of 1943 . . . useful beyond taking the course in Petroleum Geology which Walter and I had talked one of the junior professors into giving at his home for just the two of us. I didn't have to talk Kees into letting me do more and more work for him. It had not been his original game plan to have me actively participate (I was just supposed to be the "straight" front man and run no other hazard), but I was around, and it was simply convenient to give me jobs to do. Kees, who, for underground purposes, bore the last name of "de Beer", was a hilarious sort of person to share an apartment with. One peculiarity of his was that he could see absolutely no point in even a dash of occasional housekeeping, and he could argue his view convincingly.

"I see absolutely no point in it," he would say.

Neither Boetie (who went by the name of "de Wit"), nor I, was maniacal on the subject, but every month or so the mess became so great that it motivated us into cleaning the place up a little. Kees could only be shamed into joining us after we had started, though he then threw himself into it with abandon. Once only was he forced to recognize the utility of sweeping the floor. The broom I had been poking under my bed had met with resistance and had drawn forth an enormous ball of dust, inside of which I found a hat he had been looking for for months.

"Well, I'll be damned!" he exclaimed, for once at a loss for eloquence.

He was glad to have the hat back, for it belonged to his father, and he had been rather fond of wearing it around the apartment. As we had no vacuum cleaner, Boetie had devised a system for dusting furniture more efficient, he thought, than moving the dust from tables and chairs onto the floor, from the floor into a dustpan, and from there at last into a garbage pail. He would attach a rope to whatever furniture had to be cleaned and with my help lower it over the railing of the balcony. One held onto the rope, the other swept the dust off with a long broom. Our meticulous landlord never caught us in that act, to which his objection would have been firm, though doubtless polite.

Because we usually didn't go to bed until the early morning hours, we got up late, especially Kees, who was like a giant sloth until noon. For the rest of the day we each went our own way, but at times we ate dinner together at our place. Thanks to our mysterious source of money, we had those dinners brought up by one of the "meals-on-wheels" services that were common in Amsterdam at the time, the wheels, of course, being those of bicycles. Most of those enterprises were run by Chinese; toward evening you could see them pedaling through town, carrying a stack of fitted metal dishes held in a metal frame. We ate well, though at the age we were, never enough. Somehow, one's daily ration of calories had to be supplemented through the black market, and most loyal subjects of the Queen had developed ways to do so. At home, my mother was a wizard in providing food for her family—butter, cheese, eggs, flour, bacon, which she went at least once a week on her bicycle to buy at stiff prices at a farm near Eindhoven—prices no doubt bargained down by her.

The bigger the town, of course, the longer the supply line from the countryside. In cities like Amsterdam you generally had to find a local black market middleman, which upped the prices still more. Admittedly, they operated in the danger zone, and in a way deserved to get rich quick. But, in spite of the fact that almost everyone bought from them, they were generally placed on a social rung little above that of thieves. Two or three times, Boetie in spite of the risk, brought home a sackful of sugar beets, a common crop in Holland long before the war, and now put to direct use in Dutch kitchens, instead of via the detour of commercial sugar. (Toward the end of the war they, too, became hard to get, and city dwellers took to eating tulip bulbs—if they could find even those). The fresh soil on Boetie's beets showed they had come directly from the farm, but Boetie wouldn't tell. Not telling (and not asking) had become second nature. We stored them in a clothes closet, soil and all.

We had a patented way of dealing with sugar beets. The process would take most of a night. After washing the earth off them, we would put them one-by-one through a hand-operated meat grinder. The resulting pulp was then spooned into a very big, deep pot, which (this was Kees' secret) was placed directly on the gas stove, before the addition of any water. It gave a slight burn to the pulp and a delicious caramel taste to the final product, although at the price of a messy kitchen and sticky floors. For a heavy smoke would soon rise out of the pot descend to the floor and, escaping beneath the kitchen door, spread throughout the apartment, where it would slowly curl up across the furniture to mix with the dust and finally settle into a gummy layer of burned beetsoil. Even the big broom had a hard time cleaning that off. By now, it was time to add water, which would produce great sizzling and billowing dark clouds. The flame was then reduced to allow a slow simmer for several hours. When the liquid was judged thick enough, the time had come to separate it from the pulp. This was done by pouring it through a bed-sheet (pace once more, oh unknowing landlord) and into a bucket, with a final wringing of the sheet to squeeze out the last of the beet juice. The bucket was then put back on the stove until the juice had thickened into a heavy black syrup. We used it on bread, pancakes, and "poffertjes", the little fritters that are to this day the glory of Low Countries cuisine. Fortunately, it took only a single night to produce enough syrup for a month or more.

Many evenings were spent playing cards, or in lively discussions over glasses of Dutch gin, which, though almost unavailable to most citizens, we kept receiving in steady quantity in its earth-ware bottles by some underground trail or other. I never did get to like it, but it was not thought manly of a student to refuse drinking it. Not yet did I know that alcohol was like poison to my brain, scarred as it was after my hockey ball accident five years earlier. We also smoked a great many cigarettes; real tobacco ones could not be had for love or money, but imitation cigarettes were still sold freely, made of acorns, oak leaves or weeds of some sort, all equally unfit to smoke.

Enveloped in dense blue fog we got to know the Marquis de Sade, from whose works Kees, who kept them at his bedside, gave nightly readings for the edification of us all. At eleven in the evening we bent over our illegal radio to decipher the BBC news, which came in heavily jammed. Possession of a radio had been made severely punishable; it could cost you a year in Vught. But most people knew of some place where one was hidden. We had concealed ours beneath the seat of an easy chair. Listening to the BBC was an essential antidote to the incessant Nazi claims of glorious military victories in Russia, in Africa, in the air and on the high sea. They could become depressing even if you didn't believe a word of them.

Most of all, we would work till all hours to get counterfeit documents ready for distribution, along with stacks of the underground newspaper "Het Parool." Kees, after practicing a little, signed the documents. Boetie and I put the appropriate stamp on them ... of the police, the University of Amsterdam, the city's German "Ortskommandatur", the Gestapo; the SS military command, the collaborationist government in The Hague. They were then packed into suitcases for temporary storage or distribution to addresses in various cities.

In my assumed name of "Schipper" we had rented two other apartments in town, one used mostly as a depot, the other for a girl to live in who worked with us. Quite a few female students worked for the resistance, but, though some might rouse fantasies in my head, I knew they were not for touching: relationships were purposely kept as vague and distant as possible. Actually, that suited fine with both the loyalty I owed Sylvia and my cursed reticence with girls. Usually I didn't even know their names, even when I went on trips with them by train.

The trips were either to deliver packages of forged papers to addresses in Utrecht or The Hague, or pick up a couple of large suitcases filled with copies of the latest issue of "Het Parool," and heavy as lead. Only I was supposed to know the addresses, so the girl would stay behind in the train station. But it was her job to take the baggage through the station, where control was frequent and danger lurked. Females, it was thought, were less likely to be stopped by the police or SS than males. I always felt slightly embarrassed to let girls take two loaded suitcases out of my hands and past watchful eyes, for I had been taught they were the weaker sex to which courtesy was due, and protection. But these always seemed to be cool as cucumbers, able to carry their load with pretended ease. In the train we sat apart, at some distance from our baggage.

On other journeys I acted simply as a courier, carrying an envelope of some kind to a particular address, or to someone who, at an exact given hour, would stand on a certain bridge, with a dark blue hat on his head, a newspaper in his right hand and a cigarette in his left, who would ask me for a light and to whom I would say something like: "It is five to twelve on my watch—is it running slow?" And he would reply: "No, that's correct", which was the signal for me to hand over the envelope.

One trip to Utrecht turned into a major test of both my steel and the verisimilitude of my phony papers. The train was supposed to be an express, but it suddenly stopped at the small town of Breukelen, and I knew that spelled trouble. The station was swarming with SS-men. Right in front of two of them my window came to a halt, and with that nearly my heart. They made a beeline for me, knowing most young men were supposed to be working in Germany unless they possessed every single one of the many cards and certificates that permitted their presence in Holland. Buchenwald, here I come, I thought.

"Papiere!" in the usual shout to install fear!

They were all in a bulky wallet in the inside pocket of my coat, the same pocket that held the letter I was supposed to deliver. Admittedly, that wasn't very smart. The guilty letter seemed to burn in my pocket and cry out loud "Search me! Search me!" Rather than fiddling with it, I took it out together with the wallet, and put both next to me on the bench.

"Schnell!", another shout.

I handed several of the documents over. The two SS-men studied them with great care, held them up against the sun, compared the signatures with copies of the true ones they had.

"Noch!", one of them ordered. They wanted them all, and scrutinized each with the same attention. Sweat trickled down the inside of my collar. I knew my face had to maintain the right expression, neither too nonchalant, nor too scared, but showing mild concern and eagerness to be helpful. The incriminating letter glared up from the seat. How could they not ask? Hours went by.

"Gut"-and they went on.

"Not yet, not yet," said my pounding heart. "Don't stuff the letter back in, don't show relief yet—they might still look back." But they went on, and I allowed myself to collapse into the corner of my bench, whispering gratefully: "Well done, Kees!"

The train started up again. It had been a close call. In Utrecht the hot letter was delivered. What was in it?, I wondered on the way back. I would never know. Couriers were not meant to.

18

In December Jack came back from Germany, on a two-week furlough from his job in the former Zeppelin factories in Friedrichshafen. I went to see him in Eindhoven. He was holding his baby son, named after me, and he looked happy to be back in his little family. They were his source of strength. Our parents had disapproved of his marriage, because they felt sure it would interfere with the international career with Philips they thought he was destined for once the war was over. They had been dumb enough to tell him his wife, Brigette, was not welcome in the parental home, although he, of course, was. Naturally, that had angered Jack, and he swore he would come with her or not at all. So began a period of years of silence between them. When, by chance, my father would run into Jack at work, they pretended not to see each other. That conspiracy hurt us all, but doubtless did the most harm to my father, that fundamentally good man, as caring as he was stubborn.

Jack told me about his work in Germany. I listened, conscious once again, of the bond between us. He had been a great older brother to me, always a step or two ahead of me, but always ready to reach back and help me along. Memories started flooding back. Summer, when we were very young . . .

"Hey Jack, where are you?" "I'm here!" His shout came from somewhere between the bull rushes in the ditch below the dike. Our housemaid had taken us to her home for two weeks, way up north in the province of Groningen, in a farm so near-medieval that the farmer's sons, with their big, meaty hands, still threshed the wheat with a flail. We liked to climb up the dike and sit by the canal, a bull rush stalk in our mouths to pretend we were smoking cigars, watching the big boats being poled forward by a man who walked back and forth the length of the deck, while a second one on the dike strained against a rope over his shoulder to pull, or led a horse that did the pulling. At night we slept in a bed closet, centuries old, of which we could close the doors to be in a universe of our own. Back home in the nearby pine forest, we played out the adventures of the Apache chief Winnetou and the seasoned cowboy Old Shatterhand known to every Dutch boy from the novels by Karl May. Golden days they were, until I threw a wooden tomahawk at Jack that hit him in the scalp, and he ran home, wailing his head off, followed by a Winnetou in holy fear of the blood he had spilled and his parents' wrath. In later years the two of us would crawl off together through the bushes behind our back yard to play furious tennis on a dilapidated clay court, with worn-out rackets and old balls, without much style, but rock-hard, training each other until, in the annual tournament, we could beat our friends, the sons of richer parents who belonged to the Philips tennis club and had expensive lessons. Together, Jack and I had biked, summer after summer in the mid-thirties, from Eindhoven to the vacation farm near Barneveld my mother had picked out for us from "People and Fatherland", the pro-Nazi newspaper. It was a paradise for kids, but 120 kilometers away, long kilometers on a bicycle, especially against a north wind. Once, it took us over eleven hours, and toward late afternoon I was so exhausted that I sat down beside the road and cried, though I had recently turned twelve. Jack was ahead of me, battling the wind, but looked back and turned around, put his arm across my shoulders and said we could rest for a while, and then we'd spend our one dime each on a fresh roll from the bakery in the next town, Zaltbommel, our annual rest stop.

Most of all, I admired Jack for his great popularity with girls. At the vacation farm, two years in a row, he mixed it up with a girl four years his senior, Willy van der Wal, a name forever etched in my memory. Willy was a hot little number from Amsterdam, a member of the Nazi youth movement, who could wrap any young man around her little finger, and me twice. Her merest touch could leave me shaking. We would take evening walks, the three of us, and then Jack and Willy would go into a clinch in the haystack, while, raging with envy and desire, I pretended nonchalance. One stormy day the two of them were rolling around on the floor of the tent Jack and I had pitched in the meadow. Willy sat up, stretched to show off her heavenly breasts, and said:

"Oh, I'd just love some chocolate now." Then I knew my time had come, and, before Jack had a chance to volunteer, "I'll get some," I said, and through a diluvian downpour pedalled half an hour to the nearest village, and half an hour back. I must have looked as if I'd taken a long shower with my clothes on. "Here," I said, holding out my bar of Côte d'Or, shivering from cold and anticipation, but sure of my reward. Willy looked puzzled; her hair was all tousled. Then she laughed her silvery laugh and knifed me through the heart.

"You silly kid," she said, "you mean you went out in that weather just for some chocolate." No, Willy, no! Not just for some chocolate! What was it Jack had that I didn't? But no jealousy over girls could tarnish our brotherhood.

And when we started to drift apart in our interests, his in jazz, friends and the stage, mine in chess, books and classical music, that affection remained.

"At night," I heard Jack say, talking about Friedrichshafen, "you can see the houses light up across the lake in Switzerland."

"Can't you swim across some dark night? I asked. "How far is it?"

"About ten kilometers, I figured," he said, "not much more. I often thought of it?" It was clear he didn't want to go back.

"Stay here," I said impulsively, "don't go back to work for those bastards. I'll get you all the papers you need to be legal."

He hesitated. "I signed an oath back there, before they would let me go on furlough. I swore I would return in two weeks. And they told me all future vacations would be cancelled for the others if I didn't."

Earlier that year a wiry, red-headed man in Amsterdam had given me a profound lesson in how to deal with oaths and threats. I tried to describe what had happened that evening. "They are the enemy," I argued, "and with an enemy like that you can't afford to be noble. The others can escape to Switzerland, if they want." I showed Jack the perfection of my own fake documents and told him how they had fooled the SS in Breukelen. He was impressed.

"How soon could you get them for me if I stayed?" he asked. I said it might take two weeks, three at most. Brigitte took over. She was nervous, but didn't want to see her man leave again any more than he wanted to go back.

"Listen, Jack," she said, "we can go to my parents' house in Zeeland. You could hide there till you get the papers."

Jack took the plunge. I knew it was a courageous decision, and a hard one to come to: courageous because of the risk he was accepting, and hard because putting his fellow workers in Friedrichshafen in possible jeopardy conflicted with the sense of fair play our father had instilled in us. Only, this was not play, I said.

I spent Christmas with my family and went back north the next day without an inkling that Jack was going to be left high and dry to fend for himself without papers.

19

Life under occupation was becoming more and more grim. On the Dutch side, anger and disdain were barely concealed. Expressing a popular mood with wry humor had always been a speciality of Amsterdam streetcar conductors, but now that took some guts. One day a German officer standing next to me produced a scrap of paper with the name of a street on it. "Javastrasse," he said, "Javastrasse, wo ist denn das?" It was one of the stops along the route. The conductor, clipping away at tickets, came back without missing a click. "No idea," he said flatly. "Ask the Japanese consul." Laughter isolated the German from the rest of us. Small victories like that were essential for morale.

To the hatred and contempt that surrounded them, the Germans and the Dutch Nazis reacted more and more often with knee-jerk violence. On one of my missions to the Hague I saw a young man who lost control of his bicycle and slipped in front of an army vehicle. He was more dazed than hurt, but then the car stopped, two uniformed men jumped out, grabbed the victim, beat him senseless, dropped him, kicked him in the groin, and finally drove off. It had all happened so fast that the shock and rage didn't sink into me until the car was out of sight, which was just as well. Several bystanders took care of the bleeding man; I was myself too shaken to be any good to him.

Acts of sabotage by the resistance and assassinations of Nazis known as particularly vile were becoming common. Threatening retaliation, the Germans had taken a number of well-known citizens hostage. Whenever a killing occurred, they would execute in reprisal ten times as many of the hostages, or among political prisoners held in the prisons and concentration camps, and the executions would be widely reported in the newspapers and on the radio. Sometimes, they would stop traffic in a city and force people to watch victims being marched over, lined up against a wall, and shot. Another tactic was to send death squads out at night to ring the doorbells of the homes of prominent people and shoot them on the doorstep. One of those was my aunt Clara's ex-husband in The Hague. He was left bleeding to death in front of his teen-age daughter, my talented little niece Liselot.

Gradually, too, the yellow Stars of David, which had been a familiar sight for some time on the clothes of Jewish citizens, began to disappear from the streets. Jews were transported in large numbers to the concentration camp near Vught, and from there in cattle cars to an unknown, but dreaded, destiny in Germany, the full horror of which was scented by only a few of the most clear-headed ones. Organizing the deportations was a massive task, for, as defined by Nazi doctrine, Jews made up a considerable portion of the population. To be classified as a "Jude" it was enough for a single one of your great-grandparents to have been a "full-blooded" Jew. Lists of those eligible for deportation were drawn up in part by the Jewish Council, a group of eminent Amsterdam Jews, who seemed to believe in all sincerity that they could slow down the flood by cooperating, while waiting for an invasion from England. In the end, of course, they too went.

Most Jewish families obeyed the long-awaited summons when it came and, leaving everything behind, all they owned, all that had been dear to them for years or generations, all their friends, reported to their designated transport center, hoping against all evidence that things would turn out not as bad as the worst of the whispers had it. Others had already gone into hiding, most often not in the countryside, but in the cities they were familiar with. So Anne Frank and her family, by whose hide-out I must have passed any number of times. A Jewish family was sheltered across the street from our house in Eindhoven by a simple carpenter and his wife. We often bought things in their shop without ever suspecting that Jews were hiding two floors up. After the war, a girl my sister Marjolijn's age greeted her saying: "You don't know me, but I know you very well." For years she had watched us, free as we were to move about, from her little attic window. They were among the lucky ones: never mentioned, never discovered by accident, never betrayed.

For, among the many dreary aspects of life under occupation, there was the dreariest, despicable act of betrayal—denouncement not just by Nazi collaborators, but by run-of-the-mill citizens, whether for money or to settle an old score, or out of ingrained anti-semitism, or perhaps no more than pious obedience to no matter how unlawful and barbaric a government. The road was open also for small, sadistic acts of intimidation. For some reason, or no reason at all, the Geology Institute was known as a hotbed of Nazi sympathizers, among them one of the doorkeepers, a big, meaty man. One day, he tried to pester Ab Cohen, a Jewish graduate student, by blocking his way on the stairs. He had picked on the wrong man, for Ab was strong, too, and endowed with both guts and a short fuse. He knocked his would-be tormentor down the staircase, all the way across the hall, and into a corner of the doorkeeper's lodge.

After that, he left, and never came back. They got him later, though, and sent him off to one of the extermination camps in Poland.

A few of the Jews took a third option: to go on with life, hoping for the best and, above all, refusing to wear the yellow star or have "Jew" stamped on their ID-cards—death marks, both, sooner or later, as they were far-sighted enough to know. If they did not appear in Synagogue records, were not betrayed by Nazi collaborators or anti-semites, nor even spoken of as Jews by their neighbors and colleagues, they stood a chance. It was not necessarily easy for the police, even if they were zealous in carrying out orders, to find the records proving they fell within the fatal limits. Those with names often carried by Jews might have to change identity and, if they could, move into a new neighborhood. They, too, needed forged documents and food coupons.

One such person was Meck, the girl friend of my friend Victor (the one who, in more carefree days, had stuffed my pockets full of pickles). The two made, to say the least, an unconventional couple; he wore a beard, and they lived together unmarried, neither of which was exactly a traditional thing to do at the time. She was a good-looking, bright, and spunky woman, determined to be in charge of her own fate as long as she could. For a long time all went well, but then she was spotted by a disgruntled former maid in her family home at Haarlem, who denounced her to the authorities. A policeman came to arrest her. But she was lucky, for he was a good cop. Waiting for the train in which he was to take her back to Amsterdam, he said he had to go to the men's room—an open invitation for her to scram, which she did. After that, she knew she had to hide or leave. And so, one dark night she and Victor wandered across the heavily guarded border into Belgium, where they obtained false Belgian identity cards. Next, they managed to get into France, but there they were promptly arrested and jailed. Belgians were not popular in France at the time; they were, somewhat unjustly, thought not to have fought hard enough against the German Army in 1940. Once Meck and Victor proved their papers were forged, they were released with a hearty clap on the back. On they went towards Switzerland—but they were caught during a round-up in Belfort the day before they were to cross the border. Meck ended up in the infamous deportation camp at Drancy, near Paris, from where trainloads of Jews were sent regularly to Auschwitz and other extermination camps. But Meck, spunky as ever, kept protesting she was not Jewish and, amazingly, they finally released her. She went to Paris, where she heard the German Navy needed multi-lingual secretaries. Explaining she needed not only a job, but an I.D. card, an advance on her wages, and food ration coupons, she obtained all of them, left, and never came back. She managed to hide out in the city until it fell to the troops of General Leclerc.

The fates of nearly all European Jews had been dramatic in one way or another, and in most cases full of horror. It was as if the gods themselves had turned their eyes away from them. Their individual destinies were determined by all possible combinations of courage, smarts and luck (or the lack thereof), and in some cases aid from fellow-citizens willing to put everything on the line—their homes, their families, their lives. But when, after the war, I heard Meck's story, it seemed to me almost epic in nature. She had rebelled against her fate, had defied the gods, unblinking in the face of high danger, with a level head that refused the false hopes so many had embraced in desperation.

20

The night of December 26, we—Boetie, Kees and I worked long hours getting a suitcase full of counterfeit documents ready to be taken to the girl who lived in one of the other apartments in town. Her place was more or less a center of distribution. We were all three in high spirits, partly because we were drinking too much Dutch gin. Kees claimed it loosened him up the better to imitate signatures. When we were done, there was a long reading out of de Sade. Sipping gin, smoking oak leaf cigarettes, and looking philosophical, we followed the Marquis in his tortuous justifications of the abject treatment inflicted on the virtuous Justine. Idly, I thought of the girl to whom I was going to deliver the suitcase the next morning. But I knew I wasn't even a closet de Sade. It must have been close to three in the morning before we went to bed.

I woke up at eight, feeling no more than a featherweight of a hangover. By nine I was in the crowded streetcar, the suitcase between my legs. A small man boarded the car at a stop in the Ferdinand Bolstraat, and took a seat opposite mine. I saw the triangular insignia of the NSB in his lapel, the Dutch Nazi party. Did I imagine it that he was eyeing me? The streetcar lurched on, and my thoughts shifted to other things.

Suddenly, a humming sound in my ears, pounding, rhythmic, rhythmic, rhythmic pounding pounding pounding, hum-mum-mum, louder, LOUDER, HUM-MUM-MUM, mind swirling, small man's eyes drilling into my head—what? . . . panic! nothing . . .

The first thing to pierce my consciousness is legs. I am lying on a floor, surrounded by legs. What am I? My stomach feels ill, my brain in a daze, headache, headache. Where am I? Look up, there are uniforms. Jesus, SS! Mouths are moving. Far off someone says something, in Dutch, but incomprehensible. Why in Dutch? What happened? Then it hits me: the suitcase!!!!

THE SUITCASE! Where is it, where is it? Maybe this is a bad dream. If I could only throw up! Words come through to me now.

"He's waking up." Followed by unintelligible murmur. Now words again, the same voice.

"You got sick there for a while, didn't you, fellow?", spoken not unkindly. I begin to remember the streetcar—had I passed out? My head still in a fog, but holding on to the one thought: "Where is the suitcase?" Two men pick me up off the floor. "Sit down here." I crawl to my feet and slump onto a straight-backed chair. On the table I see my ID card and other papers.

"Bad luck for him," says another voice. Someone snickers. "Look" (to me this time), "look, we got your suitcase and we know what's in it, and we know your own papers are phony. So let's get this over with quick-like. You tell us where you got all that, and we'll let you off scot-free."

So they have it! Cold fear begins to set in. God, this is really it! What now? I had never really prepared myself for disaster, what to do if I got caught. All I know now, dimly, is that I have to gain time. I shake my head, mostly to clear it.

"He won't talk," the second voice goes on. "So take him over."

The next thing I knew was being pushed into the back of a car and made to sit between two uniformed men. As I left the building, I recognized it as the headquarters of the Dutch SS. What lousy luck, to have passed out just when the streetcar was passing in front of it! Why hadn't they carried me into a bakery shop or something? Any place but here. The face of that small man with the NSB pin floated up into my consciousness.

The car drove at high speed through the streets of Amsterdam, and I began to realize where we were going: the Girl's High School in pre-war days. It was now the headquarters of the Gestapo. Terrible things were rumored about that place.

They took me to a room on the second floor. Several Germans in civilian clothes were there, talking, smoking. One of my guards addressed the man at the table, who was obviously the boss. He explained the circumstances, opened the suitcase, and showed what counterfeit documents were in it. The chief scrutinized some of them, held them up against the light, and seemed almost appreciative of their perfection. I was scared witless. How was I going to keep it from him where I lived with Boetie and Kees? I had to hold out, for a while at least, till they knew I had not arrived where I was supposed to show up that morning. They would have to get out and hide for a while. I had to! But, like everyone else, I'd heard of the Gestapo ways to make you talk, and fast. They might start by hitting you in the stomach, hard, and, if that didn't work, start crushing your balls, for example, till you would faint, and bring you back again with a bucket of cold water. After that, there would be other methods.

The chief turned to me. He held my keys. Jesus God, of course, my keys—I hadn't even thought of those. Keys to what doors, he asked, amiably. "I can't remember" I stuttered lamely. He smiled and said they could make me remember, and I understood that "they" were the other agents behind my back. Keys to what doors, then? I stuttered again, and someone hit me from behind—not a hard blow, so far, but hard enough to make me think about the next one. And I knew I wasn't going to be very brave, I would chicken out too soon and give Boetie and Kees away. There had to be a ruse of some sort—anything to avoid a test of my courage. Would they fall for it if I told them I had amnesia?

"I can't remember anything at all," I said, without conviction. Another smile, another blow. But that one cleared my mind, and now it was suddenly calm and razor-sharp. I had passed out, then. I didn't know why yet, but if once, why not a second time? Turning up my eyeballs, with sagging knees, I let myself slide off the chair and under the table. O dear God, help me now!

"Da geht er wieder!" one of them shouted. They dragged me out from under and shook me like a rag doll. My tensed mind told my body to stay limp. Stay limp!

"Raus, nach unten," came the head agent's voice. Was it working? It seemed too much to hope. But they grabbed me like a sack of potatoes and carried me down two flights of stairs into the basement, where they shoved me into a prison cell the size of a telephone booth. I heard the lock turn, and then there was silence.

Standing there in the pitch dark, full memory came back, and I had time to think. What seemed to have happened to me was so similar to my father's affliction that I could not ignore the obvious: I must have inherited it. I thought of that hockey ball thundering into my head years ago, the brain hemorrhage and coma, and of the fact that my father was not allowed to touch alcohol. All that awful Dutch gin of the past month—of last night!

No good worrying about that now. What next? I might not have much time to think. Why had they given up so soon? Had they really fallen for my pathetic little act? Or were they expecting bigger fish to fry that afternoon and had no time to waste on me just then? But they would surely come back soon. I had already gained an hour or so, but I needed more. I would try the amnesia game first. If I caved in on that, I would turn into the simple courier who knew nothing and nobody, who merely received messages by phone and packages on street corners. They probably wouldn't swallow that line, but I might be able to string it out a for a while. Maybe another move would occur to me after that.

They came for me towards dusk. My heart was in my throat. Stay cool, stay cool! But now, where were we going? Instead of taking me to the second floor, they led me outside and pushed me into the back of a paddy wagon. For fifteen minutes we drove through the darkening streets. And then, when we came to a stop and they led me out, a stone rolled off my chest, for I recognized the prison on the Weteringschans, in the center of town. Hallelujah! They must have called it a day—and I had gained it! It was hard to believe, but I had outfoxed the Gestapo.

21

Second floor on the block, second cell from the corner. How often since have I looked at that window from across the canal, and searched for me on the inside. What was it like, that night? That person there, who carries my name and more or less looks like me, what is his connection to me now? What does he feel? Fear, bewilderment, anxiety? The blind eye of a barred window shuts out the scene. I remember it only as one remembers an old movie, in sepia colors.

I stand in a cold hall, waiting for something to happen. The prison guard is fumbling with his keys. At last he finds the right one and pushes open the door to the half-lit cell.

"Your new buddy," he says to whoever is inside, and closes the door behind me. Two turns of the lock, footsteps falling away. Two men get up off their cots, hands stretched toward me as if welcoming me to their home. Friends, at last!

They turned out to be officers in the Royal Dutch Navy called John and Fred. It struck me that they didn't say "former navy", or "ex-officers"—just officers here and now, in a navy that was real to them. A third person stirred behind them; he had stayed back on his cot.

"And this," said one of the officers, "is Dirk. He is a stool pigeon, so be careful what you say in front of him." Dirk grinned apologetically, but my embarrassment was greater than his.

The others plied me with questions, especially about news from the war front. What were the Germans claiming? Had I overheard anyone mentioning the BBC news? (That was a neat way of asking me, without incriminating me, what I'd heard on the illegal radio they assumed I possessed). After a while the pigeon understood the two were not going to let me talk about myself and make a mistake as long as he was there. He got up, knocked on the door, and was let out . . . a bungled spy job.

With the fink gone, talk loosened. I told the others that my father and grandfather had been naval officers, and that my father had written songs about the navy and about cadet school in the town of Nieuwediep.

"Well, I'll be damned!" said Fred, the younger of the two. "Of course, we had to learn them all!" "Nieuwediep, by Jacques Scholten," John said, and together they sang out the sentimental lines I had heard my father sing a thousand times in my life, a nostalgic sailor's remembrance of his old naval academy town when he was halfway across the world:

> Nieuwediep, oh home of all our dreams,
> Our distant journeys' long-awaited prize,
> Nieuwediep, we honor and esteem thee,
> Nieuwediep, oh sailor's paradise!

(I had always thought it was just like my father to have waxed sentimental about a sleepy Dutch brick village, where time had stood still for a century).

Someone pounded on the cell door.

The last of the ice was broken. I told my cell mates the story of my day, and they told their story. For several months that year they had been busy constructing and outfitting a small motorboat with which to flee to England to rejoin what was left of the Dutch Navy, and on a moonless night they had floated down the river past the Hook of Holland and out to sea, where they started the engine. They were halfway there when a wire burned out and the engine quit. Repair was impossible, and daybreak saw them being pushed back by an inexorable west wind. Frantic signals to overflying British planes produced no effect—the planes flew on home, missions accomplished. In the afternoon a German patrol boat passed by and picked them up. That was three months ago.

"What did they do to you here?" I asked, thinking about tomorrow "Nothing", they said. Others were interrogated, beaten, and eventually disappeared. Through the prisoner's pipe-tapping telephone system, and from furtive comments during exercise walks everyone pretty much knew what was going on day by day. The two of them seemed to have been forgotten . . . but they thought there was little chance the Gestapo would forget me.

"They'll probably call you down tomorrow, so get your story straight." For the moment I tried to put that out of my head. It was time for basic instruction into cell routine. First, food. It was distributed three times a day, they said, through the little trap door; but there would be no more today. I didn't mind: although I hadn't eaten all day, there had been too much excitement for me to feel hungry now.

Next important lesson: bowel movements. In one corner stood a pail with a lid on. That was the whole story. Once a day we were to carry it out to be emptied on the way to our exercise rounds. I must have winced.

"You'll be embarrassed at first." Fred had noticed. "It happens to everyone, but you soon get over it." In my mind I heard peals of laughter. It was my kid sister Lydia, who had just heard somebody fart. "Houbigant!" she would cry out, and collapse into herself. Thinking of her made me smile for the first time that day.

I had a hard time concentrating on those immediate problems. It takes a while to develop a prisoner's mentality, to realize the future is out of your hands, that decision-making is needed only for the present moment: bowel movements, how to get the largest bowl of soup, what to answer during an interrogation. My mind kept straying to the outside. Were Kees and Boetie safe? I had been carrying a bag that belonged to Kees' father, a well-known doctor, and now the thought gnawed at me that the bag might somehow be traced to him. How soon would my family find out where I was? It would do my father's health no good, worrying about my safety.

John seemed to have guessed my thoughts. "Let me tell you about our mail system," he said. It seemed that families were notified they were to send a second set of clothes to the prison; in fact, that was often the first they found out where we were. Once a week the dirty clothes were sent back to them to be laundered. My cell mates had perfected writing whole letters on cigarette paper in the tiniest miniature imaginable. The paper was folded over several times and sewn into the hems of clothes that would go out the following day. The tools were hidden in a mattress: needle, thread, pencil, razor blade, cigarette paper. In the same way they received "mail" from the outside; the first task after getting fresh clothes was to carefully finger all the hems until a slight bulge signalled the presence of a letter. "Because their own clothes were to be sent back the next day, I sat down and wrote my own first miniature letter to my family, and it was promptly sewn into their clothes. It was all strictly prohibited, of course, but it worked smoothly right under the noses of the guards.

While I was writing, the pipe telephone started going. Tap-tap, tap-tap-tap, in Morse code. "We have a newcomer." "What's his name?" "What did they get him for?", "Ask him if he knows my brother Dick, he's a chemistry student." John signalled quiet. It would be a mistake for me to say I knew him. I followed John's eyes to the little spy hole in the door. For the first time I had the eerie feeling of being watched by silent eyes.

The eyes moved on. Soon after, the lights flickered, a sign they'd go out for the night in two minutes. I climbed into my cot and started out on a mostly sleepless night. What would the morning bring?

Amazingly, the morning brought nothing, nor the afternoon. Names and cell numbers were called out from below in the cell block, doors were opened and closed, but not mine. Same thing the next day. It was a great relief, but what was going on? Didn't they realize everyone would have scrammed by now? Maybe there had even been time to empty the apartment.

On the third day the whistle blew below, on the main floor of the cell block, and I heard my name called, and the number of my cell. My cell mates wished me strength, told me to be cool and smart. The key turned in the lock.

22

I have never been able to understand that first interrogation. By the time I entered the room my heart was pounding wildly. A Gestapo man was sitting behind a desk. He did not look especially nasty, but still, I expected the worst. Above all, I must not give out any names! How great was my tolerance for pain? In peace time it's never much tested. I doubted I could be much of a hero.

But my interrogator seemed to think he could get more out of me by being fatherly than by being brutal. It was true I was ready for some fathering. Though not to talk, if I could help it. He offered me a cigarette. From spy novels I knew interrogators often start out that way: feel at ease, we're on your side, we won't harm you, just cooperate a little and we'll let you go.

"What was your job in the resistance?" he started out. "What about the stuff in that suitcase—where did it come from, where were you supposed to take it?" I said I was only a courier, got my instructions over the telephone: pick up a package here, a letter there, from someone in the street, and take it somewhere else. "Take it where?" "Different places, never the same." "How about this last time?" "I can't seem to remember any details. I'm still dizzy in my head, and everything seems vague." A goon, who had been standing behind the Gestapo man, stepped over and hit me. "You fucker, don't you know you're going to be shot for what you did? If you talk you may have a chance. We'll make you talk, anyway, you son-of-a-bitch." Spoken in Dutch. Damned traitor, your time will come some day! The other man held up his hand to stop the goon, and said no, there was no reason to think I'd be shot. Between the two, they played their game plan: killer and nice guy, not hard to figure out. Still, I needed to hang on to those words.

The agent seemed to think I was part of a resistance ring that had recently been broken. "Well," he said, "we'll find out soon enough which group you belonged to. We have ways of checking your story out—make the others talk.

Only you know if that's going to be bad for you or not. Meanwhile, I want you to think long and hard about telling us what you know." And, incredibly, with that he let me go. The goon took me away, muttering some more threats. But nothing could touch me now! Another day gained!

John and Fred had been worrying about me and were relieved to see me. That night I was called down again, and pushed into a stand-up cell with a bright overhead light. A slot opened in the door, eyes studied me: a fink, I thought, a fink who has infiltrated some part of the resistance and is checking out my face. The slot closed, the light went out. Waiting there in the pitch dark, I expected more to happen, but after a while the door opened and I was taken back to my cell.

The next day brought more surprises. They called for me early in the morning—for a second interrogation, I thought. But no, it was to see a doctor. He was a courtly gentleman, who introduced himself with a secret wink. Boetie's father! Amazing! I had never met him, but knew he was a physician. From a few guarded words (we were not alone) I gathered he knew who I was. He asked me to describe exactly what had happened in that car; I told him about my head injury and the disorder that afflicted my father, who had also had a head injury, and about Peter, my elder brother, who suffered from a brain tumor. The doctor nodded, tested my eyes and reflexes and confirmed what I was already half-sure of: the family curse was in me, my hockey ball accident had worsened it, I'd have to learn to live with it for the rest of my life. Although I had had a couple of days to get used to that thought, it still was a downer to hear it pronounced a medical certainty.

"I'm pretty sure you don't have a tumor," said Boetie's father. "Other than reassuring you about that, there really isn't much I can do for you here. There's no medication in this place, and in any case they won't keep you here very long. Try to avoid anxiety, if you possibly can under the circumstances. That is the only thing you can do for yourself."

He knew it was advice more easily given than followed. In any case, I figured he hadn't been asked to give medical help so much as a medical judgement to my captors. And that thought gave me a clue.

"I have trouble remembering things," I said. He nodded, and his eyes seemed to tell me he would report that partial amnesia was a plausible after-effect in a case such as mine.

Why were they so solicitous with me? Why hadn't they beaten the hell out of me to check out my amnesia quick and easy? But they tried a different way, one I had heard of: castor oil, lots of it, force-fed. How well I knew about castor oil! It was my mother's favorite prescription for all ailments: constipation, diarrhea, colds, ear aches—clean out the system, she'd say. Afterwards, she would squeeze lemon into my mouth to cut the heavy oil; but there were no lemons here, just gagging. Agony, afterwards, a terrible belly ache, weakness, humiliation in front of my cell mates. Prisoners must be made to feel less than human. And frightened. And in the dark about what will happen next.

After the lights went out that night they came for me again and locked me in a brightly lit cell downstairs, alone. No explanations, but it wasn't hard to guess why they did it. The cell must often have been used as a way station for prisoners who knew they would shortly be executed, and who had only the walls around them to express their thoughts, sum up their lives and summon their strength. There they had scrawled their last farewells, their loves remembered, and written short poems seared by the nearness of death. They inhabited that cell still. Awake for hours, I did not flee them, but searched for them on those walls and felt them close, and they carried me beyond fear to perhaps a resemblance of courage.

My Gestapo interrogator, the next morning, seemed to have accepted what was, in fact, true—that I was not the big catch he had hoped for, and did not knowingly belong to the recently broken resistance group. At that, he appeared to have lost interest in me. But he did insist on knowing where I had lived. Again those keys, dangling in front of me.

"This one, for example?"

I had to give him something this time. Four days had now gone by since my arrest. Chances were the apartment had been emptied. In any case, Kees and Boetie had lived there under assumed names, and the Gestapo was not likely to find anything to put them on their tracks. I gave them the address. An order was given, someone left the room in a hurry. I was let out, and that was the last I saw of my Gestapo man. How little he had conformed to the rumors, to the image we all had! Thinking back to it later I thought he probably was neither particularly humane, nor dumb, but simply professional. And, as a professional, too busy to spend any more time on small fry.

The last days in that prison were uneventful: daily walks in the outdoor exercise cage, from where you could hear the traffic on the other side of the wall. Showers, once. Letters on cigarette paper, seated on the floor next to the door, where you could not be seen through the spyhole. Three meals a day. Conversations with my cell mates. Or just lying on my cot, looking up to the barred window through which you could only see the sky, a pale blue wintry one that week. Trying not to think too much about Sylvia.

One day a bus drew up into the prison yard, and twenty-odd prisoners were put aboard, I among them. The gates opened, and there was the city, fast-paced, as wonderful as ever. But the glass of the bus windows shut me out. Everywhere, Amsterdammers went about their daily business, bicycling, riding the street cars, walking, laughing, and paying no attention to our bus. I already belonged to a different species, no longer part of them, or of the city I loved so much.

At the Central Station we were marched over under heavy guard to a train that said "Utrecht" on it, and made to board a separate wagon. None of us knew where we were going.

23

In Utrecht, under heavy guard, we were transferred to a wagon that carried no destination. It soon became clear we were going south, not east. That could mean only one thing: the concentration camp at Vught. No one really knew where the rumors came from about that camp, but they were all frightening—what they could do to you there and how they treated the many Jews, for whom this was only a way station to worse camps in Germany.

Soon the great cathedral of Den Bosch loomed in the distance. A little after, the train slowed down and came to a stop at a small station in the peaceful countryside. I recognized it: in another life Jack and I had often bicycled past it on our way to our vacation farm near Barneveld. We were twenty miles from my home town, my family, Sylvia. Twenty light years. They made us climb into a truck, which took us the rest of the way.

After the war, many former prisoners remembered the special terror staged for them by the SS upon their arrival at a concentration camps. I have seen it in films, also: the blinding lights, the shouting of incomprehensible orders over blaring loudspeakers, the barking of mad dogs held in rein by guards with whips who called you pigs and pushed you around. If my arrival at Vught was like that, my mind has effaced it. I only recall a bleak January day, and how tense I was, my throat dry from anxiety. What lay on the other side of the entrance gate? What would life be like there? Our little group was herded into a large building and told to undress. And there we stood, naked, lined up for an hour or more. It was the start of a continuing process of diminishment. There were also the despised uniformed women attached to the German military known by the derisive name of "gray mice." Now and then one would come close and look us over or walk behind us, but they stirred nothing sexual.

At last a prisoner entered, dressed in the striped prison suit so familiar to us today from old photos. He was pushing a cart on which similar clothing was piled high, and we were ordered (Schnell! Schnell!) to pick out a pair of pants, a jacket and a cap. I was lucky to find clothes that more or less fit me. Next, we were told to line up two by two and march out into the large square in front of the building. I was beginning to learn to abandon all initiatives of my own, to wait until someone gave an order. We crossed the square. A stiff, cold wind went right through my new prison garb. We made a left turn and continued along a dirt thoroughfare lined on both sides by barracks. Beyond, to the right, was the high, triple barbed-wire fence, with guard towers at regular intervals. Near the end of the thoroughfare we halted at a barrack carrying the number 13.

Inside we were turned over to Oswald. Oswald was the Kapo of Barrack 13, a pre-historic brute of awesome strength. Concentration camp Kapos generally were hardened criminals, who had already spent years in German prisons before the war. For them, the camps were a new lease on life, a form of freedom and a chance to exercise power. Within the barrack walls they had pretty much free rein. They could deny you food and give extra rations to their favorites. They could beat prisoners up at will. Of Oswald it was said that he had murdered his own father. He looked as if he could have hammered him to death with his bare fists. A man to steer clear of, I thought.

The barrack was built on a simple plan: an eating area with long wooden tables and benches for perhaps a hundred people and with a large wood stove in one corner, and behind it a dormitory with double-decker bunk beds. Between the two were the toilets, ten or so in a row. Oswald told us to sit down at a table and gave us a speech. If you didn't understand German, you had better ask someone who did and get wise quick. He outlined our daily schedule: wake-up time (half past five), work time (twelve hours) and lights-out time (nine o'clock—no more talk after that.) Infractions such as smoking or black market dealing would be very severely punished; only strict obedience to his rule would keep us out of trouble. Whenever we met a German in uniform we were to take our caps off and salute. He then showed us our bunks and the regulation way to make up our beds immediately after breakfast.

Back in the eating area we had to sew onto our prison jacket the cloth label we had been given. It had a number on it and a small colored triangle: black for black marketeers, orange for political prisoners, purple for Jehovah's witnesses. The Jews wore their yellow stars, but they were not meant to be seen by us. They occupied a sector of their own in the camp. Little has been said about the fate of the Witnesses of Jehovah under Nazi occupation. All they had to do to avoid imprisonment or be set free was to sign a statement renouncing their belief. But they didn't. In camp, their purple triangles made them the special butt for brutality, and a high percentage lost their lives.

I had the orange triangle, and my number, not to be forgotten for the rest of my life, was P1575. In camp, you had a name only for fellow inmates.

As far the guards were concerned, you had no name—you were addressed by your number and if you were called out, it was by your number. Humans have names, inmates don't. They should be faceless, too. A barber came in, himself a prisoner, to cut our hair and shave our heads. We looked at each other, grinned a little, and felt silly—perhaps not so much in front of each other as at the thought of our friends, and how we would look to them if they could see us. An old memory came back: the apron episode. When I was six years old (we had just moved from The Hague to Eindhoven), my well-meaning, practical stepmother made Jack and me wear aprons before and after school, to protect our "good" clothes. We hated them, of course, and were terrified that our friends might see them. But one morning, halfway to school, I discovered that I still had mine on below my winter coat. I was sitting on a bike behind my elder brother Pieter, who, day after day, rain or shine, took me to school on his bike . . . and on this day it was rain. And wind. In panic, I howled to Pieter to turn around, and in vain did he try to calm me by saying I could just take the apron off right there and stuff it into my pocket—no one would ever find out. School was a long way from where we lived the first two years in Eindhoven. But I wouldn't listen, I wasn't about to risk discovery, and the wail I set up was so loud that it left him no choice, at least none his gentle nature could accept. Around he turned, back home and back to school again, pedalling furiously to make up for lost time. That was fourteen years ago. I was a young man now, seated at a long table in a concentration camp, yet, though there wasn't a chance in the world my friends might see me in my striped suit and with my head shaved, I felt as if I had an apron on.

Anonymous, mindless, an impersonal mass of ten thousand to the camp guards: it was essential for survival not to feel what you were to them and how they would like you to feel. Your instinct had to tell you that, and also that you had to turn anonymity to your advantage. The cardinal rule was the same as for army recruits: don't stand out, don't let them notice you as smart-alecky or over-obedient—either way you invite trouble. Don't volunteer, don't forget to salute (casually, if possible, but salute), don't break the regulations too often or too obviously. There were times when I forgot about that lesson, but I was lucky and didn't get caught. Some courageous inmates refused it systematically, and some couldn't help standing out because they were very tall or very short or had red hair, or wore a purple triangle. They became automatic targets for beatings by their Kapos or the SS.

Next, we had to fill out a form officially registering us as guests of the Vught concentration camp. While writing, I felt Oswald near. He spoke to me, he was friendly, and right away I knew why, and it scared the daylight out of me. He could beat me to pulp for refusing his advances. Fortunately, his attention shifted to another young man, a big kid, really, whose response was more positive than mine. That kid led an easy life at Vught, with plenty of time and light work.

Toward evening, the inmates of Barrack 13 came in from work, and we had a chance to make our first acquaintances. The general mood was somber. Not long before all Jewish children had been taken away from their parents and shipped off in box cars. Only the realists faced the terrible fact that it was a separation for life. What it was like in the Jewish part of the camp was unimaginable.

In time, I would make some remarkable friends among my fellow inmates, all of them remembered, though I never saw any of them again after the war. There was a Protestant minister, a small man of indomitable strength who changed my view of Christianity, until now fashioned out of ignorance and snatches of unctuous sermons on the Sunday morning radio. There was nothing unctuous about this man, who spoke less about the Son of God than about the Son of Man, and who gave of his force freely and when most needed. There were also three highly intelligent Dominican monks not much older than I, who were strong on philosophy and an intellectual light in the dark life of the camp.

And then there was Kees, still another one. Kees the third was in remission from some sort of cancer. He was also in remission from something else: torture by the Gestapo in The Hague, which had nearly finished him off. Dreaded Vught to him was a resort, and the day he lived in mortal fear of was the one when he would be told he had to leave Vught, because his convalescence would be declared sufficient for a trip back to The Hague. Kees became my closest friend at Vught. He had a tenuous link with the outside via jam-pots in the food packages inmates were allowed to receive at capricious intervals. One arrived for him that contained, among other things, a jar of home-made strawberry jam. Out of Oswald's sight, Kees fished around in it with a fork and carefully lifted out a tiny package. Unrolled, it became a miniature letter from his family.

Two months later, Kees was still there, but he knew his days would soon be up. For him, escape was less a matter of life and death (for he was doomed to die in any case, either from cancer or in front of a firing squad) than a flight from torture. Together we developed a plan. There was at the time a small satellite camp at the airport "Welschap" near Eindhoven. From prisoners who had spent time there we knew that security at Welschap was fairly lax and that inmates wore civilian clothes. One described to us how it might be possible to get out of the barracks after lights-out, between periodic check visits from one of the guards. There had been no escape so far because you would have to find your way across trackless moors where the dogs could trace you easily, and no one knew where to go for help if you did make it.

When Kees found out that Eindhoven was my home town, he asked me if I knew of a place where one could hide out for a l while, and if I thought I could make it without getting lost in the dark (there would be no time for mistakes.) In my need to help him and, incidentally, show how fearless I could be, I made myself and him believe I could carry it all off. I was thinking of perhaps fleeing to Sylvia's house in the forest, where I would have her call my father's ex-navy friend Elkerbout, who perhaps owed me one for that map I had made, and who would perhaps know where to go from there, and how. It was a lot of perhapses. In fact, it was a desperate plan, with a high probability of failure, first, because I wasn't at all sure I could make a beeline for Sylvia's place without getting at least temporarily lost, and second, because the dogs would follow our track and we would put her and her family in terrible danger. I would have to get us somehow to the great canal or the river Dommel, so we could swim for a while, cold as the water might be, and the dogs would loose our track. It all made me very nervous, but for Kees there was no alternative, and he put his trust in me. There was one catch: if you were from the Eindhoven area, you were not likely to be sent to Welschap. Kees, however, knew a prisoner who had a secretarial job in the main camp office, and who could put us on the next convoy to go out there.

But the night before we were to ship out, the sword fell for Kees. When he came back from work he was told by Oswald that he was to go back to The Hague the following morning. He turned ashen, touched no food, and lay down on his cot. It was close to mine. In the middle of the night I woke up and, in the semi-darkness saw someone standing next to Kees' bunk. I heard Kees shiver with fear and fever, but through it came the voice of the minister, low but steady. The Lord is my Shepherd. But God, oh God, there was nothing I could do to help Kees! He was on his Golgotha, and I could not even fathom the depth of his terror at the cross, and I still cannot now, nor could I speak words to console him or give him strength. Only that minister could, following him through every turn of his road. Yea, though I may pass through the Valley of the Shadow of Death . . .". Wherever Kees' agony took him in that endless night, he stayed with him, and never wavered.

In the morning, Kees had calmed, his fever subsided. We said farewell when I went off to work, both knowing we would never see each other again. How is it possible, on a day such as this, that I was able to eat, talk with fellow prisoners, that I could fail to think of Kees for as much as an instant? But I did. For all I know I may even have smiled that day. And may God forgive me for having felt a twinge of relief that Kees' disappearance had made it unnecessary for me to prove my mettle and make good on my promise of courage and savvy in a desperate escape from the airport at Eindhoven.

24

The lights flick on. "Auf! Schnell!" Oswald's voice, out of a deep sleep. Everyone scrambles. "Du auch!" he yells at me, and I remember that getting up has to be instantaneous. We all grab our towels and run out into the pre-dawn, where the stars are still out and it is freezing cold. At a communal trough we wash in a hurry, and hurry back into the protective light of the eating quarters. Two slices of dark bread and a bowl of imitation coffee, good for a few hours of energy and a few minutes of warmth on the inside. Afterward, we march in step, surrounded by armed guards bellowing eins-zwei-drei-vier, to the great square in front of the central administration building, to line up by barrack and be counted.

"Block zwölf", over the loudspeakers. "Ein hundert zwei und zwanzig", shouted by one of the guards. "Block dreizehn." "Acht und neunzig." The counting done, we are marched off to our place of work. The same routine each day, including Sunday.

All of the newcomers, except Oswald's new-found friend, had been assigned to the same work unit. Our job was to dismantle allied airplanes that had been shot down, recuperate whatever instruments were still intact, and separate sheet aluminum from other metals, presumably for reuse in the fabrication of German aircraft. Somewhere between fifty and a hundred inmates worked twelve hours a day in a large hangar open at one end, and icy cold. The ones I worked with were mostly French, which gave me my first chance to try out one of my High School foreign language requirements.

In the morning we checked out our tools, metal saws, sledge hammers and the like, and from then on the essential thing was to make an infernal racket, to make the SS believe work was being done. They preferred to stay warm in the nearby guard house, and made only occasional perfunctory inspections inside the hangar. One inmate's job was to stay on the look-out and give a warning shout whenever a guard approached. Then, for a few minutes, actual work was performed, until the guard left. No one seemed to keep track of progress. Small teams of French inmates could stand around an airplane wing and hit it with their hammers for the length of a day, stopping only for the noon break, carrying on a shouted conversation above the hellish banging. One day a huge Boeing was wheeled in, still in fairly good shape—the pilot must have crash-landed it. A big Frenchman, who commanded the unspoken respect from the rest of us, took the decision. He checked out the biggest sledge hammer there was and entered the cockpit, where, with precision, he smashed away at the instrument panel to his heart's content. It must have contained the plane's radar. It was hard to believe he would get away with that, but the SS didn't seem to care what happened inside the freezing hangar, as long as we stayed in it.

To leave the hangar, go to the latrine, check out a tool, run an errand of some sort, you had to ask for special permission hat in hand, saluting smartly. Leaving without permission was risky: if caught, it could get you a severe beating on the spot and perhaps also a formal whipping at night, in front of all of Vught's inmates. For on many a night, all ten thousand or so prisoners had to march (eins-zwei-drei-vier) directly from work to the main square to be counted again. Then, the loudspeakers would blare out the numbers of inmates caught that day in some sort of infraction, who then had to rush to the front of the administration building, lower their pants, and bend forward across a wooden structure to expose their buttocks to a searing cudgel. At the top of their lungs they had to count, eins-zwei . . . and on into the scores, through the caustic pain, their voices broadcast across the field along with the sound of each hit. Afterward they could hardly walk for a day. Public punishment, of course, was meant to keep us in fear and make us remember who was master and who slave. There was one slave who kept defeating the master. Small of stature, but made of very tough fibre, he achieved fame because of the frequency of his beatings. He persisted in picking up cigarette butts thrown away by the guards and rolling up the tobacco into whatever paper he could find to make cigarettes of his own. It was, of course, strengst verboten! Time and again he would get caught, time and again his number was called out and he would firmly shout the score into the speakers, hobbling off afterward without a shred of the intended humiliation, and to our silent cheers.

The evening ceremony usually took half an hour or so, but there were times when we would stand there for two hours or more, in the cold, waiting for nothing. There didn't seem to be any obvious reason for that—in fact, I was beginning to understand that one of the techniques of terror was to keep us off-guard by erratic orders, or no orders at all. Unpredictability coexisted with the gray repetitiveness and ironclad discipline of camp life. You might come upon an SS officer who would suddenly yell at you (Schweinhund was the usual appellation) to come over, salute, and stand there till he told you to be off, or till he hit you. Or an SS-man might enter the barrack at three o'clock in the morning, the signal for the prisoner on duty to run to the dormitory and yell Attention! into the darkness, jarring us out of the heaviness of our faraway sleep and sibylline dreams—jarred back to Vught, back to immediate fear, scrambling to stand at attention besides our bunks as the hated guard walked by, fondling his whip, telling this inmate or that to step forward, to make him believe he was singled out for capricious treatment of some unknown sort, for some unknown reason.

Days went by, weeks, marked only by fatigue, cold and constant hunger. And one more thing: the never-ending lack of privacy. For everything was communal: eating, working, sleeping, getting up, washing (showers once a week)—all was done on order. Even the latrines gave no haven, so that bowel movements had to be performed in the presence of several others, seated next to you. To escape the oppressive togetherness for at least a short time, I broke my own rule against volunteering and offered to serve on night duty, which meant sitting by the stove in the eating room and keep it going for two more hours while the others slept, alert to the entrance of any SS guard. Two hours lost in precious sleep, two hours gained in precious privacy and the chance to think. Each night at midnight the inmate who preceded me shook my shoulder and I staggered into the light of a naked bulb hanging above the circle of warmth around the stove. Just to be alone. And remember.

25

At times, in the stillness of those nights at Vught, I thought of my earliest childhood, when my mother was still alive. I did not know a great deal about her, for upon her death and my father's remarriage, she had become a subject never mentioned. But she is in some of the fleeting images forever etched in my mind. A train, a canal, a tennis racket, a crib: they carry the memory of my infant feelings. I was less than three years old. We lived in Alkmaar, a provincial town north of Amsterdam, where my parents had moved after my father left the Navy to become a dealer in Harley-Davidson motorcycles.

An early fear: On the way back from a Sunday walk, my father wants me to lie down on my chest, face above the canal, and wash my dirty hands. The dark depth frightens me, I cry and draw back, and my father's coaxing only hardens my refusal. At last we come to a place where the bank dips down to the water and where it is muddy and safe. The train! Is there a thrill to rival that of putting pennies on the track with your older brothers and wait till the train roars by, spewing dangerous flames and taking your breath away? The tennis racket is my father's; I am proud as a peacock to carry it, knowing my mother stands in the doorway to wave us off. Sometimes my father sits down in a meadow and we run past him while he tries to catch us with the crook of his walking stick.

But the earliest of my memories is only a few seconds long. It is that of a crib, where I sense my first embarrassment when I hear my mother come upstairs with guests, and my infant mind knows it is "to show the baby", and I crawl under the blanket, pretending sleep. If I returned today to that house where I was born, I could walk straight to the corner where that crib stood.

Of my mother's death I remember nothing. All I have of her now is an old photograph and her entries into my "baby book." They speak of great love for her "four men": my dad, Jack, me, and Pieter, my other brother, who was a child of my father's first marriage, when he was still a naval officer. My father had fastened a sign above the front door; it said KeerIenhuis"—"Home of Fellows". He had painted it when his latest child (I, his third one) once again turned out to be male. From the little I know of his marriage to my mother, I believe they were deeply happy. They did amateur opera together. But their happiness would last only five years, for my mother was already marked by cancer. Her last entry in my baby book says that she had been away in the hospital for a long time, but was healthy again now, and able to take care of her "men". She died shortly after. Jack says she died at home and remembers people crowding into our house, and us being taken to that of a spinster lady we called aunt (then, and for many years after), who was a friend of my mother's and probably in love with my father. But what bothers me to this day is that I don't even remember missing my mother.

Soon after we moved to a suburb of The Hague, where my father advertised for a governess to take care of his children. This way it was that my stepmother entered our lives, for the governess was a beautiful and highly responsible woman, and my father married her within the year. It was difficult to start calling her "mother", after the previous "mevrouw" (Mrs.) Something seemed not right about it.

From the suburb we moved to The Hague itself for a short time, and there I burst out in tears one Monday morning because my brothers went off to school and I didn't. From then on I went to Kindergarten, right behind our house, where I felt happy, played hard, vied for the special favor of polishing the brass in the hall, and once rushed into the madness of volunteering to go the hall, where the clock was, and tell the teacher what time it was. I knew I couldn't, but made a wild stab. The teacher smiled and, to my shame, sent someone who could. Boasting was certainly a problem with me. And simply inventing, the way I invented the most terrifying, bloodthirsty dreams to recount at the breakfast table, just to see the effect on my parents and brothers.

My stepmother brought with her a ready-made family. That was just as well, for Jack and I had, in one fell swoop, lost half of ours when my father remarried, just as Pieter had lost his mother's side several years before. My new grandfather had recently retired from the sugar factory he had owned and managed in Indonesia. He had a big, white moustache of the kind popularized by Kaiser Wilhelm III and called "est is erreicht" because it was so difficult to achieve. He also had an enormous, fire-engine red Chandler convertible that could seat nine people on its leather benches and bucket seats. In later years, when we had moved to Eindhoven, he and my grandmother would sometimes drive down to pick us up for a weekend in the Belgian Ardennes or the German Eifel Mountains. (It was there that I saw my first anti-semitic banners and smashed Jewish store windows.) My grandfather was a slightly built man, but he looked terribly impressive behind the steering wheel, with his leather coat and gloves, honking the rubber klaxon to his left, his moustache flapping in the wind. His wife, my new grandmother (Oma to me), was perhaps the only grown-up I was conscious of loving as a kid. She actually seemed to love her new grandchildren, perhaps more than she had loved her own children—I think my stepmother felt it that way, no doubt with pain. She was full of humor and spell-binding tales of witchcraft in Indonesia, to which, on dark winter nights in Eindhoven, we'd listen by the chimney fire, shivers running down our backs. And when my stepmother decided to give a big Indonesian dinner party, it was she, our "oma", who did the cooking. She would put on her beautiful sarong and, for two or three days, sit in a tropical heat on a stool in front of our immense wood-burning kitchen stove, softly singing Javanese songs in Malayan while tending to a score of little pots with bubbling sauces that would eventually come together in something indescribably delicious called "Rijsttafel" in Dutch. If you came in, then, she would hardly notice you, and you knew her mind was thousands of miles and four decades away, in the remembered dream life of her beloved Java.

And then there was Uncle William, their elder son. By the time I got to know him he was already condemned to life in a wheelchair by some mysterious disease of which no one ever spoke. He had been in the merchant marine, a bright young man's life ahead of him, when "it" struck and paralysed his legs. "It", no doubt, was polio, I later realized. Embittered, he spent his days in an upstairs room in his parents' house, avoiding contact with his family if he could help it. Except for me. I was only a little tyke, but we made great pals, talking endlessly (about what? I wonder) during long hikes to the dunes, he in his hand-propelled tricycle, I running alongside. Aside from a few friends his age, only I was allowed inside his room. One day, my stepmother came to the door, looking for me because it was dinner time. But Uncle Wim, who had warned me in conspirational tones not to make a peep, had hidden me beneath the lid of his giant roll-top desk, and told my mother he hadn't seen me for hours. He also made me a terrific slingshot, for which, however, he needed two pieces of leather. He told me to bring me a pair of shoes from his parents' bedroom closet on the floor below. In the closet I fell upon an embarrassment of riches, but decided that patent leather would look great on a slingshot. Uncle Wim resolutely cut off the inside flaps and warned me to keep the slingshot in my pocket inside the house. Fortunately, my grandfather seldom wore those shoes and didn't discover how they had been maimed until months later, by when the track of the crime had gone stale. How could one not admire an uncle like that? Only as an adult did I understand that the door to our friendship was open because it never occurred to me to pity him. Pity can be hard to swallow. To me, he was just Uncle Wim, whose wheelchair was as much part of him as my grandfather's walking cane with its silver knob went inseparably with him.

His sister, my stepmother, was a woman of many contradictions, at the same time tough and caring, showing her affection more easily by deeds than by words or touch. It is hard for me to imagine her actually telling my father she loved him even during their courtship, though there was no doubt she did, and she might tell others so. The tough strand in her character was at times hard on my father, but she also possessed a natural gaiety that could make her break out into peals of laughter, and which alleviated my father's somewhat overly serious nature. Those qualities, and a robust sense of responsibility, made her well equipped to take care of the three children so suddenly thrust upon her, and to look after my father and my brother Pieter during the difficult period of their protracted illnesses. Pieter had developed a brain tumor in the early thirties, and over the next fourteen years suffered the awful consequences. His left eye was enlarged, pushed out by the tumor. Then he had to quit school because, although a brilliant student before, he could no longer keep up. After that he started working for a gardener, until paralysis crept up his legs and his epileptic attacks became too frequent to go on. At last, he had to stay home, where he took care of the aviary in our back yard with its twenty-five colorful songbirds. As with Uncle Wim, I didn't pity him in his affliction. Pieter stayed Pieter, with whom Jack and I had gone on camping trips in the Ardennes as long as he was still able. But seeing him decline in that way was almost more than my father could bear, and worsened his own condition. All of that was hard on my stepmother. But she had great energy and resourcefulness, and also courage. On any of her frequent war-time bicycle trips to the black market farm, she might easily have been arrested.

Did I love my parents—as a boy, I mean, rather than in retrospect, away from home? Not consciously, I think. Love is a big word. I certainly had a sense of belonging, even if I sometimes envied my friends for belonging to a different family. Some of our mores were odd, and so embarrassed me that I rarely dared ask my friends over to the house. Parental authority was not open to question. I chafed, but accepted it the way one accepts the weather, rain or shine, in the absence of an alternative. Across the gulf between our parents and us, their children, we could see they cared, and that the Navy-like discipline that ruled our daily life was not capricious, but imposed upon the whole family. Every evening before bedtime, my father, who might have preferred an extra hour with his newspaper after a tiring day, would ask us what subjects we had been given for homework, and then he might say: "Bring me Algebra and German." If we did not know it, we had to get up at six the next morning to study some more.

Time, to him, was an all-important thing. Coming home sixty seconds late from the swimming pool meant finding him at the door, watch in hand, ready to send you upstairs, sometimes without supper. But only one time did

I really feel hurt, because principle had been given priority over affection. The final match of the annual tournament of Dutch "wicker-ball" (a fore-runner of basketball) had gone into overtime. The High School team I captained finally won on a shot sunk by me, and the winner's cup was presented by Mr. Philips Junior. Full of pride and fear I raced with Jack across town and against my father's watch, but my heart sank as I rounded the corner into our back yard and saw the family at table. It was my birthday, and what they were eating was my birthday dinner. When I got sent to bed, oma, who lived with us for years after her husband's death, left the table to weep in the hall. She wept for me, and for the dumbness of unbending discipline. Parents do these things, even good ones, and it is fortunate that most kids, in the end, recognize aberrations for what they are, and don't hold grudges.

26

The weeks dragged on at Vught. Exhaustion began to creep in from lack of sleep, lack of food, from the constant cold and the unremitting dreariness of camp life. A low fever stayed with me, enough to make me feel sick. But to stay away from twelve hours of work or be admitted to the barrack that went by the name of "hospital", your temperature had to be above 39° C (102° F). I have always had trouble convincing people that I was sick, because the thermometer would rise little if any above normal. Now, violent stomach cramps made each day a trial. One morning, at last, the mercury hovered at 38.9°, and they said I was close enough. At the "hospital", an orderly stuck a tube down my throat and pumped out my stomach. Feeling immediately better, but weak as a raggedy doll, I fell down on the bed they showed me and was asleep on the spot.

I don't know for how long I was out, but it was dark when I woke up to a shout of Attention! The lights switched on and a young SS officer came in barking incomprehensible orders. As a newcomer, I wasn't sure what bed patients were supposed to do, and I wouldn't have come close to guessing if I had been asked. Because the Kapo seemed to yell something in my direction, I looked around and saw that my fellow sufferers had all stretched out stiff in their beds and were saluting. Saluting! Again the Kapo yelled, and I understood I was the Schweinhund he was addressing. So I, too, stretched out and saluted. Slowly, the officer made his way between the beds; here and there he asked a question—temperature was what seemed to interest him the most. He scowled at mine, but to my relief moved on. For fifteen minutes we stayed immobile, looking straight up to the ceiling and saluting. Finally, he left, the lights went out, and I fell back into more sleep. When I woke up again, both fever and exhaustion were gone. They allowed me to stay for the rest of the day, a day punctuated by more salutes, but by evening I had to go back to Barrack 13.

Back to the rest of the winter, to cold and hunger. I absolutely had to do something about food. One slice of dark bread in the morning, two at noon, and a bowl of dubious watery soup at night was not enough to keep going. I lost weight and thought about food all day long during work. Only sleep brought relief.

Our work place was on one side of a wide thoroughfare near the edge of the camp. We knew what was on the other side: the Jewish compound. And another thing: a large shack where prisoners made radios. It was a dependency of the Philips factories, only twenty miles away. Philips employees imprisoned for one reason or another were often put to work here, and I was sure there were people from Eindhoven whom I would know. Philips, being important for the German war effort, had some pull at Vught. Every day a truck arrived from Eindhoven, and big kettles of soup were unloaded for the inmates on the other side. I had visions of my bowl being filled with Philips soup. But the kettles stayed over there. "Do something," growled my stomach.

Then, providentially, I got to know someone in the enormous shed where I worked who had found a way, and was willing to let me in on it. At noon he would eat his bread on our side, amble casually over to the wide open doors as if to take a breath of fresh air. There, he would watch intently to the left and right, and when he thought no one was looking he would sprint across the 40 meters or so of empty space to a ditch on the other side. From the ditch he would crawl unseen to the nearest barrack. But he still couldn't go to the soup-line, because the inmates on our side had lately been given different clothes—civilian clothes confiscated from Jews who had been sent away on transports. A large circle had been cut out of the back of each jacket, and a piece of brightly colored cloth sewn in. But on the other side, the Jewish prisoners still wore the striped concentration camp uniforms. My new-found friend had obtained one of those and kept it in a storage room. Every day he would crawl to it, change clothes, proceed to the soup-line, eat, change again, and run back to our side. He said he could get me a striped uniform—tomorrow.

"You're crazy," I said.

"Yes, but not hungry," he replied. "Are you coming?"

Two days later, with thumping heart I, too, stood on the look-out. I thought of that cudgel and knew that only disgust at my cowardly heart could drive me across. I saw my friend diving into the ditch. No one seemed to be watching and I ran across. In the ditch he whispered "Follow me", and together we crawled to the storage room. Fifteen minutes later we took our loaded stomachs back to our side. Every day it worked like a charm, but it wasn't hard to believe that sooner or later we'd get caught. And then I saw Mr. Polis.

The Polis family lived not far from our house in Eindhoven. Mr. Polis was an engineer at Philips. Our families were not all that close, but we knew them well. For a time, whenever I was back from Amsterdam, I would go over to their house to listen to the BBC News, which began each time with the first four notes of Beethoven's Fifth. Ownership of a radio was by 1942 "strengst verboten," but the Polises, at some risk, kept theirs concealed in their attic. Just to hear Adolf Hitler referred to as "Herr Schickl-Gruber" delighted me. Once or twice I heard the voice of the Great One himself, Winston Churchill's, so gravelly heavy that all the German jamming and squawking could not reduce its magnificence or drown out its morale-boosting message. One day, Mr. Polis disappeared. It was said he had been arrested and sent to Vught. But he was among the few who was let out after a while, probably through the good offices of Philips, Inc. He then became a liaison between Eindhoven and the tiny radio factory at Vught.

I saw him just as I was waiting till the coast was clear to cross over. I was sure we weren't supposed to talk, but no one seemed to be around, so I stepped forward from the shadow of the work-shed, took my hat off (for obscure reasons I must have felt that that would make it less of an offense, though I felt silly talking to a family acquaintance with my head shaved bald), and waited till he was close and saw me. From my parents he knew, of course, that I was at Vught, so we did not need to waste time on explanations. We spoke quickly, briefly.

"I would like to work in the Philips compound—could you arrange that?"

"That may not be easy. The Germans consider the work you are doing (pointing to my work shed) as 'essential'. I'll try. Wait. And stop running across (how did he know?). Too risky. I'll tell your parents I saw you." And he was off.

I walked back with a lump in my throat. Coming so suddenly upon someone from home, from that other world, had gotten to me. I waited, hungry again, for I followed his advice. It took a while. Then, ten, perhaps twelve days later, my number was called off during work. An SS guard told me to follow him. My heart beat in wild joy. "Soup!", was all I could think. Soup it was. Heavy soup.

My new work place was more pleasant. For one thing, it was warm. As I had expected, I saw people from home. One, with a twinkle in his eye, called me over and introduced me to someone I did not know, but who looked familiar.

"Rob Scholten, meet Rob Scholte." Of course, the singer of popular songs, whose name was a household word in the Holland of the thirties!

The Jews spoke with infinite pain of their children who had been taken away and shipped off. How could anyone encompass such unmeasured sadness?

I was put to work on a radio assemblage line, soldering wire connections. In little time I became a fairly expert solderer. But the radios were shipped to Germany, perhaps for war usage, so the important thing, and also the daily fun, was not only to work slowly, but to slip as many poorly soldered parts through the line as you thought you might get away with, hoping that some day on the

Ostfront a critical radio message would dissolve in crackles and a crucial battle would be lost as a result. The camp authorities didn't seem to have the means or the interest in strict quality or quantity control. For the better part of the day we simply gabbed. One inmate was put in charge of the window, and would yell Boutenkoning! whenever he saw a camp guard approaching. The word has no meaning in Dutch, and I wondered who invented it.

Towards the middle of April there were a few days of breathtaking early spring. I stood outside at noon, taking in the sudden warmth of the sun. In the distance, Allied planes flew high through the pale blue sky, and the familiar cream puffs made by anti-aircraft bursts started to appear among them. Suddenly, there was high drama in that limpid spring sky. A plane was hit. Slowly, it spiralled downward, and then, just before it went into a straight nose dive, three parachutes opened up—no, two, for the third one stretched out long as a cigar and its ballast plummeted to earth. Did the man scream in that space of a few seconds before death, did he have time to think of his wife or his girl friend, his parents, his boyhood in Kansas or Virginia? Someone had told me once (wrongly, I know now) that you lose consciousness at the speed of free fall, and I prayed to an unknown God to let that be true, or else to sustain the man in this awesome moment. He disappeared from sight. From afar I could see the other two swinging gracefully from their ballooning umbrellas, grateful, no doubt, that theirs had opened (as they would later relate countless times to their children and grandchildren.) Then they, too, disappeared, and the sky once again looked innocent. I felt as if I alone had witnessed the aerial tragedy, all of life and all of death in the wink of an eye.

—

Winter returned for a last gasp. One day I received a clandestine gift during work, no doubt through the good offices of Mr. Polis. It was my stepmother's favorite sweater jacket—kashmir, colored in squares of light and dark brown. I put it on directly over my prison underwear and kept it on that night. The warmth it gave was more than physical.

The next morning one of the inmates of Barrack 13, whose bunk was close to mine, was shivering uncontrollably. I thought he might be starting in on a flu and gave him my mother's sweater to wear that day, just before we were marched off for the morning count on the main square. On some days they called off the numbers of certain prisoners, who, at the instant, had to break rank and run on the double to the administration building, usually not to be seen again. I wasn't paying much attention. There was a freezing wind, and I thought of that sweater; but I knew I would soon be close to the wood-stove in the radio shack. Suddenly, P-1575! over the loudspeakers. Good God, me!

From the shock I nearly fouled my pants. But I ran to the front, where several others were already waiting.

With the usual shouting we were herded into an ice cold room in the central administration building, and there waited for something to happen. I regretted my sweater, knowing I had seen the last of it. After a while we were each handed back the meager belongings that had been taken from us upon our arrival. I even found an old pal, my wrist watch, which I hadn't expected ever to see again. Nazi prison life never ceased to surprise. What would come next? The question was on everyone's mind, but no one told. Freedom seemed unlikely, Buchenwald too scary a thought to entertain for very long.

A bus was waiting at the camp gate, along with a handful of armed Dutch police. As we drove off I took a last look back at the camp and at the slogan over the gate: Arbeit macht Frei. Freedom in slave labor . . . was there a more cynical way of distorting language? The Nazis were great at such sayings. Strength through Joy (Kraft durch Freude) was another: the Nazi's version of Schiller's "Ode to Joy." "Seit umschlungen, Millionen!" Not until after the war would the world learn of the darkest of meanings Schiller's words had acquired in mid-twentieth century Europe, that the embrace of millions was an embrace of unspeakable death and mass graves for millions in the sodden soil all over the land of Beethoven.

27

In the bus, the Dutch police collaborators acted reassuringly. We were going to the central prison in Utrecht, they said, and there, after a few formalities, we would be set free. Our relatives were waiting for us there even now. All of us knew they were lying through their teeth to keep us quiet, but all of us also kept a small corner in our hearts where we could shelter belief in their words.

Under a low, gray sky the bus drove up to the front of the small train station of the village of Vught, and we were escorted to a waiting room emptied of all other travelers. There we sat for twenty or thirty minutes. A train rolled in—it wasn't ours, but suddenly I was awash in a flood of confused thoughts, impulses and doubts. The train was heading south, away from Utrecht, towards Eindhoven! What if . . .? Could I . . .? Were they . . .? Just now the policemen were not looking my way—would I have a ghost of a chance if I walked out onto the quay and into the train as soon as the station master with his red cap blew his whistle, just before the doors would close and the train would be off—but then, inside, what would I do? Ask someone for his hat to cover my close-cropped, prison model hair, and for his coat to conceal the bright tell-tale circle in the back of my jacket, hoping he would understand and have guts and would not be sitting near any Nazi sympathizers? It was crazy, but . . . and at that moment one of the policemen looked around and guessed. He shook his head slowly. The train was off.

The prison in Utrecht was a heavy, dour-looking building. I had two cell mates, both of them black market racketeers, who had been there for some time already, and would probably be freed eventually. One, a thin, sallow-faced man with slow motions and dull eyes, had been the longest occupant and, by the generally accepted prison code, was more or less in charge. It was, above all, his privilege to stand by the door when you could hear the soup kettles being dragged across the floor of the hall outside, and it was he, therefore, who would be nearest the door hatch when it was finally opened with a great clanking of keys, and would receive the three bowls of soup thrust forward by an unknown hand. He would inspect each bowl to see if the soup was thick enough, and hand it to the rest of us if it wasn't. I sometimes wondered what I would do if I were number one, but, fortunately, was never put to the test.

My other cell mate, whose name was Joost, was a lot more fun. He was in for black marketeering, but not on any ordinary scale. His operations were on the scale of Robin Hood and the Three Musketeers. Not for him, stealthy trips to the countryside or whispered back-door deals at city dwellings under the cover of night. No, my new fellow prisoner was a true patriot, a friend of the people and enemy of the enemy. His deals were big and always at the expense of the Germans, and the tales of his exploits were as thrilling as they were hilarious. As far as I was concerned, he could tell them over and over. But the one I liked best was about The Great Tobacco Heist. Joost had found out that great bales of tobacco were stored in an abandoned church in Amsterdam. Resolved to get them out, he cased the lay-out for days. He saw that a soldier was stationed in front during the night, but not during the day, so he decided the job would have to be done in broad daylight and in sight of whoever cared to stop and watch. One pitch-dark night he and a friend climbed up a drain pipe at the back of the high house adjoining the church, and from its roof they managed to get into the loft of the bell tower. After stuffing the bells with the packing they had brought with them, Joost slithered down the bell rope into the black abyss below. But, holy Jesus, when he came to the end of the rope, he still hadn't come to the floor! How far below was it? Five feet? Twenty-five? He had no idea, but he didn't dare to let go. In despair he hung there, wriggling like a fish on a hook, lacking the strength to climb back up. He whispered to his friend to pull up the rope, but he was too heavy for that. And then, slowly (because of all of that pulling and wiggling), the rope began to sway, forward-backward-forward, with ever-increasing amplitude, until (Joost swore) he was swinging from wall to wall.

"What the hell are you doing?", whispered his accomplice from above. "The rope is too short," he whispered back in panic "Drop, damn it, drop!" said the other.

At last his grip gave way and he let himself fall to a near-certain death on the pews below. But he fell all of two feet onto a soft bale of tobacco. His mate then joined him, and they slept peacefully till morning, when they unlocked the doors from the inside, opened them wide, and loaded the bales onto a truck driven by a third conspirator—workers no doubt employed by the German army, the passers-by must have thought. They got them all, those bales, and without a hitch drove off into the noon sun. How my creative friend was finally caught, I can't remember.

April passed slowly in Cell 96. Looking upward from my cot I could see a small rectangle of transparent sky through the top of the barred window, with slowly drifting clouds. Spring had come, and I thought of long Sunday walks along the Amstel River to a bucolic restaurant called, for unknown reasons, The Little Calf, and of the smell of the pine woods near my home town. Sylvia! She must be worried. I missed her, though not sexually. For it was a fact of camp and prison life that sex took a back seat to hunger and fear, and remained mostly as a fond memory, but without torture. Prison talk, camp talk, was mostly about food, not women. Priorities had been reordered.

One thing the prison in Utrecht had over the one in Amsterdam was easy access to a fairly good library. One book a week was not much, but a lot better than seven empty days. My cell mates were not readers, and became so bored that they volunteered our cell for one of the manual jobs that were available. For hours on end they made clothes pins, mountains of them, and when they were finished with their share, they took on mine. I didn't mind chipping in for an hour or two a day; it gave me a chance to gab, and listen to them gab. But mostly I read, and re-read—novels, biographies, books about countries and other people. Three times over I read a long biography of Leibnitz, sitting on my cot, my knees scrunched up, back against the wall.

By the middle of the month I was called out and taken to a room. I had a visitor! It had to be my father, I thought, and that gave me a jolt. My father it was. He had heard, somehow, where I was, and had applied for a "Sprechschein," a visitor's pass. The amiable Herr Liese, object of my knee-jerk dislike, had helped him get it. My father did not look well. So proud he had been of his three sons, so full of hope and expectation. And now, one lay dying slowly of a brain tumor, another was estranged and had strayed from the brilliant career my father had envisioned, and the third was in a Gestapo prison, perhaps in jeopardy of his life. I tried to reassure him. The war, I said, was bound to be over soon (again!). I would be released from wherever they would send me, and I could certainly hold out that long. "Don't worry, dad."

But my dad, though understandably anxious, was not a weak man. When the occasion demanded it, he knew how to act. And he brought news—news which finally explained what I was doing in Utrecht. Most inmates of Vught, I knew, were simply put on transports going east and disappeared into some German concentration camp, and that had been my own expectation. A few, however, were apparently kept for show trials before German civilian judges that were meant both to intimidate and give the appearance that a judicial system was operative in Holland. One such trial involved the Resistance commando that had attacked and burned the labor register for all of Holland, led by that intense, red-headed man I had met so briefly a year ago. From some of the questions the Gestapo had put to me during my interrogations in Amsterdam

I had had the impression they were trying to prove I was part of that group. Or some other group, perhaps. The Germans were infiltrating the Resistance network. In Vught I had met some other members of the Resistance, who were now also in Utrecht and were in for much more than I. I had never had any idea how I had fit in, which was, of course, on purpose. In any case, my father informed me I would go on trial in late May and that I had the right to an attorney. He had asked a lawyer from Rotterdam, Mr. de Jongh to represent me. He was the older brother of a High School friend of mine, and a distant nephew of (who else?) Mr. Philips. Mr. de Jongh would visit me in the near future.

When the fifteen minute visit was over, we both had a difficult time. It may be I had never before been as aware of the depth and constancy of his love.

Back in Cell 96, I read the letters he had brought. The first I tore open was the one that carried the handwriting I knew so well and loved so much—Sylvia's. What she wrote was neutral, as it had to be, but every line seemed to carry unspoken thoughts and deeper meanings. Then there were letters from my two sisters, Marjolijn and Lydia, and from my mother. Suddenly, they were all close again: my family in Eindhoven, Sylvia, my friends in Amsterdam, my cousins in The Hague. Hardened as I had become these past few months, those letters and my dad's visit had been unsettling. I knew I had to guard against depression.

28

Mr. de Jongh's visit came towards the end of the month, by which time I had recovered from my slump. He made only a few points. I would be tried under martial law. There would be a prosecutor and three judges, all German. The case against me was being a front man for an illegal organization, distributing illegal documents and newspapers, and acting as a courier. In my favor was that no accomplices had been caught, so that it was difficult to make a major case out of me. (At that I felt a little proud, thinking of my successfully simulated faint in front of the Gestapo). I should plead guilty to those charges, since all were known to be true, and I should act contrite in front of the judges.

"Contrite?" I exclaimed. But Mr. de Jongh cut me off by reminding me that most heroes are dead, and I might consider swallowing a little pride to avoid the firing squad. He would plead leniency because adolescents are easily led astray by the thought of heroism in lost causes (here I swallowed a big chunk of pride). If I cooperated, and I didn't draw hanging judges, he did not think I would get the death penalty, but I should expect to remain imprisoned for the remainder of the war. He seemed to know what he was doing. I liked him and agreed to do my part; there was little choice, in any case. Before leaving, Mr. de Jongh said my family and some friends were allowed to attend the trial, perhaps to speak to me for a short while afterward, and to bring as much food and as many cigarettes as I could consume on the spot. At that he left, telling me to stay up-beat.

There were more weeks of waiting, reading, gabbing, making clothes pins, and plain idleness, wondering about the future. Then, on the fifteenth of May, I was told my trial would take place three days later, May 18. A Thursday. Soon I would see my family, after almost half a year, and perhaps some friends, too! I was excited by that, but there were also moments when, in spite of my attorney's confidence and my self-imposed optimism, I couldn't keep a few bubbles of anxiety from rising in my chest. What if I did get hanging judges?

I tried to get used to the idea of the end of my life, just in case—but how rehearse a script that hadn't been written? Better go back to reading.

On a gray morning they came for me, and in no time a paddy wagon took me to the court house. From a distance I saw my father and mother, and then I got a glance of Sylvia. I had been near-certain she would come. If her presence should hint at a bond between us that might puzzle others, Sylvia was not one to care. In her paleness, she looked more beautiful and lovable than ever.

There was no time for talk. Mr. de Jongh whisked me away to a waiting room for a last minute rehearsal of how he wanted the trial to run. Suddenly my name was called, and we were in the court room, decorated with enormous swastika banners and a large portrait of Adolf Hitler. A nervous silence hung in the air. At last the judges entered and took their seats. What did hanging judges look like? The charges were read. No one asked if I pleaded guilty or not. The prosecutor, a thin, venomous looking man with steel-rimmed glasses, took charge. He outlined the circumstances of my arrest and the proofs of my guilt, but then he went further, saying I was one of those students who had refused to sign a simple statement forswearing illegal acts against the security of the occupation forces and the Dutch government in The Hague. The fact that no one else had been arrested in the case was proof enough that I was part of a sophisticated conspiracy among those students to do what they had been asked to renounce. Such people were a menace to the German State and deserved the severest punishment martial law allowed.

I was beginning to feel edgy. Were things going out of control? I glanced over at Mr. de Jongh next to me, but he remained impassive. The prosecutor continued. There was, he said, one mitigating circumstance: the fact that I was still a minor. As the German people were compassionate by nature, he would not insist on the death penalty for a minor, but demand imprisonment for life at hard labor.

I tried to suppress a heavy sigh of relief. My twenty-first birthday was four days away! There was living ahead of me. Even the rearguard action my lawyer was now getting ready for had lost its importance: "life" was as good or as bad as a month: in any case I was not going to get out until war's end and only needed to survive in whatever place they were going to send me.

Mr. de Jongh and I did our rehearsed little act. I cringed once more at the words "adolescent" and "remorse" and almost inaudibly said "yes" when one of the judges asked if that was really what I felt. For the sake of Sylvia (though not my own) I would have preferred to go down in flames, to make an impassioned speech about "tyranny", and "duty", and "resistance to death", rather than casting myself at the mercy of the oppressor. Behind me, was Sylvia ashamed of me? The judges withdrew for a few minutes. When they came back I was told to stand, and my sentence was read: five years of hard labor. I heard gasps behind me, but in my heart I smiled.

Afterward, only my parents were allowed to see me. They were moved, and so was I, but we tried not to make our farewells too hard on each other. They knew I was going to need to be tough in the time ahead. "Don't worry," I said again, trying to sound convincing. "I know I can make it. I've learned a lot already—about myself and about survival. I'll find friends, and I'll think a lot about all of you." "All the time," said my father. "Be strong!" My mother gave me a hug. She had baked a cake for me, and there were cigarettes. While we talked, I ate and puffed as fast as I could. Soon time was up. A last hug, and then they had to leave, while I was led down the hall to the back door.

The police van was waiting a hundred feet or so from the door. Suddenly I realized no one was holding me. I was a pretty fast sprinter—should I run for it? Just then I caught the gleam of a gun in the hand of the policeman to my right. Why did his face look familiar? Would he shoot? After the war I read that a police collaborator called Oosterbaan was tried for gunning down a fleeing prisoner. Oosterbaan had been Holland's pride in the Berlin Olympics of 1936, where he had run the hundred meter sprint only one-tenth of a second behind Jesse Owens' new world record, earning him the bronze medal. Everyone knew his face. At his trial he pleaded he had been forced to shoot because he had been unable to catch up. Reading that, I wondered then if that cop in Utrecht two years earlier had looked familiar because it was Oosterbaan. Probably not. But something in his face had told me he would shoot. I renounced, and walked to the police van.

For a week nothing happened. Back in Cell 96 I wondered where I would end up. In Buchenwald, perhaps, or some camp like it. I would have to start all over again to learn the rules and the ways to get around them, find out what the Kapo was like and how to avoid him, try to make a nest for myself as at Vught, stay away from the SS as much as possible, not let myself be noticed, and never, never forget about the arbitrariness of the peril in camps like that, where any SS-man could beat the hell out of you if he felt like it, or kill you without having to account for it to anyone. It was likely to be worse than Vught.

On a drizzly afternoon at the end of May the guards came to take me out to the prison yard. Other prisoners were already waiting, a dozen or so, and more arrived. Once again, a long wait, once again a bus. The guards had pulled their guns. At the train station, another wait. The drizzle had stopped. A wind had risen and broken the clouds into shards, glowing red low on the horizon. A train pulled in, a short one, mostly freight cars, but with one passenger wagon. We boarded, six prisoners to a compartment, armed guards in the corridors. A mournful whistle from the locomotive seemed to send a shudder through the train, which slowly, jerkily, started rolling. Behind us, Holland's sky gave us a flaming farewell.

PART II

GERMANY: BEHIND BARS AND BEYOND

29

I looked around. Five faces, five pairs of eyes, turned inward, lost in thought. It was as if we were all listening to the droning of the wheels on the rails, to each click-click that sent us closer to the hated land, hated and feared. Perhaps we became conscious, now, of loving what we left behind. Outside, the telephone wires rose and fell, rose and fell.

Now it was dark. I could make out the Big Dipper, and remembered, almost with a smile, how Sylvia and I used to have a pact: when we were apart, I in Amsterdam, she in her forest home near Eindhoven, we would look at the same star, the second one in the handle of the Dipper, at 11 o'clock every night. It was like a caress, out there in the Universe. Already, it seemed as if that was part of a previous life.

Something attracted my attention. The window! It was closed, but was it locked? If not, one could shove it about a third of the way down, maybe more—enough of an opening to crawl through! The train was moving fast—jumping at that speed would be near-suicidal. But I had heard of the technique you were supposed to use—dangerous, too, but with chance of surviving without breaking your neck. You were supposed to lie down on the running board, feet forward, and roll off. At ninety kilometers an hour? It seemed dubious to me. Could you hit the gravel without hurting yourself so badly that you wouldn't be able to go on? What if you fell face down? If one of the guards passed by, he'd shoot you, for sure. Would one of my fellow prisoners alert them, afraid of punishment if he didn't? Too many questions, too great a risk.

Still no one spoke. We entered a town, blacked out and under curfew, as all other European towns, every night for years now. Under the moonlight it looked deserted. As we raced by the station, I could make out the sign: ARNHEM. Half an hour later I told myself we must be in Germany. How far would we go on?

Not much longer, it turned out, at least not on this leg of our journey east. The train slowed down and came to a halt, puffing as if exhausted. KLEVE. Just across the border. German prison guards were waiting on the platform. It seemed almost by instinct that they started yelling out incomprehensible orders as soon as we stumbled out of our wagon. For the first time in my life I was manacled to someone else. The soldier who did it was almost apologetic—a flicker of decency under the swastika. Through the silent town we marched to the local prison, where they locked us up, seven to a cell meant for two. There were mattresses on the floor. We had had nothing to eat since noon, but within seconds sleep conquered hunger.

In the morning we became acquainted. The only cellmate from Kleve I now remember was a tall, saturnine man, who, unlike the rest of us, looked well-fed. There was a reason: he turned out to be a pastry chef from Haarlem. An anxious pastry chef, who seemed to have a hard time understanding what he was doing here. He hid his anxiety under a torrent of talk, but what talk it was! He mesmerized us all, for what he did, in his lugubrious voice, was build cakes, multi-layered pastry cakes. Layer after layer he built them, right there in the cell in Kleve, using his soft, white hands to spread out the creams, the chocolate paste, the almond paste, the nougat, the jellies and jams and sugars and slices of strange fruits from Oriental lands.

"Some of my cakes," he said, "I start with a layer of hard caramel. On that I spread a thin layer of very heavy whipped cream of just the right consistency"—a pause to let it sink in—"then a layer of fine pastry batter. The fourth one might be of coffee or chocolate cream—Belgian chocolate, of course, mixed with Grand Marnier, or else Dutch orange-flavored chocolate. Then again cake batter."

On droned the voice, infusing the cake with delicious, long forgotten tastes. Strawberries, bananas, more whipped cream, delicate tear drops of dark chocolate on top, or tiny crystals of colored sugar to catch and reflect the soft candle light. At last the cake was finished, but one final ceremonial sentence remained to be pronounced, and here it came, the same one after each cake. The pastry chef folded his hands in satisfaction, lifted his eyes, and said, his voice now expressing reverence: "And all that with the finest, the very finest unsalted butter."

It was unbearable. Lunchtime came and went without food. We were weak with hunger, but listened again as our chef prepared to bake still another cake. At last, as the sun set on Kleve, we were rewarded, each of us, with a bowl of sauerkraut soup, the first of many to come, and a slice of rough dark bread.

The chef looked worn out and seemed suddenly dispirited. Looking at him more closely now, I thought he looked flabby and was afraid he might not last long. As it turned out, he didn't. A few weeks later a dead man covered by a sheet was carried by me on a stretcher. I was told the body beneath the sheet was that of the pastry chef from Haarlem.

30

After a few days we were marched back to the train station, once again handcuffed to a partner. It was early morning, a fine day—summer was in the air. But I was in no condition to appreciate it. In the last 24 hours a carbuncle had appeared on my right leg and quickly grown to an impressive size. Because of the pain I could only limp along, and had a hard time keeping up with the eins-zwei-drei-vier.

Another freight train was waiting for us, but without a passenger wagon, this time. We climbed into a cattle car. With a carbuncle and handcuffs, that was no easy task. We were told to sit down on the bit of straw that covered the floor and not to get up during the trip. The sliding door was slammed shut and bolted on the outside. Soon we started rolling.

Light entered through a slit on the long sides of the wagon, at eye level if you stood on your toes. Now and then a pair of prisoners stood up to stretch and look out, reporting back what they saw. Nothing of much interest. Hours went by. My stomach told me noon was approaching, but it was obvious we weren't going to be fed for a while. Suddenly, there was a shout: "Hey, take a look at this!" Everyone scrambled up. By now I was in such pain that I would have preferred to stay down, but my partner in manacles wanted to see what the others had seen, so I slowly hoisted myself up with him, and looked out.

The sight was amazing. We were passing through a fairly large town, or what had been one. Much of it lay in ruins from bombardments. The sweetness of revenge quickened our war-corrupted hearts. "Hurray!" we shouted, and we would have danced if we could. The German language may be the only one that has a word for what we felt: Schadenfreude, joy in misfortune—the other person's misfortune, or course. No one had a thought for maimed civilians (if we'd had one we would have figured they were all Nazis, anyway, and had it coming) or for the children that must have died here. I had to sit down again, and, reluctantly my partner sat down with me.

In the middle of the afternoon the train stopped, the door was unbolted and slid open, and we climbed out. SIEGBURG, the sign said. I had no idea where we were. Was this our final destination, or just another stop on the way? The SS was there to greet us with the usual shouts. We were counted, lined up two by two, and walked out into the street.

It was raining. We were all weak from hunger. The people in the street were openly hostile. Some jeered at us. The SS yelled to hurry up ("Schnell!") I hobbled along, and with every hobble my carbuncle sent daggers up my leg and into my brain. An acute colic was twisting my insides. "O Lord," I prayed, "let me get quick to wherever we're going . . . before I have to let go." We were following a long, high brick wall. A gate creaked open, and we were inside the yard of the Siegburg prison. It was a forbidding building we entered—dark, huge, somehow more menacing than the prisons in Amsterdam and Utrecht. In the hall a table was covered with files that had our names on them, and a large brown envelope was attached to each file. It looked as if we were meant to stay. I surrendered my watch, my only possession, and bade it a silent farewell as it disappeared into an envelope. "Well," I told myself, "this may not be the Ritz, but it's bound to be better than those camps in the east, so count your blessings."

For I already knew what I would realize even better after the war was over: that, after all, I had been very lucky compared to most of those who had been arrested. Because I had been selected for a trial, I had entered into the German legal system. My sentence was an official state act, and from then on I had to be accounted for and would not be sent to one of the concentration camps set up outside the legal system, where, as we all learned in time, no one had to be accounted for and no one was accountable. It was this that kept me out of Buchenwald or some other mindless camp built for nameless destruction somewhere near the Polish border. I had been condemned and saved by the same sentence—saved from unspeakable horror and probable death. In Siegburg, at least, you stood a chance.

31

My intestinal cramps were now so violent that they almost took the pain away from my leg. I told a guard about it, but he told me to shut up. After a while, our handcuffs were taken off and we were made to strip and line up again—a score of stark-naked men who now eins-zwei-drei-ed it to the showers, where we were given a minute to wash. Then, at long last, a cell! It was a very large one, a holding room for new arrivals waiting to be assigned to regular cells or to be shipped out somewhere. The place was swarming with prisoners from all over Europe. There were no bunks—just a thin mat on the floor. Although I had had six months to get used to performing bodily functions in public, sitting in front of such a crowd still had the power to embarrass me. But far greater than that was the power of my cramps.

At six we received our slice of bread and a bowl of (what else?) sauerkraut soup. I was told it was between that and rutabaga soup, with an occasional treat of pea soup. Something still had to be done about my leg. By now, it really looked awful and menacing. But to whom could one turn? The inmate who ladled out the soup showed little interest; there probably was nothing he could do in any case. I found a corner of the mat to lie down on and slept fitfully. The next morning a guard entered and I managed to get a word in. He didn't react much, but an hour later my name was called and I was taken to the infirmary. A prisoner in his thirties appeared. From my name he knew I was Dutch, and he addressed me in Dutch. I assumed he was some sort of paramedical orderly (a Sanitäter, as the Germans called them), but he turned out to be a physician from Utrecht. Dr. Helberlein: tall, close-cropped hair, a no-nonsense type, but with kind eyes.

He gave a low whistle. "Your poor fellow," he said. "That must be hurting like hell!" I assured him it was.

"Alright," said the doctor, "I don't have much to work with here, but I'll have to lance it. It'll be painful. Hold on." And, before I knew it, he was doing it. I almost passed out. He dressed the wound and told me he would come by my cell in two days. He had a pass key. The pain hung on for quite a while, but after a few hours I began to feel chipper enough to chat with some of my fellow inmates. As usual, no one knew what was going to happen next. I gave up guessing.

After a second night I was taken to an ordinary cell, already occupied by three others, Dutchmen all. It was for a day only, but it was there that I had a shock so intense that I can still conjure it up today. Something itched on my lower abdomen and made me take my shirt off. And there it was: a louse, part way buried into my skin. Revulsed beyond words, I ripped it out. Right away my cellmates told me that was the worst thing to do. If the louse was infected, the infection would enter your bloodstream and could cause typhus. The best method was to burn its back with a lighted cigarette, if somehow you had one. In the absence of a cigarette, you had to squeeze the louse out of your skin between the nails of your two thumbs. I shivered with disgust.

But where had I picked it up? In the communal holding cell? From my new cellmates? They read my thoughts. The lice, or louse eggs, they said, were hidden in the seams of the supposedly clean change of clothing we received once a week. Therefore, the first thing you had to do was go through all of the seams and squeeze them dead one by one between your nails. And you had to repeat that every day. In time, louse-hunting became a routine exercise, and you became expert in the different louse species: round gray ones, flat translucent ones, tiny red ones, burrowers and non-burrowers, lice that sought out body hair, others less particular. The most I found in a single inspection was over a hundred. You did the job while carrying on a conversation with your neighbor. But that first experience went down hard.

The next day Dr. Helberlein came in. The swelling on my leg was way down and the boil was starting to dry up. "You're okay" said the doctor. "But now I want to ask you a favor. You can refuse if you want to. There is a man from Amsterdam on the ground floor who has just recovered from diphtheria. Except for one thing: he is becoming paralyzed, a highly exceptional after-effect, but he has it. He needs help—with eating, with going to the can, and also to lift his spirits, for he's all alone and getting awfully depressed. Are you willing to do it? There's no danger you'll catch diphtheria yourself, for he's over the infectious stage."

He looked at me hard, clearly not expecting me to say no. And why should I? In no time I was transferred to the ground floor cell, where I met the doctor's patient, whose name was Henk. He lay in bed, no longer able to stand up for long. In his mid-twenties, I thought. He looked as if he might have been athletic once, but he was thin now, and listless. We talked, he in a low voice because talking tired him out.

"I'm scared, he said. "The doc doesn't want to tell me I'm done for. He says this will go away, but I know it's just to cheer me up." His look showed the doctor had failed. I lied, and assured him the doctor had told me the same thing.

"Come on," I said, trying to hide my own doubt, "you have to believe it to get well again. And the war will soon be over."

He wanted to talk about his life and family, and I talked about mine. Food arrived, and I fed Henk. I had hoped they'd give us a little extra, but it was again just one bowl and one slice. We talked some more, and I helped Henk to the can, after which he was exhausted and just lay on his bed, staring at the ceiling.

The following morning Henk was called out, and I had to go with him to hold him up. Clothed only in our bed shirts we were made to line up in the ice cold hall, and there we waited. The German prison doctor would come to examine the sick people. Barefoot, we stood there, along with twenty or thirty other inmates. Some looked as if they were at the end of their rope, exhausted, with dead eyes, and so emaciated that you could have circled their legs with one hand. When no one was looking, they leaned against the wall for support.

For the first time I had an overall view of the prison. It was built on the plan of a cross, almost like a cathedral. We were at the end of the nave. Administration offices and lookout posts were at the intersection with the transept. There were four stories. I estimated there must be about five hundred cells.

We stood for an hour, maybe more, waiting for something to happen. And then, something did happen, something momentous, a lightning bolt. News! From where it came was impossible to say, but no prison wall, no barbed wire could stop it from leaking through. It was what we had all been anticipating for so long. Someone told it to one of us in the line and, like an electric current, it raced from one end to the other. Just a few words: "The invasion! Yesterday! In Normandy!"

I felt my eyes misting over. God, oh God, was it possible. All this misery, all this pain and suffering and humiliation—would it finally come to an end? "The invasion, the invasion, pass it on!" Yes, it had to be true. The arrogant Nazis would be driven back, beaten, locked up, humiliated in turn, and we would be free again. "Pass it on, pass it on!" How could we hide our joy from our captors. We couldn't, we didn't, we smiled the victor's smile. Thank you Churchill, thank you Roosevelt, thank you, England and America, oh thank you, thank you!

The prison guards watching over us knew we knew, and became angry. So much the better—it could only mean the news was true. One of then came over and started to taunt us. "Ha, you think they landed, don't you, you

Schweinhunde! Sure they landed, those Amerikaner friends of yours, and they got their stupid noses bloodied, just as at Dieppe. They've already been driven back into the sea. It's over, it's a failure. No one can beat Germany, no one can touch the Führer!"

He may have believed what he was saying—he was probably repeating what he heard on the radio. But we didn't believe him, not for a moment. Nothing could drive the Allies back, with all their planes, their ships, and their countless tanks and hundred thousand troops. How sure we were of that—and how little we knew that defeat still hung in the balance in Normandy that day.

32

The German doctor finally arrived—an old, bald-headed man with a look of distaste on his face for our little group of louse-ridden inmates, ridiculous-looking in our long night-shirts and bare feet. With a guard barking out an order for us to stand at attention, the doctor hurriedly walked past us, hardly looking at us. And that finished the medical check-up for which we had waited a good part of the morning.

In the days that followed, Henk's condition rapidly worsened. He could no longer get up. I had to help him with a bed pan, which he had to use frequently because he had less and less control over his functions. Because his voice was getting too weak to call me at night, if needed, I put a table next to his bed with a spoon on it, with which he could tap to wake me up. Dr. Helberlein came in several times a week to check up on him and assure him he would get well again in the end. But Henk, who did not believe him any more than I, became somber and depressed. His paralysis seemed to affect his muscles only, not his nerves, for he was in constant pain.

One day, the door was suddenly flung open. Two men entered, carrying a stretcher. Without saying a word, they picked Henk up by his legs and armpits to put him on the stretcher. In terror and pain Henk made his voice rise to the nearest thing he could muster to a scream, and then he broke out in sobs, saying they were going to kill him. With the little force he had left, he tried to hold on to his bunk, to the table, the door. "Help me, please help me, please, please!"

The door slammed shut. Silence. I sat down on my bed, shaking, afraid they were really about to do away with Henk, who had become a hopeless nuisance to them and to whom they were not about to give any real medical care. What lousy luck, not just to catch diphtheria, but to be among the tiny fraction of a percentage that end up with paralysis. The invasion had come too late for him, I thought.

Feeling depressed myself now, I lay down and stared at the ceiling. "Don't let it get to you," an inner voice warned me. But it was hard not to. I wanted desperately to talk with someone. Night fell. Sleep came at last.

Several days passed. I assumed they were not going to let me stay in solitary for very long, but nothing happened. I let my thoughts wander wherever they would: to my father (was my imprisonment affecting his health?); to my two fun-loving sisters, clear-eyed Marjolijn and rambunctious Lydia, both still in High School; to Jack, whom I had left in the lurch without documents (how was he dealing with that—was he in hiding?); to Sylvia in her forest home; and to my friends in Amsterdam, Walter and my other classmates, and Kees and Boetie. It gave me pleasure to picture those two carrying on their underground work, though I was more aware now than I had been of the danger they were in.

I also thought back to my hometown of Eindhoven and surprised myself at finding a real soft spot for that not especially beautiful industrial city, that cultural backwater where quaint, centuries-old customs had lingered on, resisting modernity. When there had been a death in the neighborhood, a tall, sepulchral individual, dressed in black and carrying a top hat, would make the rounds, knocking on every door and in a sententious voice repeating the same solemn news in the same solemn words. Periodically, too, a public announcer would make his appearance to call out municipal messages. Stopping at every street corner to toll the heavy bell he was carrying, he would unroll an official-looking scroll and, his voice pitched to a single high note, ring out his formal tidings in the broad, soft-edged dialect of Brabant: "Early tomorrow morning there will be a public sale of two hundred twenty pounds of pork meat at sixty-nine cents per pound, of three hundred seventy pounds of beef at eighty-five cents per pound, and of two hundred fifty pounds of mutton meat at one guilder and five cents per pound"—here he would pause to take breath and make sure everyone was listening—"in the Municipal slaughter house"—another pause for dramatic effect, then, his voice dropping a fourth of an octave for the last two syllables—"at Tongeren!" Tongeren was where we lived, an old village long-since engulfed by the spread of Eindhoven. Not far away was a wide canal, and next to it the gypsy camp. Now and then the gypsies would come by, knowing that my mother, herself in touch with occult powers and, moreover, hopeful always of better times to come, was fair game for palm reading. The old gypsy woman would tell her we would come into a large sum of money from an unexpected source, and that there were fabulous journeys ahead, and then my mother would be happy, nodding her head in shared knowledge of mystiques from which the rest of us were excluded.

My mother—what a bewildering bundle of complexities: full of goodwill, but anti-semitic, down to earth, but as familiar with ghosts, spirits, and visions as with the price of potatoes. My post-adolescent habits of reasoning were constantly baffled by the stunts she pulled off. One morning she appeared at the breakfast table very upset. "Miss von Motz had a car accident last night," she said, "and she's in a hospital." Miss von Motz was my piano teacher, who came once a week from Amsterdam to give lessons in Eindhoven. She had a lot in common with my mother, and the two had become fast friends. But we all knew she was just now on vacation in Morocco. So how could my mother know what had happened to her last night? Never mind, she knew—and, of course, turned out to be right. Many years later, shortly after my arrival in Ann Arbor, USA, I got a letter from her describing in detail the apartment I shared with a Swedish student. And later still, when she herself had moved to America after my father's death and she came to visit us for a week in Pennsylvania, she said to me one day: "You know, you have a house ghost here." Long used to such surprising utterings, I asked: "Where is he?" There, on that chair." "What is he like?" "A nice, elderly man," she said, "slim, with graying hair. He says he used to live here, that he died in this house." I pricked up my ears: "What's his name?" My mother strained to listen. "He's telling me," she said. "I'm not sure I'm hearing it right. Could it be White?" "Not far," I exclaimed, "not far. It's Wright." Cal Wright had been head of Penn State's Department of Fuel Technology and had lived in our house till he died in it from a stroke two years before I moved into it with my family. How was a young scientist supposed to deal with spiritual stunts like that? I didn't try, as I had learned not to, long ago in Holland.

During those days in solitary I thought, too, about life after prison (for I never really doubted I would come out of it alive.) Most of all, I wanted to see the world; it was an unbearable thought to me that there were countries, people, customs, mountains, forests, deserts out there that I might never see. Uruguay! Why Uruguay? I don't know—maybe I just liked the name. Tibet! How alien a place, but what attraction! I had read a book about Tibet from my mother's mystical library, the same library that introduced me to such visionaries and charlatans as Ouspensky and Rudolf Steiner, Madame Blavatzky, Annie Besant and Bishop Leadbeater—all rejected with a sneer when I shifted into reverse as a university student and was taught to trust reason only ... and made such a nuisance of myself at home during vacations, parading my new-found enlightenment to all who wanted to listen and all who didn't, that my exasperated father politely suggested one summer that I return to Amsterdam by the first train. Only Krishnamurti, among the authors from that library, wise, strong, gentle, reasonable Krishnamurti, stayed with me all my life, a seed half-forgotten, but always there.

I wondered, too, how the invasion was going. Were they getting close? Cut off from the outside, I had no news at all.

One morning, I woke up with a fever and a scratchy throat. Dr. Helberlein came in, took one look and shook his head. "What is it?" I asked. "Diphtheria, I'm afraid," he said. "I'm sorry—I didn't think Henk could still give it to you. You're going to have a very high fever and a very soar throat for a few days. Hang on! You're young, you'll weather the storm. And don't worry about paralysis. We've already had our one case in a thousand."

For nearly a week I lay in a half-daze, my face turned to the wall, burning with fever, my throat on fire. It was as bad as the time my tonsils were taken out back in The Hague, when I was five: cold turkey, in the family doctor's office, my dad and a nurse holding me still. I couldn't eat, not then, not now; mere swallowing was torture. Twice a day Dr. Helberlein came in, but there was really nothing he could do to help. At last the fever abated and the fire went out. Weak as a wet towel, I crawled out of my bunk to take a few steps, a few more the next day, until I could march back and forth for fifteen minutes several times a day, thin but recovered.

Still nothing from the outside, other than noises in the hall, the scraping of the big soup cans across the cement floor at mealtime, the hand that passed me my soup bowl, and one evening, to my astonishment and deep emotion, the incongruous sound of a violin. Who was playing, where, why, whose idea was it, this message from the world outside, carrying the memory of moments better than today, a promise, perhaps, of a better time to come? Who was it that sent us this reminder of what was eternal and could not be humiliated, maimed, destroyed? Gounod's Ave Maria. It came from somewhere in the central area where the watch-posts were. It came, cascading down the hollow prison halls, washing up the concrete walls, permeating pure and clear through bolted iron doors, filling every inch of space and my still incredulous heart. Never had I heard anything so beautiful, so rending, so healing. "The voice of a weeping angel," the Dutch author Aart van der Leeuw had written once about the violin . . . a voice that brought me now the near-forgotten gift of quiet tears.

33

At last the door was opened. A prisoner came in, apparently to stay. Solitary was over. It had not bothered me so much to be alone for several weeks, but still, I was glad to have a companion again. In awkward German, he introduced himself as Jean Juliot, from Normandy. A Frenchman . . . what chance! I would be able to polish my French, of which I had had seven years in grade and high school, and which I had occasionally spoken with Sylvia. Jean was delighted to find out I could understand him without difficulty and, though with more difficulty on my part, could converse. He, too, was recovering from diphtheria. Jean was full of fun and energy. He was a train engineer by profession, and had been arrested because he kept derailing his locomotive, and the Germans had caught on that there was a purpose behind his high accident record. Jean laughed out loud, his eyes sparkling. That evening his friends passed by in the hall on their way back from work, and spoke to him through the door, asking him how he was, and if his new cellmate was French, as they hoped for his sake.

"Mais pas du tout, pas du tout," Jean exclaimed, "c'est un hollandais sympa, qui parle très bien français." I felt considerably flattered to hear that Jean thought highly of my French.

We had a great time together, Jean and I. No one bothered us, no cell inspections, no call-outs to stand at attention in the hall—the guards were still too scared of catching diphtheria and probably remembered what had happened to Henk. I taught Jean chess. With a spoon I scratched a chessboard on the floor, and we tore up pieces of toilet paper to make chessmen, fashioning them roughly to resemble kings and queens, knights and bishops, and rooks and pawns. Jean had a quick intelligence and caught on in little time. When he lost, he would exclaim: "Nom de nom de nom! Encore!" We played for hours each day.

Jean told me a lot about his country, which he had traversed so often in his locomotives before he started derailing them. France seemed like a beautiful place, listening to him. And Paris—ah, Paris! There was, he said, a night club in Paris where women, married and unmarried, would go to make some extra money. You would go there and sit at a table, and the women circulated bare-breasted, hawking napkins, each her own color.

"Cing francs cinquante, la femme et la chambre," they would call out. For five francs and a half you would buy a napkin from a woman you liked, and later she would come to sit at your table, spotting it by the color of the napkin, to talk and drink and smoke, and then you would go up to the promised chamber. With the flair of a Toulouse-Lautrec, Jean described the scene, the bright lights, the little round tables with their wine bottles, the women—blond women, or dark skinned, or oriental (Jean preferred the black ones)—the whole smoke-filled atmosphere of the place. I thought of the swimming pool back home, with its strip of water dividing the men's part from the women's, and felt like a country bumpkin. "Cing francs cinquante": that was living! But the burning desire I felt was not for sex, but to see fabulous Paris. For in camps and prisons sex was not a subject that came up. Food, yes, all the time, and family, work, hope, cold, sickness, lice, krauts, air raids, how to get a haircut, the technique for cutting your fingernails with a razor blade, all or that and more, but never sex. Not that the subject was taboo . . . it was simply irrelevant to our existence, in which the primary urge was for food and the primary instinct how to protect yourself against all sorts of dangers.

"But," I heard Jean say, "it's no longer the same". "Now, there is blackout, curfew, 'boches', food coupons." That took us to comparing notes about rationing back home.

"The worst," Jean sighed, "absolutely the worst, is how little wine we get." "How much?" I asked. "A bottle a week, or what?" Jean looked at me as if I was mad. "A bottle a week?!" he cried out. "Are you kidding? We'd all be dead! By the time I was arrested it was down to a litre a day, and that's bad enough. How much do you get in Holland?" Not much, I told him—in fact, none at all. Jean really did think I was kidding him. "Come on," he said, "tell the truth. How much?" "Do you think wine is all that essential?" I asked. "Mais évidemment," he said, affirming the obvious, "Of course it's essential! How else are you going to make red blood cells?" Since I wasn't sure just how you did make red blood cells, I didn't pursue the question.

Dr. Helberlein had stopped coming in. We were considered recovered, and he was needed elsewhere. But we did get a visit from an unexpected person, who unlocked the door himself. He was a Catholic priest, a stocky, round-faced, pleasant-looking man. He chuckled when he saw our surprise. "Don't worry," he said, "I'm not here to take your confessions. I know that you (looking at me) are Protestant, and you (turning to Jean) are French, so probably a Communist." He laughed out loud as if at a private joke, and sat down on a bed. You couldn't help laughing with him.

"As for me," he went on, "I've been the regular prison priest since long before Adolf Hitler (did I see a faint look of distaste on his face?). They haven't yet dared take my passkey away, so I can indulge my old habit of visiting the sick and convalescing." Had he come in just for a chat? I wondered if he would tell us about the war. He guessed that thought. "Well," he said, "I can't give you the details, but it looks as if you aren't going to be here for many more months." I was burning to ask him about those details anyway, but realized he couldn't compromise his position. Prison news may travel fast, but can sometimes be traced back to its source. So I didn't push, but inwardly rejoiced, for it was clear he had meant to say Germany was losing the war.

"I know you're hungry here," said the priest. He sighed, but then seemed to remember something, and his eyes expressed merriment again. He's hiding something, I thought. What is it? Just then the priest dug his hand beneath his frock, and when it emerged again, it was holding a package. He handed it to me. "From your family," he said with sudden quiet.

I looked at him, dumbfounded. No one received packages here, not even mail. "Letters," he said, "plus a few edible surprises, if I'm not mistaken. Go ahead, open it." Inside was a thick envelope, unmistakably carrying my father's handwriting. The edible surprises were a pre-sliced pound cake, a small bag of shortcake cookies (my favorite kind, called "sand cookies" in Dutch) and several bars of chocolate . . . food for kings!

"How is it possible?" I asked. The priest raised his hands. "Don't ask me," he answered. "Now and then, presents just fall into my lap somehow." I didn't push him on that, either.

"Alright," our visitor said, getting up. "I must be on my way. I suppose both of you know these things must not fall into the hands of any of the guards. Read them, eat them, hide them, and find a way to get rid of the wrappings, and of the letters, too, once you've read them. I'm sure you people have learned how, and don't need me to tell you."

I thanked him, but he waved it off. "Thank rather the Lord," he said. "And while you're at it, ask him if he couldn't end this terrible war as soon as he sees fit, or sooner yet. Prayer never did anyone harm." He was at the door now. "Until then, hold on as best you can, and may Christ protect you. I doubt"—the old merriment creeping back into his blue eyes—"I doubt he makes much difference between Catholics and Protestants, or, for that matter, Communists." He laughed out loud again (his private joke), shook our hands, and was gone.

Still bewildered, I opened the envelope. There were letters from my sisters, from my father, from Sylvia. I scanned them quickly, before putting them away under the mattress, like storing candy, for future enjoyment. Marjolijn and Lydia's letters chatted away about Eindhoven, the latest happenings in high school, about missing me. My father's tone was more stately, as usual, barely concealing his concern and love. He also explained in a few words that the package the priest had delivered was being sent through the good offices of (what else?) Philips, Inc. They really did have their tentacles everywhere, I thought. My mother added a few words, hoping the cake she had baked (with how much black market butter, I wondered?) would please me. Would it ever! Nothing about Jack: he must be in hiding. Sylvia's letter was short and non-committal, as it had to be, but to me glowing between the lines.

I unwrapped the cake and, with Jean, stared at it in wonder. We promised each other and ourselves not to eat it all at once, after which we took a slice, and then another, and soon we had eaten it all at once. It was the next best thing to liberation! After that, self-control took hold of us, and we hid the other edible surprises beneath our mattresses.

Early in August I was called out. It was late afternoon. They handcuffed me to another Frenchman, and together we climbed into the back of an open pick-up truck. The guards hoisted themselves into the cab, a soldier drove. Where next? Northward, the setting sun told me. The road was in bad repair, and so was the truck's suspension. Even at our slow speed, we were shaken like a rattle. After a while, we stopped in front of a roadside bar. The guards got out, told us to stay where we were, and disappeared into the bar. My partner and I stood up to stretch and look around. Twilight was falling. The countryside looked desolate, as if abandoned by man and beast. But no, someone was on the road, up in front, on a bicycle. It was a woman in a light summer coat. Approaching the truck, she saw us.

And then that German woman did something exceptional, an act not to be forgotten in a lifetime. She stopped behind the truck, leaned her bicycle against a tree, and put her hand in her coat pocket. She looked around, then walked quickly to the back of the truck and put an open cigarette pack on the flatbed. Cigarettes! They were almost as precious to civilians as to prisoners. Just as quickly, she turned and walked back to her bicycle—but before she got on it, she turned around to look back at us, and put a finger to her lips. Don't talk! She rode off and disappeared into the dusk. It had all taken less than a minute, but in that minute she had offered me the greatest of gifts, greater by far than the value of those cigarettes—a reminder that there are faces to the enemy, that Germans can be human, too. I have often wished, after the war, that I could find that woman to tell her what her act had meant to me. She had made a small, spontaneous personal atonement for the sea of suffering her people had caused.

34

The guards and the driver came back from the bar, and we drove another hour or so. It was dark by the time the truck stopped in front of what looked like a factory. They took us to barracks behind the building and into a crowded common room, where my new fellow inmates were standing around or seated at long tables, talking, yawning, checking their clothes for lice, or just staring. A prisoner who seemed to be in charge was called over; he took us to the sleeping quarters and showed us our beds. Soup time was past, but they gave us a slice of bread.

I sat down on a bench, weary from the trip. To the right of me an inmate started talking to me in Dutch, and I found out that I was in a small concentration camp at a place called Porz, a suburb of Cologne on the east side of the Rhine. The inmates were mostly French and Dutch, more than a hundred of them: half of them were right now working the night shift in the building across the yard, a factory for the manufacture of small parts of Messerschmitt airplanes. Others joined us, and I had to tell how I came to be a prisoner, what was happening in the outside world, especially on the military front. I could not tell them much: in quarantine I had been out of contact.

One of the inmates spoke up. "So you're a university student! You'd want to meet our Professor. Just wait here for a minute." He was soon back with a man perhaps fifty years old, slight of build, with sandy hair and quick, attentive eyes. It was Professor Baas-Becking, a biologist of some repute in Holland. Among the books he had written was one called "Geobiology"; it dealt with the relation between the geological environment and the organic world.

The Professor sat down cross-legged on the table and started asking me questions about myself, what role I had played under the occupation, what I had done about the "loyalty oath." Then we talked about the Allied invasion, and he told me the western front had been securely established, that Allied troops had taken most of France. "The air war is getting hot, too," he said. "We get alarms several times a week, daytime and night-time raids."

I asked him about the camp we were in: what was it like? "It could be worse," he replied, "except for the food. There's so little of it, and it's so bad. We're all sort of weak. And people get sick. They're not a bad lot at all, with a few exceptions. Of course, if you're starved for intellectual nourishment, this is not the best place, but there is at least one exception. I'll bring him over, hold on."

The Professor returned with a man who looked to be in his sixties, straight-backed and vigorous, with graying hair and a face that looked somehow aristocratic, though I would have been hard put to say why. Perhaps it was not his face so much as his bearing, which expressed a strong sense of self. Not one to take lightly, I thought to myself. He was introduced as the Comte de Coucy, from Paris. Later, I found out he was a designer of aircraft and automobiles.

For as long as I stayed at Porz, it was Baas-Becking and de Coucy that I could count on for discussions on any number of subjects. I hadn't had any like that since those monks in Vught. Unfortunately, they were both in the day-shift, whereas I was soon assigned to the night-shift, so I didn't see as much of them as I would have liked.

The night shift ran from six to six. They put me to work at a small tool machine. Above my machine, on the wall, a glorious slogan had been painted in large gothic letters, condensing the whole crazy Nazi mystique in five words: Der Führer hat immer recht . . . the Führer is always right. To understand that, I thought, you had to do more than read German: you had to be German. The supervisor showed me how to fabricate a thread on the inside of steel and aluminum nuts. It was not particularly difficult. For each shift, you were supposed to produce a set minimum number of whatever you were making, called the pensum. For steel nuts, the pensum was nine hundred, for aluminum ones eighteen hundred. From our point of view, the important thing was to produce less, if possible much less, and to mix in a high percentage of bad ones—nuts too wide, bolts too narrow by a fraction of a millimeter. Prison guards and SS-men walked around to make sure you were working, so you had to keep eyes in the back of your head. They also made random checks of your product, and if they happened to come upon a bad one, they would yell at you and threaten you, and you had to pretend your machine was giving you trouble. But, as at Vught, it astonished me to see how little they really seemed to care about quality control. After all, someday, somewhere (or so we hoped), a Messerschmitt fighter might spring a couple of bolts and drop out of the sky.

The only one who did care was the company director, a dyed-in-the-wool Nazi. He wasn't around much, but looked dangerous. I ran into him at the end of my first shift. Hands down, I was beating the record for least productivity by newcomers, who, after all, had the best excuse to offer: unfamiliarity with their machine. I had made thirty six aluminum nuts in twelve hours, a record that stood for the duration of the camp at Porz—though honesty impels me to play down the heroism of my non-achievement and confess my machine did act up, and I was all thumbs trying to adjust it with a home-made contraption of strings and rubber bands. My mechanical skills had never been great. In my family they always started laughing as soon as I proposed doing something with my hands. Once, Jack and I had tried to construct a tandem bicycle by putting the steering column of my bike onto the rear axle of his. We actually rode it once, and I can still hear my stepmother, who was watching us from the front lawn, emit piercing shrieks of laughter because, being a three-, rather than a two-wheeler, it wouldn't round corners, and we had to get off each time to do it. She finally crumpled down on the grass and nearly fainted. That disaster remained one more stain on my record, although Jack's contribution had been as great as mine. For all that, cutting a thread on a nut here in Porz was a feat even I could have mastered quickly with a little goodwill.

Suddenly the director was standing next to me, looking at my machine and my basket with its thirty-six nuts and speaking to me in tones of ice-cold anger far more menacing than the usual shouting. As helplessly as I could, I pointed to my machine. He inspected my contraption in utter disgust, ripped it out, pushed me aside, and adjusted the machine himself. I had to give it to him: he knew his business from the ground floor up, for it worked perfectly after that. When he was gone, a fellow inmate came over and warned me to be careful with that man. "He's a snake," he said, without further explanation. I believed him.

Soup time and a half hour break came at midnight, and at five-thirty in the morning you had to take your box with whatever you had been making to the central weighing station, where one of the prisoners, the "secretary", weighed the number you had produced and wrote it down in a log book. After that, back to the barracks, where the others were just getting up, bread and imitation coffee, lice-searching, and at last bedtime.

The only thing that broke the routine was the air war. Several times a week, a loudspeaker blared out a warning that Allied planes were in the region, and if they seemed to be heading towards us, the sirens would begin to wail, and nervous guards and SS-men would hurry us into the basement of the factory, with much schnell-schnell and much drumming of sticks on the backs of prisoners too old or weak or sick to run fast. Mostly, the planes just flew over on their way to some other destination, but once in a while they bombed the enormous railroad complex close to our factory, Porz being the principal switchyard for the Cologne area. Usually, it all came so fast, that the bombs were already falling while we were still running. Each alarm was hard on the nerves ("was it going to be us, this time?"), yet, when several days passed without one, we became impatient—the more raids, the sooner freedom, we thought.

The memories I have of those night shifts at Porz are oddly cozy. I got along well with my fellow workers. Behind me worked a light-hearted, silver-tongued Frenchman, who bore well his name of Rossignol: all night long he sang like a nightingale, and he gave me an enduring love for the French chanson, of which he knew an endless number. Rossignol was a small fellow, but he could be tough. One morning, a countryman of his, who worked the machine behind Rossignol's, brought his box to be weighed, and it turned out he had produced over twenty-two hundred aluminum nuts—probably out of sheer boredom. Rossignol, incensed, walked over to him and knocked him around several times until the poor man fell down in a corner, and then told him he hoped he wouldn't have to do that again. He didn't.

Rossignol also gave me a lesson one night. The "secretary" had been sent somewhere else, and one of the guards, a man getting on in age, whose whole career had been that of a professional prison guard, decided I would be the perfect replacement. He thought that because once, in a genial mood, he had struck up a conversation and asked me what I'd been doing before I was arrested. When I told him I was a geology student, he beamed and said he was a Roman Catholic. I didn't know what to make of that non-sequitur, but he winked at me meaningfully and, in a low voice, started chanting a Gregorian hymn. Only then did it occur to me that he had understood me to say "theology." He eyed me suspiciously when I didn't join in on his chant. Was I an impostor? Holy cow, how could I get out of this? Experience had taught me that few even knew the word "geology", and that explanations usually roused incredulity that anyone could devote his life to so useless a thing as rocks. (The common follow-up question was: "Yes, but what do you really do?", after which the best thing was to say you were looking for gold.) Hopeless, I thought, so I, too, beamed, and nodded with dignity. And that was why, now that the time had come to select a faithful shepherd to lead his flock, the guard remembered the theology student from Holland. No more machine work for me! I could loiter, gab, cut my finger nails, or dream through the shift until morning, when the workers came to me to account for the fruit of their labor, and I sternly weighed their product and entered the calculated numbers into the log book, next to their names. Power, at last! And, why, here came little Rossignol with his box of steel nuts! I weighed, figured, and frowned. "Five hundred sixty-two," I said, disapproval in my voice. "Is that all?" It was then that Rossignol saved me from the corruption which, in a single night, the puny privilege of my position had already made to seep into my soul.

"For whom are you working?" Rossignol asked, blandly.

It was like a punch in the nose. Good grief! I was working for them, the Enemy, and was putting my heart into it! I walked over to the Gregorian guard and told him I wanted to go back to my machine on the next shift, that I was making too many mistakes as "secretary." Reluctantly, he let me go, probably figuring that an unwilling secretary would make an unreliable one. He never came back to talk, or even chant. But no matter: I went back to listening to Nightingale's songs, and felt grateful. To this day.

35

The fall days were beginning to get short . . . and cold! It was promising to be a bad winter. The factory was poorly heated, and in our barracks only the living quarters were heated by a coal stove. Everyone took his turn around it to warm up a little. Inevitably that led to quarrels when somebody tried to hog the stove for too long, but on all but one occasion violence was squashed quickly, as if we all knew that it would make a breach in our armor of solidarity, our only defense against low morale. The exception occurred on a Sunday in October.

Sundays gave us our half day off. The night shift finished at midnight Saturday, and day-shifters were done the following noon. On those free afternoons we could wash up, change clothes and bedding, have our hair cut, even get a shave from a French barber, a fellow inmate, and get together with friends from the other shift. Everyone looked forward all week to that brief release from discipline and monotony, those few hours or companionship. But on that October day, companionship and solidarity donned an ugly cloak. An evil-doer had been seized—a bread thief. Some of the prisoners had the habit of saving a slice of bread till later, when hunger was at its worst, hiding it under their pillow or blanket. Now and then, it would disappear, to the impotent rage of the famished owner. And now the thief had been caught, red-handed.

He was carried into the living quarters by four or five fellow Frenchmen, squirming and loudly protesting his innocence. He looked scared, as he had reason to be. Two inmates took his pants off, and they put him face down on one of the tables. Someone brought a rope to tie him up (from where did he get it?), someone else a solid stick from the bin where kindling wood was kept. The bread thief took one look at the size of it and started screaming like a stuck pig. Everyone of his countrymen but one took his turn, encouraged by the others with howls of hate and pleasure. It was awful. Two SS-men came in to see what the commotion was about, and left again, satisfied that prisoners were settling their own scores and beating up on each other. I stood next to de Coucy. He was pale with anger and disgust. "Dégoutant, dégoutant" was all he could bring out between clenched teeth, and he turned around to go to the sleeping quarters, pushing his way through the hustling waiting line, with me in tow. The door now closed behind us, the yelling subdued, he spat out one more word: "Animauxl"

I had a great admiration for de Coucy, and a great liking. To me, he was a pillar of strength. He could speak German, but always pretended he didn't understand, or answered in French, when guards or SS-men addressed him. And he had a way of looking through them as if they didn't exist that infuriated them—a French aristocratic way, I thought, that came from the time of Louis XIV or before. It amazed me he never got a severe beating. The insult of his bearing also seemed to be his protection.

De Coucy talked to me about Baas-Becking. He was worried about him, and, in a way, so was I. The Professor was developing signs of a Christ complex: he seemed to want to give of his body to feed others. At night, sitting next to me, he would push his bowl over to the inmate across the table, pretending he couldn't eat. But I knew better. All you had to do was see him stare at that bowl as if transfixed, his eyes following every movement of the spoon, from bowl to mouth and back to bowl, till all the soup was gone. Sometimes he would even give his slice of bread away. He was beginning to look emaciated, and at times his eyes could glow like hot coal. He often talked about Christ, too. When I told him he owed it to himself and his family to take care of himself, he brushed me aside, saying he was fine. And it was true that much of the time he was fine—his usual talkative, interesting, humorous self. I didn't know what to make of it. De Coucy's worry, however, went beyond his friend's health. Thoroughly Cartesian, he found Baas-Becking's behavior disquieting because simply unreasonable, and in that sense he was no doubt right. We tried to tell others they shouldn't accept the offered soup, but it was clearly unreasonable on our part to expect results from that.

We were just too hungry not to be greedy. Though even greed had its bounds. One Sunday, the soup arrived late, and when it finally came, it tasted terrible and was obviously spoiled. For all but one of the inmates the limit had been reached: we didn't, couldn't eat. But one inmate, a Dutchman, sat down by that kettle of rotten soup, took it between his knees, and started eating it right out of the barrel. He ate, and ate, and ate, slowly, deliberately, for an hour, two hours, maybe more. We watched him in disbelief. I went away for a while, and when I came back he was still eating. By the time it was getting dark he was at last scraping the bottom, licking his spoon—and went to bed to sleep peacefully all night, waking up in the morning with no ill effects that I ever heard of.

And then, one mid-October day, it was suddenly over with Porz. An air raid—the usual wailing of sirens, the usual running to the factory basement, the never-to-get-used-to scare, the detonations coming from the adjoining switchyard. Suddenly, an enormous explosion shook our building. I sucked in my breath. The lights had gone out, and we were in total darkness. We all waited for the next bomb. I tried to control my shaking. But there was no next bomb—not this time. The siren sounded the "all clear", and still nothing happened. We spoke in low voices, as if the pilots might hear us and come back for us. In the darkness no one was sure who was listening, anyway. Time passed, and still nothing. But at last the basement door was opened, and a voice shouted at us to move. They led us out the front of the factory and lined us up against the high wall surrounding our compound, watched by SS with automatic rifles at the ready. The rumor spread that our barracks had taken a direct hit and were totally destroyed. If so, where would they take us?

Night had fallen, and the waiting continued. No food today, I told myself; the others must have had the same thought. It was cold. Then we heard engines, the gate in the wall creaked open, and several trucks drove in. Cattle trucks. The sight of them had a Pavlovian effect on the SS, who immediately started yelling at us, schweinhunding us just to get themselves ready for herding their human cattle in. In we went. The door was latched behind us. We were off. Goodbye, Porz! And thanks for not being too hard on us.

36

In spite of the air raids, I had begun to feel at ease at Porz, and regretted leaving it for an uncertain destination. I had always had anxieties about major transitions. Later in life I almost forced myself into them, perhaps to put the genie into the bottle, but in my childhood I was wary of them: what lay ahead, where and how would I carve out my new role, how would I cope?

Looking back now, I can see that major personality changes occurred in me after sea changes in my environment, as between school in Eindhoven and the University of Amsterdam, and even between schools in Eindhoven. In grade school I had been a bully, plotting with friends how to organize the rest and terrorize the defenseless. In second grade, already, I had set up a "Play Club", proclaimed myself President, and in a rule book wrote down its laws, all of which described reasons (such as disobedience) for the President to throw out members, but none of which provided for admission. I did not have the talent to keep that role going in high school, where other qualities were needed for success. Suddenly introverted, I sought refuge in studying, which got me the approval of the teachers and a form of appreciation from my fellow students, especially if they needed me to crib exams for them. In time, I learned the difference between that and friendship. I really did not make close friends in high school, unlike Jack, who had them at his fingertips, boys and (oh!) girls alike. He was good at sports, too, but so was I, especially field hockey, ping pong, and, of all things, baseball: for it was our school that introduced baseball into Holland in the thirties—into Europe, for that matter, where it is now alive and well as a sport.

Our high school, the Lorentz Lyceum, was a private school. It was located in two rented houses, so the place looked homey. I felt content inside its walls. Where learning was concerned it was a demanding place. Many students had to duplicate at least one year before they got their diplomas. I took to all subjects except, for some unknown reason, botany. Foreign languages, especially, I absorbed like a blotter. For German there was a holy terror called Mrs. Tinbergen, whose single look of reproof could freeze you in your seat. To this day I can recite without stumbling all the German prepositions (mit-nach-nebst-bei-seit-von-zu-entgegen-ausser-aus-gemäsz und gegenüber) that take the dative. Not knowing them was unthinkable. English was taught by Dr. Kalma, a Frisian poet whose large frame and frantic menaces gave him no protection against our disgraceful torments, but who caused me to read "The Merchant of Venice" at sixteen, instilling in me (though I understood it dimly at best) a life-long love for Shakespearean language and wit. And then, of course, there was our swashbuckling French teacher, who impressed us all because he went to Brussels every weekend just to have his hair cut (or so he said), though we never saw much change on Mondays.

In Porz, I had reason to be grateful especially to those three, for they had prepared me to communicate with fellow inmates from other nations, and find friends among them. On the whole, it was not so much cultural differences that kept them apart: we knew we were all in this together, that there was only one common enemy. In our own way, we formed a community. But for the great majority, the language barrier was hard to overcome, except through the little German all would eventually learn by osmosis, but which no one liked to speak. So I had a role to play, that of interpreter, citizen of the world.

Among the French-speaking prisoners, there had been Jean Juliot in Siegburg, and here at Porz, Rossignol and de Coucy. There was also a hotel owner from Luxemburg, a hearty fellow, who must have been big before the war, and who now sorely missed his wife and children. And there was a Belgian kid, barely seventeen years old, who kept singing a nostalgic French chanson popular in those days: "Je n'sais pas pourquoi j'allais danser, au Saint Jean la musette . . ."—over and over, until it was grafted into my mind, remaining to this day an immediate reminder of wartime whenever I hear it. I also befriended Mario, an Italian communist factory worker, who had lived in France for years, and in Porz was made to pay for Mussolini's stab into the back of France in 1940. Ignored and isolated, he looked sad and perplexed, and sought out my company not only because I could talk with him, but would. The really odd duck in the bite was George, an Englishman of all things. He was from the Channel island of Jersey, occupied by the Germans, but to me he seemed so quintessentially British that he might as well have been from Oxford.

Those, and others. There were Russians, too, quite a few of them, apparently, but they worked somewhere else in the factory and had their own barracks. I never met any, except dead.

In the dark of that cattle truck, rumbling once again to another resettlement, in a place unknown, I wondered if I was now going to lose my Porz friends. I made a resolve to look them all up once the war was over, to stay in contact. Life rarely works out that way, of course. Of all of them, de Coucy was the only one I would see again after the war. But all my life the memory of them has come back to me from time to time, and I have thought of them with special fondness, as if a bond still united us.

Eindhoven: My father, Jacques H. Scholten ca.1938 in front of the building on two floors of which, for the benefit of visitors, he had spent years making a miniature of the giant Philips industrial complex. The building was destroyed in the fall of 1942 in a British air raid.

Alkmaar: Jeanne Scholten-van Gennep, the mother I lost in 1926, just before my third birthday.

The Hague: My brothers Pieter and Jack (l. and r.) and I (center) with our new mother, Henriette Elisabeth Scholten-Kromhout ca. 1928.

Eindhoven: *De Haven*, the family home from 1930 to 1953. I moved out in 1940 to study Geology in Amsterdam, but spent part of vacations there until my arrest in December of 1943. The last time I saw it was in 1950 after four years at the University of Michigan. Inexplicably, the gracious house was destroyed some time later.

Amsterdam: My student digs at 110 de Lairesse street from January 1941 to May 1943. The arrow marks my roof window from where I could watch the searchlights and aerial anti-aircraft explosions at night.

Amsterdam:
My new I.D. card issued by the police in July, 1943, when I said my original one was stolen, a pretense made because the alteration of 3 to 5 in my critical year of birth, 1923, was too obvious.

Amsterdam:
Students in the Resistance. One of its leaders, my new friend, Kees Rübsaam, with whom I was to room from May, 1943, to the day of my arrest, December 27, sits on the ground (l.) with me (r.)

Vught:
Concentration camp ("K.Z. Lager")
Permission slip for a day in the sick ward
on February 23, 1944, after my fever rose
at last to 39C (102F),
the required minimum.

Vught:

Concentration camp
An order for me, prisoner P1575, of Work
Barracks 3, to report to Barracks 43 in the
separate section of Camp Vught set up by
agreement between Nazi authorities and the
Philips Corporation to produce, among other
things, radios. Philips succeeded in improving
living conditions for imprisoned Jewish and
some non-Jewish ex-employees. Going there
represented a welcome change.

Siegburg, Germany:
In the summer of 1944, recovering from
diphtheria in a prison cell, I received the
miracle of a package from home,
thanks to the Philips Corporation and a
local priest. It contained, food, letters,
and, from my brother Pieter, a hand-
written copy of a well-known poem,
which his deteriorating mind was
still able to comprehend.

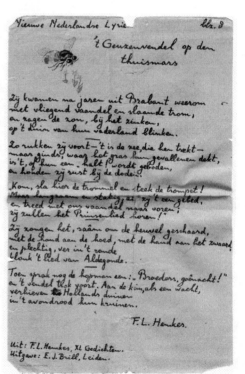

Wetzlar, Germany:
In 1945, the millions of liberated foreigners (Displaced Persons, or D.P.'s) received an I.D. card from UNRRA, the U.N.'s Repatriation and Rehabilitation Agency. In the spring and summer I worked as interpreter for this agency and U.S. Counter-Intelligence.

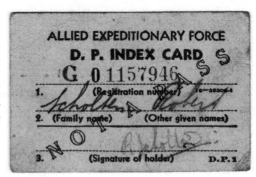

Amsterdam:
My first passport picture, 1946, for geology excursions to ravaged Belgium and wealthy Sweden, a personal side trip to glorious Paris, and in August the great adventure of a year at the University of Michigan that was to stretch to a lifetime.

An honest attempt by the German government in 2001, some 70 years after the fact, to come to a manner of resolution by offering payment of 7669 Euros for forced labor during World War II.

37

After two days in the main prison in Siegburg, they packed some of us off to a camp not far away, at the "Zellwolle" factory just across the Sieg River. I had heard it was a bad place to be, and went with much apprehension.

The plant manufactured an artificial fibrous material used as a substitute for wool. The fiber was produced in an acid solution circulating in elongate open troughs. They put me to work at one of those. Again, I drew the night shift. My immediate supervisor was a Ukrainian prisoner, who showed me what to do. He wore long rubber gloves for protection against the acid. I had to work with bare hands. After a while, the Ukrainian left to hobnob with the guards for the rest of the night. He lived well.

The tricky thing in my job was to judge when enough fiber had formed in the acid, and then to reach down into the trough, grab a bundle with two fists, pull it out, and swing it in one smooth motion across the first of several huge cylinders overhead that rolled into each other as in the old mangling driers. Between them, the rollers squeezed out the liquid, and what came out was a wide, flat ribbon of cellulose material, the Zellwolle, which, from there, moved like a high transport band across the factory, out of my sight and responsibility, drying in the process. The work could be painful—after a while, the acid burned your hands red and put any cuts you might have on fire, and the fumes stung your nostrils and lungs. It could also be perilous. Some who had had this job had got their hands caught in the mangle and been pastured out to different jobs. That danger was greatest when you didn't throw the fibre just right, so that, instead of following the proper path between the cylinders, it started making a bungled mess. What you had to do then, and quickly, was pick up a big, sharp knife and cut through it. The Ukrainian had warned me not to let the knife get stuck in the fibre, but it happened the very first week. By instinct, you hold on to that knife, you try to pull it out to keep it from disappearing between the cylinders. I felt it pulling me in, and let go with only a fraction of a second left. The Ukrainian yelled at me, less because I had almost lost my hand than on account of the crushed knife. A German guard came over and hit me—not very hard, really, but it made me so mad that I forgot my primary safety rule ("don't get noticed") and shouted back at him to keep his damned hands off me. To my amazement, he walked off. Nothing was ever predictable.

It was cold in the factory. The lonesome twelve-hour standup shifts were tiring and seemed endless. It was cold in the barrack, too, which was heated only by a small central stove, on which we all took turns warming up for a minute, or grilling our slice of tasteless bread. The place was overcrowded, but washing facilities were so rudimentary and sparse that it was hard to keep clean. It was a haven for lice. At Zellwolle I established my all-time record of one hundred twenty lice crushed in a single search. Until now, I had not had fleas, but here everyone had them. There were armies of them, hiding and breeding in our filthy straw mattresses, coming out at night to bite you in your sleep or keep you awake, scratching. Everyone looked pale, worn-out, withdrawn. There was none of the sense of community that had made life bearable at Porz. Instead, there was a climate of distrust and fear—the whole atmosphere was sinister, threatening.

There was good reason to be fearful. The commander of the camp was a high-ranking, fanatical Nazi, who didn't care if we lived or died. Periodically, he had prisoners flogged at the mere suspicion of some minor infraction, or because they had become too ill and weak to snap to attention or work fast enough. A short time before my arrival, I was told, he had personally ordered and supervised the hanging of a Polish prisoner for the sin of "talking back", and everybody had been forced to watch. "There have been prisoners here since 1940," one of the inmates told me, "but no one has lasted more than two years. And most don't last that long." "And don't even think of escaping," he added. "They have bloodhounds to track you down. The ones who tried have all been caught and been beaten to pulp and starved in solitary and then sent off God knows where." After that conversation I knew I had to find a way to improve my condition, as at Vught, or somehow get out of Zellwolle altogether.

I had heard there was a means to get extra food. You could volunteer to do overtime work on a farm, digging potatoes. It was a trade-off: fresh air and extra food against precious hours of sleep. I had to try it. At the end of the next night shift I joined a small group of men and climbed into a truck.

It felt good to be out in the countryside, the sun a hand's breadth above the horizon, your skin stinging from the cold of morning air, your nostrils filled with the smell of earth. The farm was half an hour away. We were led out into the field and started to dig. It was hard work. Bent over like that, hurrying from row to row to keep up with the others, you felt sure your back would break if it went on much longer. But at the end of three hours there was a whistle, and at the farmhouse we could at last sit down. Bowls of hot boiled potatoes were set out on long trestles, three or four potatoes for each of us—a feast! I had forgotten what it felt like to have a full stomach. It was good, also, to see Germans other than our guards, who, by and large, were a sorry lot, whose enjoyment lay in being feared. These farm folk seemed to have nothing to do with the persecution of Jews, with shouting and intimidation, or crazy notions of a pure Aryan race and German lordship. It was difficult to see them as enemies, and that momentary contact with common decency and release from hatred was itself a balm. They knew all of us stuck potatoes into our pockets, which we would later roast over the flames of the stove back in camp, but they didn't try to stop us. By noon we were back in camp, bone-tired, to eat our noon soup I and drop off to the few hours of sleep before the night shift.

It was an impossible routine to keep up for long. No doubt each of us burned more calories in the field than those few potatoes gave us back. The benefit was mostly psychological. As it turned out, I did not have to decide whether to go on with it or not, for I was reassigned to work in the factory's warehouse section. That daytime job not only put an automatic end to the farm option, but left you too exhausted for overtime work.

Warehousing meant carrying big sacks of Zellwolle on your back from the factory to a large shed, and then up a ladder to stack them in the loft. We were like a line of worker-ants, watched over by soldier-ants schnell-schell-ing us across the factory yard, faster-faster, stumbling, all muscles aching, weak from fatigue and hunger, thinking you can't go on. Two days of that, three days, and I knew I had to do something, or else I wouldn't last. I still had potatoes hidden away in my flea-bitten mattress but one evening I found them gone, stolen—and I knew the thief was the unpleasant fellow who had the neighboring bunk and who was now blatantly roasting one in the fire. The loss of precious food was bad enough, but the moral blow was worse: we lived in a jungle, and our laws were the laws of rats, every rat for himself. The following morning I asked to see the "Sanitäter", a prisoner who had been a doctor in Vienna.

It was the only thing I could come up with: play the same card I had played with the Gestapo in Amsterdam, use my physical disorder (which had not recurred since that fateful day of my arrest) to escape from imminent danger. I told the Sanitäter about my head accident, my brain hemorrhage, about losing consciousness in the streetcar. "And now," I added, "more and more often I have spells of dizziness, I feel myself sliding off, nearly pass out. Just this week I've felt it four or five times. If I black out at the wrong time . . ." The doctor heaved a heavy sigh. "Unfortunately," he said, "there's no medication here—nothing. So what can I do?"

"Couldn't you tell the camp commander that I need to see the prison doctor in Siegburg?" I asked. "To see if I should be reassigned?" I added, hopefully.

He nodded sympathetically. "It's true that this is a bad place for someone with your problem," he said. "A very bad place. I'll try. It might work. You can never tell with these people. There is no system. What they decide depends on how they feel that day. In any case, it must all be in your file, so they can check it and see it's not a made-up story. I'll see him today."

The result was immediate—and catastrophic. At noon, while we were eating our sauerkraut soup, the camp commander entered, in full Nazi uniform. An orderly called out my name and I shouted: "Here!" I felt triumphant, sure my trick had worked again. Goodbye Zellwolle! Only then did I notice that the Nazi officer's look was not one of goodwill towards man. He glared at me. "Of course," I thought, "I forgot to salute." I saluted and stood at attention. But he looked angrier yet, and started out on a fair imitation of the Führer himself, talking first in a low, menacing voice, then working himself up into a frenzy for the better part of three minutes. But what made me freeze were his last words: "I have your number now," he yelled, "and I promise you I won't forget it. I'll get you one way or another, and soon." With that he turned and walked off.

He left me shaking. "Chicanery", he had called my act, which, of course, it was. How could I have been so dumb? I had called attention to myself, and now the fat was in the fire. A fellow inmate walked over and said: "Man, you had better watch out! There's no telling what that bastard will do to you."

It was time to go back to work, but with my panicked mind racing in circles, I could hardly keep up. I felt like a caged rat. I was a caged rat! How could I save my skin? Try to escape?

An hour later my name was called out. Good God, so soon? "Schnell, schnell!" With fear in my heart I ran over, expecting the worst. A small group of inmates was standing by a truck. We were ordered in. What were they going to do to us? At least, I thought, I've not been singled out. There was some comfort in numbers. But where were they taking us?

The truck left the camp and turned up the highway, going north. Why, that meant towards Siegburg! Sure enough, soon we were driving through streets that were starting to look familiar. Only then did I dare to believe that we were going back to the main prison, where I would no longer be in the power of that psychopath who had it in for me. A stone fell from my heart. Saved by the bell! Wherever they would send me next, I could at least begin with a clean slate—become anonymous again.

But why had this happened? The mystery was soon cleared up. We were told the barracks at Porz had been rebuilt, and we would soon go back there. How could I be so lucky? It was the next best thing to freedom. In the week past, the memory of Porz had begun to take on a glow of old gold in my mind. Porz was safety, the simple life, Porz was easy work, enough sleep, a wooden table beneath soft light, good food, good friends, casual conversation, friendly guards who chanted Gregorian chants—in a word, Porz seemed all that Zellwolle was not. And now I was to go back there. Hurray! Goodbye, Nazi bastard, and may you get an apoplexy when you find out I'm gone! But you, my guardian angel thank you, oh, thank you, thank you!

38

Because air alarms were more and more frequent, almost daily, in fact, the city of Siegburg had decided to construct a community bomb shelter. In the center of town stood an isolated hill, the lower part of which was a park. Here, a long tunnel was being dug into the hill, and the digging was done by prison inmates. Temporarily, I was put to work on that project.

From the prison to the park was a twenty minute walk through town—a town I had disliked from the day of my first arrival, under a drizzly rain and to the jeers of some of its citizens. It had seemed ugly and grim, then. Now, beneath a cold, clear sky, it seemed less drab, though still hard to warm up to. Many years after the war, on a hot summer day, I finally went back to Siegburg and was astonished to find a pretty, appealing German town. In a small square at the foot of the hill I sat down on a bench shaded by trees, and in this place of hunger ate the most delectable pastry I have ever tasted. It was impossible to merge my wartime and postwar images. To this day, Siegburg remains two towns, carrying the same name, but otherwise unconnected.

Digging the tunnel was strictly a manual affair, done with pick-axes and wheel-barrows. I worked in the wheelbarrow squad. It was pleasant in the park. The work was hard, but not crushing. If I felt tired, all I had to do was think back to Zellwolle. Now and then you could stop to rest for a few seconds without getting threatened by one of the SS-men who were watching over us.

During one of those rests, returning from the place where I had just unloaded earth and rock from my wheel-barrow, I heard someone calling—a woman's voice, coming from an upper story window of one of the high, stately row-houses across the street from the park. Two women. They had opened the window and were beckoning me to come closer. The SS were talking, not watching. I came down a little, and then both women started throwing things into the park. Apples! Red apples, sailing across the street and tumbling down into the grass. The coast was still clear. I dashed over, feverishly stuffed my pockets full, dashed back to my wheelbarrow. From there, I waved my gratitude to the two women. They waved back . . . another sign that decency and kindness were not dead in this country. I hid my apples behind a tree for later distribution among our group of inmates.

The following morning one of the SS-men called me over: "Du, da!" Two well-dressed women were standing next to him, talking to him. "Diese Damen möchten dir etwas geben," he said to me. One of the two women spoke asking me where I was from. "Holland," I said. She nodded.

"Yes," she said, "it must be hard being away from your family. And hard for your family." "You see," she went on, "I have a son your age. He has been drafted into the Army and is now in Russia, on the east front. He even looks like you."

I was not sure why she said all this, but she soon made it clear. "Now," she said, "the amiable Untergruppenführer here (turning to the SS-man) has given me permission to give you something." From under her coat, she produced a parcel and handed it to me. "I would like you to have this," she said, "but, you understand, it's just for you—because of my son. So you mustn't give it away. Will you promise?" I promised, and the SS-man told me to go back to work.

I opened the package during the noon break. It contained cake and cigarettes, and we had a feast.

While pushing my empty wheelbarrow back up to the tunnel opening, I often looked up to the top of the hill, which seemed shrouded in mystery—you could see old walls, of a castle, perhaps, surrounded by high trees. From below, it was something dreamlike, far removed from the war, from yelling, arrogance and debasement, from killing and destruction and all the Nazis had created. Now and then, from afar, you could see a few people walking around under the trees. It all breathed tranquillity, so that just looking up gave you a moment of peace. On my postwar return, I discovered that the walls were those of an old monastery, and here, only here, the two images, wartime and postwar, came together, for the tranquillity I had felt then, I felt again now, walking into the courtyard, where birds were singing and all was peace.

But, who were those people you could see walking around in those days of tunnel digging? Someone said they were British and American airmen, shot down over Germany and wounded, and that they were temporarily hospitalized here. So English was spoken up there! That thought alone, and the idea of the nearness of Allies, even as prisoners, was terribly exciting. English—the language of freedom, and of the certain victors over the people who spoke that other language, the German we had come to despise.

Certain victors—perhaps not even the Germans doubted it by now. But in the sky above us, some of them were still paying the ultimate price. One time, several planes came into sight. We could watch them from the opening to the tunnel, where we scurried at every alarm. High puffs of cloud appeared among them where shells had exploded. And then a plane was hit! It started trailing smoke, began its fall to earth, at first twirling like an autumn leaf, silently, as if in slow motion. "Jump! Jump!" I begged. "For God's sake, jump! But no one jumped, and then the plane began its nosedive, and it was too late to jump. Another time, several crew members did jump, and sailed down gracefully in their parachutes.

A week later I was back in Porz.

39

The barracks had been rebuilt exactly as before, there were the same guards, the same machines, and little by little the same inmates came dribbling in, most of them glad to be back, depending on where they had been the past few weeks. But, although the conditions were the same, there was something different in the air, an imminence of change, and an expectation. It came from the scraps of news some had picked up, and from which we could form a notion how the war was going. We learned Paris had been taken by the Allies, and northern France, perhaps even part of Belgium. Were they in Holland, too, I wondered? Might they even now be pushing into Germany? But where—through the Alsace, or towards the Ruhr? It had to be all over in a few weeks, we thought, or not more than a couple of months. What would our liberation be like? I didn't have the haziest idea what a front line was like—but it was bound to be exciting.

Winter had really set in now. In the ill-heated factory and barracks the cold was with you all the time, down to the bone. Christmas was approaching, and we were told we would have a day off and get white bread on Christmas Eve. As always, incongruity was the only thing that made prison life halfway foreseeable. White bread, no less! But when the day arrived, the white bread didn't. It was a disappointment. Still, work did stop for the night, and we spent it together with the day crew in the living quarters, talking, singing songs in three different languages. Next to me, Baas-Becking sat cross-legged on the table and sang an English song of many verses, a forlorn lass's plaint to her mother about her sailor-lover who had abandoned her. He did the Cockney accent to perfection, and acted it out so well that he got a round of applause and was asked to sing it again, even though most had not understood a word of the text.

At midnight something astonishing happened. The camp commander, an SS-officer we rarely saw, suddenly entered the room. He seemed ill at ease.

The place fell still. He started to speak slowly, groping for words to express unfamiliar feelings to unfamiliar people. It was hard to believe, but he spoke of peace.

"It looks as if this terrible war is not going to last much longer," he said. "You people didn't ask for it, and many Germans didn't, either." (Did he include himself? Then why that uniform?) He went on. "In this season of peace, we may at last think again of peace, and the end of killing and hatred. Before long, you should be back in your own countries and with your own families. That is my wish for you, and for all of us."

It was unsettling. How should we react? Sympathizing with him seemed unthinkable. He was a Nazi, and he was probably just out to save his skin, hoping his belated benevolence would pay postwar dividends. And still, and still, I felt moved, as if, for once, I could see through the hated uniform and into the man's heart, and found sincerity there, perhaps even torment, and never mind if they were new found. Should one reply, after all? No, still unthinkable. But someone did speak up. It was Baas-Becking. He spoke briefly and without a trace of fawning, thanking the camp commander for his Christmas wishes and expressing the hope that we would all find our way back to humanity. The camp commander listened, nodded, turned, and left.

You could hear a pin drop. I looked over to de Coucy, knowing he would be furious. He was. Baas-Becking had put us on the same footing as the SS-officer. He had implied it was not only they, but we, too, who had lost touch with humaneness. I walked over to the count.

"What's the matter with him?" he exploded. "What does he mean, all of us? Does he absolve the boches?" He searched for words to go on, to condemn his friend, but held them in. "C'est inexplicable. C'est inacceptable!" was all he added. "Tu comprends ça, toi?"

I waffled, feeling I ought to share his indignation. What held me back was the certainty that, much as I understood de Coucy's anger, it was Baas-Becking who had just expressed the highest values of western civilization, and that it was he who was far ahead of the rest of us.

That incident was the beginning of a falling-out between the two. Baas-Becking was either unaware of the chill, or above it. In the count's eyes he soon heaped insult on injury. One of the guards had fallen ill, and it was he, the famous biologist, professor at Leiden and Stanford Universities, humanist, our "Sanitäter", who now acted In Imitatione Christi. For days and nights he took care of that man, who, in high fever, lay on his bed in the guards' barrack. He sat by his bed, wiped his brow, changed his compresses, and coaxed him back to health.

For de Coucy, and just about everyone else, that was too much. The kindest thing he could say about his former friend was that his mind must have snapped. In the end, I was one of the few who still spoke to Baas-Becking. I couldn't help admiring him and liking him. He didn't talk at all about what he was doing. Although thin and pale, he still had verve, and was already making plans for life after prison. In that, he was well ahead of us, too. At one point he said: "When all this is over, and the borders of Europe are open again, why don't we do some traveling together? Italy, Spain, Greece, maybe Egypt, too." The thought was so startling to me, that it made my head swim. He played down the novelty of it; but then, he had already done a lot of globe-trotting, and I none. But we were inmates! Was the time really near when you could do that sort of thing, move around as you wanted to without being told? Psychologically, I had acquired the mind-set of a prisoner, of most prisoners, always waiting for an order. It was hard to imagine an end to our state; so hard, that, when our promised white bread finally arrived on Christmas Day, slightly stale, and I had savored it slowly, I caught myself looking forward already to the next time we'd get this special favor . . . a whole year away. As if prison would go on forever.

Shortly after Christmas, our guards and SS-men, who had been looking more gloomy by the day, suddenly became triumphant. They were burning to tell us the good news, that the fortunes of war had now definitively shifted in favor of the Third Reich.

"We have driven die Engländer und die Amerikaner back", one of them said. "They are fleeing, and in a day or two the German Army will retake Paris. After that, it will be Dunkerque all over again."

They were lying, lying! They had to be lying, just to pester us! But then, why were they smiling so? Could it be true? After the war, I heard about the bloody Battle of the Bulge in Belgium, and understood the Germans had not sucked all of the story out of their thumbs. But then and there, around New Year in Porz, we kept telling each other that they had fabricated it all out of thin air and were faking their smiles on orders from above, to demoralize us and keep us in line. Before long, the smiles disappeared.

In January, for unexplained reasons, we exchanged air raid shelters with the Russian prisoners. From then on, it was they who ran to the factory basement, while we ran to a quonset hut covered with a layer of sod, one to two hundred meters away from the factory. And it was there we raced on the evening of the twentieth of January.

40

The loudspeakers were still blaring out that planes were over the Siebengebirge, well south of us, and heading east, when they were already on top of us, filling the air with their awesome droning until the sky itself seemed to vibrate in unison. A major attack! Hundreds of them, without any doubt. Where were they going? Just then the first bombs whistled overhead and exploded in the direction of the switchyard: they were after Porz! Quickly we hustled into our shelter.

The inside was lit by a few candles only, just enough to push total darkness into the corners and show the outlines of the tables and benches. Behind us, the door was closed, and locked from the outside. No one spoke. The whistling of the falling bombs was all around us, followed by strings of explosions that shook the shelter. There seemed to be no end: phiiiooo-phiiiooo-phiiiooo! Boom-boom-boomboomboomboom! More, more, more. Holy God, this could be dangerous. It was night, it would be easy to miss the target by a thousand feet or so, and hit somewhere near the sod-covered aluminum roof that was our only protection. Listening to the sky, now, you could make out a sound different from the continuous droning of the engines and the intermittent whistling of the bombs. It was a muffled rumble, which seemed to come from the carpet of bombs when first released, dropping to earth and heading for a still unknown destination. Drrrrrrrrrrrrrrrr. The overhead whistle came after that and was actually reassuring: these bombs, at least, were not for us. No, it was the rumble that was frightening—the waiting for the whistle.

On went the attack, on and on. Time was in split-seconds, the raid without end. But now the droning waned, the wave spent. Everyone breathed deeply. Smiles reappeared, and some started talking. Saved again! In the near-dark we waited for the "All Clear" siren. But it didn't come. The Germans must be shaken up, we said. More waiting. And then, far away, the same ominous buzzing in the sky. Another wave? Porz again? It was, and once more we fell still and dug our nails into our palms. It was near freezing, but I didn't feel the cold. Only the bombs counted—those, and the fear . . .

———

Now the second wave recedes. Silence again. The smiles are weaker this time. This is hard on the nervous system! Is it over now? How long have we been in here, anyway—one, two hours? It must be near midnight. IS IT OVER NOW . . . IS IT OVER, OVER? No, Jesus-God, it isn't! Another wave is approaching. Is that me, shaking like that?

And now, all hell breaks loose. Earthquake after earthquake. The explosions are ear-renting. It seems this time the target is our factory. They must be done with the switchyard. Drrrrrrrrr—Jesus, where are these going? Is this the end, now, now, NOW? Phiiiooo-phiiiooo—relief again, boomboomboomboom. Rumble again—drrrrrrr—phiiiooo-boomboomboom. How long can this go on? How can they keep missing our lousy shelter? A man starts screaming in the dark, as if he'd been hit—Aaaaaaaaahhh!!!—till he runs out of breath. Someone talks to him; now he only whimpers. I want to duck, hide under the table, where it seems safer. The uselessness of it makes me stop. Or is it the ridicule? Must stay calm! Remember my dignity. But I bury my head beneath my clasped hands, as if that would help. I want to pray, and, though I know the hypocrisy of it, still I pray, for protection, for not really believing, for not having prayed before. After a while I look up again and turn around. In the corner, by the light of a candle, four French inmates are playing cards as if they were sitting in a bistro on a boulevard in Paris. Only the limp cigarettes are lacking, and the glass of Pernod. How can they be so cool? I may seem cool, but I'm not. I am a bundle of nerves packed in nothing but jelly. On it goes, drrrrrrrr—phiiiooo-phiiiooo-phiiiooo! What is it like to die? That last fraction of a second of consciousness before you are torn apart and all is dark? Will it hurt? "Mother, why isn't there NOTHING?" Phiiiooo-boomboomBOOM!—an enormous explosion, deafening, the end of our quonset hut caves in part-way. There is yelling, but no one seems hurt. That was close to a direct hit! Thirty feet, forty? And still it goes on. God, oh God, if I survive this I'll never again be upset at anything or mad at anyone—promise! "PROMISE!!"

Suddenly, it is quiet, except for the faint buzzing of planes in the distant sky, on their way home. Are these the last? Don't hope, don't hope yet, be quiet, or they'll come back! We wait in silence, an eternity. Then, at long last, it comes, the high, single-pitch squeal of the siren: ALL CLEAR.

Hours later, the key turned in the lock. We were ordered out, stumbling into the gray, unpromising light of dawn, onto a scene of utter destruction, lit by the flickering of a last fire. The factory was blown apart, a rubble of bricks and concrete and burnt wood. Part of a single wall was still standing; it carried a slogan: Der Führer hat immer recht. I recognized the place where I had been threading my steel and aluminum nuts. "The Führer is always right." Several corpses were lying on the frozen ground: Russian prisoners, killed in the place that had been our shelter until a couple of weeks ago.

Trucks were waiting. They packed us in, and we left Porz, this time for good.

41

In the thousands of pages written about Nazi prisons and concentration camps, Siegburg occupies no more than a footnote. There was no counterpart in western Germany of the torture and famine, the foul debasement of the human spirit, and the ultimate destruction of the will to live inflicted upon Jews and non-Jews alike in the extermination camps of eastern Germany and Poland. Beatings could be severe, but were not systematic torture. Our hunger left us weak, but was not famine. Our guards threatened and yelled to make us obey, but not many spirits were broken. There was death, death from disease and undernourishment, from the shooting of escaped prisoners, death to set an example and maintain a climate of fear, but not planned death on a mass scale. Our condition was bad, but not so abysmal as to undermine all sense of fellowship between us—at least not at Porz.

Looking back, what astonishes me is that I remember no feuds, no real animosities between all those inmates, with their different tongues and cultures. There were flare-ups, but they were soon quelled. Once, I almost came to blows with a Polish prisoner, for a reason now forgotten, and within seconds several Poles were by his side to back him up, if needed. But others came and kept us apart. Collectively, we had spun a social fabric that would not tolerate destructive behavior, and also kept us from falling into a sense of inferiority to those, who, in their raucous voices, called us Schweinhund. I believe we felt stronger than they, many of us.

I thought about Europe, then . . . the New Europe that would arise after the war, a shining continent of unity and hope, in which centuries-old hatchets would at last be buried. For had we not suffered a common fate, had we not been tempered by the same terrible fire and gone through the same katharsis? The Allied countries of Europe first—they would form the nucleus. In time, when Germany and its partners had expunged their unforgettable crimes and a new generation had arisen, untainted, they, too, would join, and we would have a true United States of Europe. Yes, yes, my brothers, my sisters, we will do it, all the old faces will be swept away from the scene of European politics, and new ones will arise in each country, we will see to it—fresh ones, with new ideas and new ideals and the same overriding commitment: to bring this about, and soon, before they are lost, those memories of our joint fate, before the gossamer web of our comradeship is torn apart, blown away . . .

When none of this happened, not in 1945, nor the year after, when the old faces did come back and even the new ones talked like them, about nationhood and patriotism, about socialism and conservatism and party loyalty and economic independence, and no one spoke of the New Europe, I knew the momentum was lost for decades to come, and lost interest in changing the world. Europe now seemed old and stale. For youth, excitement and opportunity, you had to go overseas, I thought, to Canada, the U.S. or Australia. Many in Holland began to think and talk of emigration, and I was glad with the profession I had chosen, for as a geologist I could go to the far corners of the world, if I wanted to. So that, when, in '46, I had a chance to go for a year on a scholarship to America or Switzerland, or perhaps to Sweden, the choice was easy.

But in the early months of 1945, all of that was still unimaginably far from my mind. The only important thing at hand was to survive the war. I don't think I really doubted that I would survive it, but still, there was danger all around. With luck I had escaped the rain of bombs on Porz. I would need more luck to get home safe.

42

The truck that took us away from Porz had brought us back to the central prison in Siegburg. The place was crowded, and soon became overcrowded, as the pressure of war forced the closing of more and more of the satellite prison camps in the region. Soon we were six to a cell, locked up all day long with nothing to do. Only a few dozen inmates got out during the day to do the minimal work necessary to keep this small city-within-a-city going. We had little news from the front. Where was it now? What took them so long? Sometimes, from far away, a western wind carried a muffled rumble into our cells, and we knew it was the sound of canons. The front-line... our still unthinkable freedom! But the rumbling didn't seem to be growing any louder. Were they stalled? Our glimpses of Germany outside the prison walls showed a country so dilapidated by now, that we could not believe a modern, well-equipped army could not just plow the enemy under. Of front-line realities we knew little, and our impatience grew by the day.

The cell was oppressive. I felt the need to move around, and after a while had my way. Some of the Porz inmates were called out and put to work repairing bombed railway tracks at the vast switchyard of Troisdorf, several miles north of Siegburg. To my delight, I spotted de Coucy there, and sat down next to him during our noon soup break. He seemed pleased, too. "Bienôt la fin, mon jeune ami," he said. "La fin pour les boches. Un nouveau début pour nous." His indomitable disdain for the Germans was as obvious to them as ever. They sought to humiliate him by refusing to allow him to go to the latrine, forcing him to squat down in the snow in front of them and the rest of us. He barely shrugged his shoulders and performed his function with casual grace. It might have been the king of France relieving himself in front of his courtiers. He talked to me about the work waiting for him back home, and again invited me to Paris. It remained unreal to me. Reality was the cold in the early morning, the bleak landscape, the dirty snow along the tracks, the armed guards around us, and the double-tailed fighter-bombers I came to know after the war as P-38's high in the sky above us. Periodically, they would swoop down and drop bombs, undoing our day's work, while we ran like hell. You had to watch out, for they deserved their nickname of "Lightning", and came down near ground level to strafe us before we knew what happened. One day, I had to stay behind in my cell because of violent stomach cramps. In the afternoon I heard a distant rattling of machine guns and a long series of heavy explosions from the direction of Troisdorf. On that day, several inmates were killed, I never found out how many.

Meanwhile, the sound of the canons had grown steadily louder, and with it grew our excitement. From the few snatches of news we managed to get, scraps of newspaper or veiled comments by our guards, we gathered Aachen had fallen. In my cell, from memory, I had scratched a rough map of western Europe on one of the walls to keep track of where the front-line was. How, where would the Allies cross the Rhine? How soon would we see our liberators?

But as the guns grew louder, we had for some time heard another sound, one we could not place at first. It was like that of a plane, yet different, very even, and it usually came at night. Then we were told: Germany, it seemed, had developed a powerful new weapon, a pilot-less, armed guided missile called the "V-1", hundreds of which a day were sent to England, sowing panic and havoc wherever they fell. England stabbed in the back, straight in the heart! The people were reeling, and were demanding capitulation, our guards assured us. No one believed that, but the droning did sound terribly ominous in the dark of night. Once, it woke me up, and I listened to its approach until it seemed straight above us, when it suddenly stopped. I held my breath, waiting for the explosion. Inexplicably, the silence continued. That gave me hope that most of them were duds or didn't make it to England—or, for that matter, to Holland.

The Germans at last saw the uselessness of our daily track repair job. Very few trains managed to sneak through in the brief hours one of the tracks was actually cleared. So we were pulled off the job, and I was back pacing my cell whenever someone else wasn't pacing it.

And now we all came to know a new enemy, dangerous, invisible and unfamiliar, which could strike indiscriminately and without warning, and against which no one was safe, not even the Germans. Typhus! At first, there were only rumors of isolated cases, but in little time it became epidemic. Infested as we were with lice, it was a wonder it hadn't broken out before. One of the wings of the prison was set aside for typhus patients, and there you went if you ran a fever and complained about it, or if it showed on your face. The dread, therefore, was not just the typhus, but any simple flu, which could get you into that wing, where you were sure to get it. None of the sick was treated there: on your own you lived or died. After the war, I heard that great quantities of disinfectant powder were discovered in the prison, which we could have used to kill the lice. Our clothes could have been changed more frequently, and could have been boiled. The prison authorities had good reason to be afraid for their own lives, but the only preventive measure they took other than quarantining the sick was to have us all shaven bald—the first time I had been bald since Vught. Other than humiliating us temporarily, it had no effect, for we had body lice, not head lice. We were sitting ducks for the typhus bug. All there was to do was sit, sleep, talk, walk, stink up the air in our cramped quarters with the windows shut against the bitter winter, and hope liberation would come soon. Hoisting myself up to the barred window, I could look out across the dreary prison yard, where inmates were carrying corpses to a small building to be piled up for later burial. Day after day. It became depressing. It was March.

43

It was March. The Allied troops had crossed the bridge at Remagen, less than fifteen miles south of us. We didn't know it, but we knew something was different. The canon fire now came from the south, no longer from the west, and that could only mean that our troops (for we thought of them as "ours") were on the east side of the Rhine! By the middle of March it sounded as if they were only a few miles away. Any day now, we said to each other, but no one had any idea of the form our liberation would take.

Then I was called out again, to be part of a new work squad. The prison's water supply had broken down. A temporary hand pump was installed along a tributary of the Sieg River. It had two large T-bars on opposite sides which had to be moved up and down, like a see-saw, from above your head to below your knees. There were four of us to each side, pumping river water through a hose towards a large tank in the prison yard. I wondered if we were now actually drinking raw river water. In any case, we had no choice. The work was not hard, and we were all glad to be out during the day, especially now that the weather had improved. The sun had come out, and there were days when you could believe that winter was over.

At the end of the first day out, I stopped by de Coucy's cell on the way back to my own, to ask how he was doing. He was sick, one of his cellmates said; I froze. But having heard my voice, he got up, and for a few seconds we spoke through the closed door. "Ce n'est pas le typhus, ce n'est pas le typhus," he said, his voice shaking with fever. It was like him, to deny with all the force of his character what was most probable: that he, too, had come down with the dreaded disease. The next day he was gone from his cell, and for a long time I was afraid that he, too, might have died there. After all, he was no longer young. But I had underestimated him. I found out after the war that he had indeed had the typhus, but had beaten it ... beaten it, I felt, with no more than the tenacity of his will power.

The pumping job lasted a few days only, and literally came to a crashing halt. We had become aware of a light plane circling above us all morning. Towards noon there was a whistle overhead, the sound of an explosion, and a plume of smoke somewhere halfway between us and the prison. Another whistling, another plume, halving the distance again. Suddenly it hit me: that was an observation plane, and those were smoke grenades launched to zero in on us. "Run!" I shouted, and all of us, guards and prisoners alike, sprinted away from the pump till we thought we were far enough. We hunkered down against the bank of the stream. The sound of hellfire reached us from where we had come. It was tense, but it was also terribly exhilarating to know we were being shelled by "our" artillery. The front-line, at last! They must be sitting on the south side of the Sieg River, practically within sight! The pilot of that plane must have radioed that he was observing a strange war machine, an anti-aircraft gun, a howitzer, or whatever, and they weren't taking any chances. When the shelling was over, we returned cautiously to what had been the pump. It had been blown apart, the main part lying in a deep shell crater. And that was the end of the pumping squad. I have no idea where we got our water after that.

Next, they put me to work for a few days building a brick wall in the prison yard, between the main building and a smaller one. I knew enough, now, to keep one eye on the sky, but I wasn't ready for an attack at roof level. All at once, there was the roar of a plane engine, and almost simultaneously a fighter swooped in over the wall and started strafing us. There was no time to run, so we just threw ourselves on the ground against the wall. No one was hit that time, but when it happened again, one of the inmates lost his leg. The town of Siegburg itself was also getting it on the chin. It was overcast, so that no planes could be seen, but the sky became a droning sounding board and bombs started falling from the clouds as if the gods themselves were throwing them. They were heading for the area where I knew the railroad station to be, and within seconds an enormous fountain of rubble rose up from there. It was awesome. And not just rubble, I was thinking. There were people living there, many of them. Der Führer hat immer recht!

But where were the troops? Why weren't they coming? We didn't know then that we were just inside the southern edge of what came to be known as the "Ruhr-pocket", a large region left alone while the main Allied armies rushed for Berlin. All we knew was that our liberators were almost within shouting distance, but weren't moving. It was incomprehensible and frustrating. The typhus bug was working away: Sometimes, at night, there was machine gun fire not far off, and we thought: "Now!" But it was not now, it was not an offensive—they just seemed to be sending in probes, always to turn around and go back behind the line. The prison itself became an occasional target for Allied artillery, in spite of the big white crosses that had been painted on the roof. Could a shell penetrate our prison walls? No one knew, but it was on everyone's mind.

When the brick wall was finished, I had to spend my days inside again. Often, I climbed back up to the cell window to look out. The prison yard was nearly empty now. Very few prisoners were still working outside, mostly to carry out the dead. People seemed to be dying like flies now. Four inmates had stopped by the corner of the building to chat for a few moments; soon they broke up and went back to work. Just then, there was an earsplitting explosion and the sound of breaking glass. Cell windows were blown in everywhere, and a shard of flying glass cut my left index finger. But it was not the pain or the blood that made me catch my breath, it was the shell hole in the prison yard. It was at the exact spot where the four prisoners had been standing just a few seconds before.

Two days later the finger had become swollen and was throbbing. I showed it to the guard at mealtime, and a little later was led to the door of a room to have it disinfected and dressed, and was told to wait in the hall. After a while the door was opened, and to my amazement it was a nun who came out to invite me in. A woman! I remembered then the rumor that nuns from a nearby cloister had volunteered as nurses for the typhus ward, and had been required to have their heads shaven first. This was a young woman, with warm, lively eyes. When she took my hand in hers, I shuddered and felt tears welling up. It had been a year and a half since a woman had touched me, and it sent a deep current through me. It moved me, too, to know that she was putting her life in danger to take care of typhus patients from enemy countries. She did her work efficiently and told the guard he should bring me back in a few days.

The infection must have been deeper than she had thought, for the inflammation began anew. But by then I had grabbed an opportunity to spend my days outside again, and I didn't want to loose it by complaining about a little wound. One of my cellmates had an enviable job. He spent his days away from the pesthole our prison had become, to cut wood for the kitchen in the forest near Siegburg. Every morning they came for him at half past five. But one evening he came back with a fever, and the next morning he was too ill to get up when his name was called. Would the guard notice if I stepped out instead? My hesitation lasted only a second—after all, what could they do to me if they discovered? Even one day in the fresh air would be welcome. I stepped out. The guard hardly looked at me.

Down below, at the intersection of the three wings of the building, about ten men were already waiting, all French. I joined the line-up, and soon two armed guards were marching us through town to the forest. It was wonderful! Spring had arrived, and a bright sun lit up the first shoots on the branches.

Sun-dappled, we looked as if we wore camouflage clothing. I took great gulps of air: it was like drinking cool spring water after months of smelly pollution. We worked two men to a saw, resting whenever the guards were not looking. That night, my sick cell mate had been taken away. His misfortune was my good luck: I took over his name and became a permanent member of the saw squad.

44

April 9, 1945. In the early morning hours artillery fire became almost continuous. Machine guns rattled away in the distance. Something was up—this had to be it, the day of our liberation! I wanted to be out there, in the forest, if the front line was going to come through, not locked up in my cell, where I could see nothing. But I was anxious: would the saw squad be allowed to leave? In the dark I waited for the footfall of the guard.

There it was! The key turned in the lock, and in a second I was outside. The guard looked glum, if not downright scared, and said we would certainly not go out that day. In the line-up we waited. Looking up to the glass-encased control room, I saw a discussion going on, and kept my fingers crossed. At last one of the wardens stepped out and shouted an order to the guards below. We were going!

Outside, we ran through the empty streets, ducking into entryways of stores and houses whenever we could, for shells were coming in hard and fast. There were pamphlets lying on the streets everywhere, apparently thrown from planes during the night. Running, I picked one up and read it in the next doorway. It said American troops would move in to occupy the town and warned the population to stay inside, or they would be shot at.

In half an hour we reached the end of the town, and soon we were in the forest, where the war was only a distant rumble. And there we worked, ready for adventure and high drama—the drama of the front-line, and our liberation. It came around eleven o'clock in the morning. Sawing away at my log, I got a glimpse of something moving among the trees. I looked again, and then a tremendous shout came out of my breast, freeing many months of pent-up anxiousness, years of impatient waiting. It was over!

"Les Américains!" I yelled to my French work-mates. Everybody looked up at the extraordinary sight. Three G.I.'s in battle dress. Though they held their rifles at the ready, they approached us as if they were on a casual stroll through the woods.

In most people's lives there probably are a few high points of total exhilaration, engaging their entire being, which will stay with them all their lives and, all alone, are almost enough to justify living. The first time I managed to make love to Sylvia was one of them. After the war there was my first sighting of America from a ship, and, several years later, the first time I embraced the girl who was to be my wife and murmured: "I want to marry you," and she did not say no. There was also the morning I received a phone call from Michigan telling me I had become a father. And the splendid moment when, under a stark blue sky, I was standing on my skis on top of Madonna di Campiglio, next to my ten year old daughter, and took a deep breath and said: "Let's never forget this is one of the best moments in our lives." And so it was with the arrival of our liberators.

The instant was too overwhelming to think of much to say. I rushed up to them and spoke my first English words in months: "Oh boys" (I didn't know what to call them: "guys" was not in my vocabulary, and I did not think of "fellows"), "oh boys, we've waited for you for such a long time!"

They seemed surprised to see us. Sent out as a patrol to look for the enemy, the last thing they expected to find was twelve gaunt-looking men waving saws. Who were we? What were we doing here? "And who," said one of them, pointing to our armed guards, "who are these jokers?" It was great to hear them called jokers. The guards did not know what was being said, and looked uncomfortable. I suddenly felt important, because I was the only channel of communication. When I had explained the situation, the platoon leader scratched his neck and said" "Tell you what. Take those birds up the trail a ways, and carry their rifles. In a few minutes you'll find our troops. Tell them who you are and hand the rifles over to them. Ask to see the captain. He'll take it from there."

That did not seem a good idea to me at all. "I have survived camps and prisons and disease and bombs," I said. "After all that, I don't want to be shot at by your troops because I carry rifles." The platoon leader scratched his neck again and looked dubious. "Aw, I don't think they'll do that," he replied thoughtfully. But that wasn't good enough for me, so he said "Okay, show you what we'll do." And he disarmed the guards, smashed their rifles and pocketed their hand guns. "Now just go up the trail," he said. "We have to move on. By the way, are there any krauts nearby that you're aware of?" I guffawed. It was the first time I had heard that name for the Germans, and it struck my funny bone because of all those gallons of kraut soup we had had to digest for so long. I said there were no krauts in the forest to my knowledge, and our liberators were on their way. How often have I wished since that I knew their identities!

I explained what we had been asked to do. And then an amazing thing happened. Our two now toothless guards started ordering us to line up two by two to march in unison up to the American troops! Eins-zwei-drei-vier! It was hard to believe. A torrent of abuse poured over them from my French workmates. "Salaud!" "Fils de pute!" "Sale boche!" "Va te faire foutre!" This was real freedom! It was lucky for the guards they hadn't been too hard on us before, or else the French would now have beaten them senseless. They looked bewildered when I told them they were our prisoners now. They had a hard time understanding that, but saw themselves surrounded by unfriendly faces and kept quiet.

Up the trail we went. As we got out of the woods, we saw ahead of us a few dozen soldiers lying in the heather, smoking and sunning themselves. This was the front-line? I could not have come up with anything like it had I been giving a hundred guesses. If I had not been so terribly excited, it would have been positively disappointing.

When they saw us coming, some of the soldiers got up, rifles in hand. We didn't know enough to raise our hands or even to shout that we were friends, but they didn't seem overly worried and eyed us with curiosity more than suspicion. I picked a soldier with two V's on his sleeve as probably the most important, and approached him.

"We were prisoners of the Germans, sir," I said. "We're civilians, mostly from France, and these two birds here (I was catching on to the lingo) were our guards. We were set free by three of your men back there in the woods. They told us to follow this path to find the American troops."

"Well, I'll be damned" said the important soldier, but that was his only comment. He motioned to me to follow him, and we walked to the top of a little rise, where another important soldier (certainly an officer, this one, I thought) was sitting on a folding chair in front of a camp table, studying a map.

"Captain," said the first important soldier to the second, saluting, "there's a bunch of civilians down there that came out of the woods. Seems they was French prisoners. They brought their Heinie guards with them, those two over there in uniform. This man here is Dutch. He speaks English." He couldn't have summarized the situation more succinctly.

"Well, I'll be damned," said the captain, and scowled. He seemed irritated, and let me know why. "Don't you people read? There's thousands of pamphlets we threw out all over this town, to warn everybody to stay inside."

I explained we'd hardly had any choice in the matter, although in my heart of hearts I knew I wouldn't have stayed inside if I had had the choice.

"Okay," said the captain, "it's okay. It's just that I don't know what to do with you here." He relaxed, and looked me over.

"Prisoners, eh?" he asked of no one in particular. "And you're Dutch? Nice country, Holland. We came through it on the way here. Nice people—made you feel like home. Good milk, too, for once. We've got a lot of Dutch back in the States, you know." Was there really a war going on around us? Well, yes, just then the captain came to the point.

"Now that you're here," he went on, "maybe you can help us." He pointed to the map in front of him, a detailed map of Siegburg and its immediate surroundings. "Tell me what you know about this town. Military installations, things like that. And did you see any troop movements, any German military?"

Much as I would have liked to join the war effort and act as a valuable informant, there was not much I could tell him. Except for one thing. Pointing again to the map, the captain asked: "What about this building here. We've been shelling it, but we can't figure out what it's really for." It was hard to believe: he had his forefinger right on top of the prison. "But that's it!" I exclaimed. "That's us, the prison. It's got big white crosses painted on all the roofs."

"Well, I'll be damned," he said again. "White crosses don't tell you much. Sorry, though."

Someone gave a yell. In the distance a kid was running away from us. A soldier gave a warning shot into the air, but he kept running. "Aw, let him go," said the captain, and the kid disappeared among the trees. Thereupon the captain called over one of his men and told him to take us into town to the colonel, minus the two Germans. With light hearts we set off, and after a while came to a four-lane highway. The "Autobahn." I had heard about Hitler's highways even before the war, but never until now knew I had been living almost next to it. The Siegburg exit was nearby, and we followed a road crowded with infantry, tanks, armored cars, Jeeps, howitzers on wheels—there seemed no end to it. I thought of the day the Germans had entered Eindhoven, almost five years ago, but that was like nothing compared to this! I couldn't get used to the idea I was now on the Allied side of the front-line. It remained a thrilling thought: this was my team! I waved at the tank crews, but most of them didn't wave back very heartily, and I realized they had no way of knowing we were Allies, their brothers-in-arms. To them, we must have been "krauts", and odd ones, at that: krauts welcoming the enemy.

To the colonel, when we arrived, I was a bother more than a brother. I got another lecture about staying inside. There was heavy fighting going on in town, he said. I gave the same answer I had given the captain, after which we were taken to a school house and told to wait inside till it was safe to go somewhere else. And there we waited, milling around until late afternoon, hungry but happy. When they came for us, we were told to follow a Jeep, and we marched out of town, southward, to an unrevealed destination. We were in high spirits, which was a good thing, for the Jeep forced a brisk infantry pace on us. Before long, we started lagging behind, too weak to keep up. Our wood-soled, prison-issue shoes were not made for as much walking as we'd been doing since we had left the prison at dawn, an eon ago. The blisters on my feet had long ago broken when the pain made me give up and call out to the driver to, please, slow down. He did, to a snail's pace, but it was still too fast, and he got the message. He got out, flagged down an Army truck and spoke with the driver, a jovial black G.I., who nodded his head in sympathy and shouted over at us: "Hey man, you can't go on walking like that—get in here!" And with much relief we clambered into the back of his truck.

Our destination was a prisoner-of-war camp, nothing more than a broad field near a farm, surrounded by barbed wire. It already held thousands of German soldiers, and more were arriving all the time. We climbed out. Our driver spoke to an officer, who told us to line up and went to tell the commanding officer about the unexpected arrivals. The commanding officer bore the same insignia I had seen on the one in Siegburg: another colonel, I thought, and immediately disliked him. He was arrogant, and of arrogance I had had my belly full. The colonel looked us over with distaste, and began to interrogate us, starting at the other end of our line. He spoke flawless German—another count against him in my estimation.

"So what were you in for?" he asked of the first man in line. The Frenchman hesitated. "Come on, what for?" the colonel prodded him with impatience. In his halting German, the other explained he had been in the black market. "So, you're just a common criminal," said the officer in a biting voice.

What was going on? Who was this sneering man. It was as if we were prisoners again, less than twelve hours after our liberation! No doubt we were a scruffy bunch, but, damn it, we were Allies! The Frenchman looked embarrassed, probably for the first time since he had been sent to Germany. No one amongst us had been held in contempt because of the nature of his offense to the enemy.

The colonel went on down the line and had a scornful comment about everyone. Now he was addressing himself to me, still speaking German. "Und du?" he asked. I felt my blood boiling, and didn't answer. He repeated his question: "Und du?", and at last I managed to say: "I will speak with you in English, not in German. Now, what was your question?" He looked at me for a few seconds without speaking, then turned around and walked off.

"Qui est ce salaud," my companions asked me, their voices filled with anger . . . who was that bastard? "A German-American," I said. "I bet he was born here . . . his German is too perfect. I bet he likes Germans better than us."

We stood around, waiting for something to happen. At last someone took us to a corner of the camp they had cleared out for us. And then something wonderful occurred. A Jeep arrived, stacked with cardboard boxes containing what I got to know later as C-rations. An American candy bar, among other delights. And three American cigarettes! Long live America! It went a long way towards making us forget the colonel.

Night had fallen, and still German soldiers kept streaming in. It was marvelous to see them now in defeat, after so many years when they had lorded it over us. My thoughts turned to the prison: had it been liberated? How had it occurred? Were my friends alright—Baas-Becking, whom I had not seen for some time, and de Coucy, Rossignol, Jean Juliot, and the others? What would the Americans do about the typhus epidemic? They would have to put the entire prison in quarantine. I felt lucky not to be inside. After the war I learned all prisoners had been kept inside for six more weeks, and that they worried more about me than I about them, for there was a rumor I had been taken by the SS and shot.

Surrounded by spotlights, the PW-camp was a lone bright spot in a dark and cold night. Few of us got any sleep, not only because of the cold, but because we were all too excited. We exercised our new found freedom by walking back and forth, turning right or left as we pleased, without waiting for an order. It had become a very unfamiliar sensation. And we talked, endlessly, about the past and what we would do in the future, and about family, and freedom. Once, I lay down for a moment and gazed up at the jewelled sky. And the stars, that night, seemed more brilliant than ever before, as if to celebrate the momentous joy in my heart.

45

Worry returned the following morning. Where would we be taken next? Would we be sent back to the prison, which was presumably liberated by now? None of us wanted to go back to that nest of infection, but if word came back about the typhus epidemic, they probably would not want to take any chances and put us there in quarantine. It was a dismal thought: barely free, and now back for weeks of confinement. The morning dragged on without anything happening, and we became increasingly nervous.

Pacing around, I suddenly saw our two guards from the day before, standing at attention in front of the flawless-German colonel. I left our corner of the camp and, behind the colonel's back, came as close as I dared. One of the guards was talking. What was he up to? I edged closer still, and heard him mention the prison. Then he pointed over to where the rest of our group were standing. He was saying we all had lice, and that our presence here was a danger to the American soldiers. The bastard! Suddenly concerned about the health of the enemy! I could see their game: have us sent back to Siegburg, and them with us, in the hope they wouldn't be shipped off somewhere else, perhaps even of passing themselves off as civilians employed as guards, not really part of the Nazi system, and be let go. Then they were led away. I took a deep breath and approached the colonel, who was about to walk away . . . hoping he would not remember our exchange of the night before. It was our only chance.

"Sir," I said, "I couldn't help overhearing what that Nazi guard was telling you, about typhus and us having lice and being a danger to your men. They're just inventing that to get out of this camp and back into town, along with the rest of us. There has been no typhus in that prison, and we hardly ever saw lice."

I don't know how I managed to tell those bald-faced lies with a straight face. It seemed as if I could feel a crawling on my body while I was talking. "You can believe me," I added for good measure and with as much conviction as I could muster. As he had done the previous night; the colonel stared at me for a while without comment, and then walked away. I went back to my group and reported what had happened. It produced another stream of invective, addressed to the American colonel as well as the German guards. But now we were really tense. What would they do?

Shortly after noon an Army truck drove up to our corner. The driver got out, opened up the back and said: "Okay, fellows, we're going to take a ride." Where to, where to? Going out through the camp gate, the truck followed a dirt road. We saw we were heading west. A few minutes later he stopped at the highway. We held our breath: right meant north, back to Siegburg, left meant freedom in the south. The truck jerked back into motion and we felt it turning, and then we knew: it was heading south! A loud cheer went up, and we slapped each other on the back, overjoyed. What a good guy, that colonel!

After that, things happened fast. The truck stopped; ahead of us was the wide Rhine, and a pontoon bridge across it, protected from low aerial attack by a forest of cables held up by blimps. It must have been close to Remagen. We had to cross the bridge on foot, and in my eagerness to be the first one I was not watching my step. A soldier standing guard grabbed my arm. "Watch it, buddy," he said, and pointed to a shallow hole with a land mine in it. I jumped back, and circled it with respect.

On the other side of the Rhine we were taken inside a long tent and asked to strip naked and hang our clothes on a line. Wonders were not to cease: we were asked to walk past a row of soldiers, each holding a large canister. "Left arm up." Psss-psss—and a jet of powder was sprayed into my left arm pit. Next soldier. "Right arm up." Psss-psss—the other armpit. "Close your eyes, bend your head." Pssssssss—a long spray across the scalp. "Legs apart." Pssssss-pssssss. Two other soldiers were spraying our clothes. At the other end of the tent were showers. How great it felt to be clean! The last soldier in line gave us each a pamphlet advertising the wonders of DDT. What a country, I thought: commercial publicity following right up behind the front line! And what efficiency—how could the Germans ever have hoped to win? Now we were outside in the sun, putting our clothes back on; the whole operation had lasted less than five minutes. I never saw another louse.

Someone told us we would be on our way soon. "Back to your country by tomorrow," he added, and those simple words gave me a sudden shock. Somewhere in our minds, I think, we were all still in prison. Was it possible that in twenty-four hours or so I'd be back in Eindhoven? It didn't seem real, it was all going too fast to adjust to. But there it was: a truck took us away. We were following the Rhine, going north. From the east side came the booming of artillery, and you could see fires raging and plumes of smoke rising to the sky. We entered a city, or what had been a city. Isolated, blackened walls, the ravaged remains of homes and buildings, rose like ruined teeth above a sea of rubble in silent testimony to Nazi madness. I thought of Rotterdam, five years earlier. "Der Führer hat immer recht!" In the midst of the wasteland stood a great cathedral. I recognized it at once. Once, when I was little, I had been allowed to go with my father and a group of Spanish Philips dealers on a bus trip to Germany, and I had been struck with awe by the immensity of the Dome of Cologne. In its sole splendor it now looked more immense yet. How had that cathedral escaped destruction? Was it any wonder that Catholics believed in miracles?

Now we were again rumbling through the countryside, heading west—towards Aachen, I guessed, close to the Dutch border. This was the country I had seen flying by from the bucket seat of my grandfather's big red Chandler convertible on those child-remembered weekends, when his white moustache and my oma unexpectedly showed up in Eindhoven and our family drove out to the Eifel Mountains. Now, town after town was a site of destruction. I began to understand why it had taken so long for the front to move from the border to the Rhine. The fighting must have been fierce every step of the way.

The sun was already low on the horizon when our truck came to a halt in front of a large building in a town that seemed still largely intact. By now we were dead tired, not just from the long trip, but from not having slept at all the night before: une nuit blanche, as my French companions called it. We were very hungry, too, for all we had eaten was another C-ration. Inside was a milling crowd of men from all over Europe, liberated forced laborers and inmates of German prisons and camps. The staff was Anglo-American, part military, part civilian. Dinner was called—soup, of course. But it had little in common with the watery prison fare we were all acquainted with: not a shred of sauerkraut, and seconds all around. Then we each got a blanket, and we settled in for the night wherever we could find a place to stretch out. Within minutes I fell asleep on top of a table.

The next morning a line of trucks pulled up and it was announced a convoy would be leaving for France, and that later in the day there would be trucks heading for Belgium and Holland. I had a lot of translating to do, for not many in the crowd spoke English and there was a lot of confusion. Soon, the French were lining up to go and I said farewell to the companions with whom I had shared the great events of the last two days. Then they were gone.

Alone now, sitting on a table, I began trying to imagine what the rest of the day would be like. Would I really be home tonight? It was still impossible to grasp. Perhaps see Sylvia tomorrow? Still less plausible. Prison life had pushed family, old friendships, love and sex first onto the back burner of daily consciousness, and then into a world of remembrance only, a world you would visit as if paging through an old photo album, in which you see a person at ease with the people and places around him, and that person seems to be you. But now those phantoms would reenter my life. How would it happen? No one was expecting me that day. Should I act nonchalant and just stroll into the kitchen, saying: "Hello, here I am"? Or should I be dramatic, throw out my arms crying "Mother! Father!", and sob my heart out. Or be pale and taciturn and secretive because so much suffering could not be put into words? It all baffled me.

"You're the one who speaks English," came a voice, stating a fact more than asking a question. I hadn't noticed someone had entered the room. I looked around. An Army lieutenant stood by the doorway. Intelligent eyes looked me over. "From where are you?" he went on.

"I'm coming from Holland," I answered, and he laughed. "Don't say it that way," he said. "The progressive tense means you're doing it right now. It's special to English. People who don't know English very well often misuse it."

It was an unusual time and setting for a lesson in English grammar. The progressive tense—impressive he knew that. I'd have to remember not to make that mistake in the future.

The lieutenant came in. There was something rakish about his casual walk and the jaunty angle he wore his cap. He reminded me of Arl, the much younger brother of my stepmother, adored by Jack and me for the dissolute playboy life he managed to lead and the beautiful girls he always attracted. I decided I liked the lieutenant.

"Okay, so you are from Holland," he continued. "What are you doing here in Germany?" I told him I had been a political prisoner. He nodded, apparently satisfied. "I suppose you speak German, then," he said. "This morning I heard you speak French." He thought for a while, then said: "Would you mind waiting here for a moment? I'll be right back." He was back in a few minutes. "Just follow me."

Captain Smith rose from behind his desk when we came in and introduced himself. "Sit down," he said, but remained standing himself. He was a burly man, and what struck me about him was not only his politeness, but something kind in his face. Why did he want to see me?

"I'm sure you are looking forward to seeing your family," he began. I said I was. "So are a lot of other people," he went on. "Millions of them, in fact, all over Germany—ex-prisoners, like you, and forced laborers, all trying to find their way home. It's chaotic, and we have to deal with it, fast." He walked back and forth a little, and then seemed to change the subject. "Have you heard of UNRRA?" he asked. I hadn't. "Have you heard of the United Nations?" I hadn't. He sat down at his desk and told me about the new world organization. It was interesting, but why was he telling me this? He came to the point: "UNRRA," he said, "means United Nations Relief and Rehabilitation Agency.

The lieutenant, here, and I are both assigned to it. It is supposed to organize the repatriation of all those displaced persons in Germany. It's a mammoth job. A terribly important job. This place here is one of the first way stations that have been set up, but it's only a small one. There is a huge camp farther east, in Wetzlar—twenty thousand people and already overflowing. New camps have to be organized, and very quickly. We need all the help we can get. We need interpreters." He stopped and looked at me. "You could be a great help to us," he added.

I felt as if I knew, suddenly, why it had seemed so unreal to me that I would be back with my family that very night. Unreal, because it was not destined to happen so soon. There would be a time of adjustment to the idea. I didn't hesitate. "I'll be glad to help if I can, sir," I said. "But is there a way I can send a message to my family in Holland, just to tell them I'm safe?" The captain's face broke out in a big smile. "Great!" he said. "We are leaving for Wetzlar in a couple of hours. The lieutenant will get you some Army clothes and shoes. Write a letter to your folks and I will give it to the driver of the truck that is leaving for Holland today and tell him to make sure they get it."

We were off by noon on my first ride in a Jeep, Captain Smith next to the driver, the lieutenant and I behind. Proud as a peacock in my uniform, I felt as if I now belonged to the Allied armed forces.

46

The UNRRA Center for Displaced Persons had been set up in an enormous camp of German Army barracks at the edge of the town of Wetzlar. Our driver carefully piloted the Jeep through a thoroughfare crowded with people, almost all men, finally stopping in front of a low-slung building that seemed to serve as administrative headquarters. Captain Smith ushered me inside and introduced me to some of the staff, part military, part civilian, mostly American and British, but a few from other countries. That was how I met Vera.

Vera was Russian. About my age, she functioned as one of the camp's interpreters, the only one available to the thousands of Russian inhabitants. "Hello," she said, holding out one hand while passing the other through the curls of her chestnut-colored hair—rebellious curls that seemed to warn you her petite stature did not contain a petite spirit. It was clear she was fully conscious of her sex-appeal and her good looks. If I had been at all resensitized to carnal desire I might have been aware of the fullness of her mouth and the outlines of a perfect body beneath her smart WAC uniform, but I wasn't, not yet. This was the second time a woman had touched my hand in a month, but only the second time in a year and a half, too, and I was again shaken by the experience. I was sure she sensed my confusion and enjoyed it. It showed in her eyes, eyes I would come to know as the weathervanes of her shifting moods, mocking, as now, or sparkling with conspirational laughter, but at other times flaring up in anger or dissolving into sensuous languor—willful eyes, too, that lost their determination only in moments of darkest foreboding. But of that I knew nothing as yet.

Vera's English and German were excellent, better, perhaps, than mine, and better by far than that of the two other interpreters, one a Dutchman in his late twenties, the other a young Belgian. They showed me into the adjacent dormitory for male civilian UNRRA personnel, where I selected a cot. Selecting choosing, deciding, acting—it all was still very new to me. The habit of waiting for an order would take a while to wear off.

Dinner was announced, and the four interpreters sat down together in the mess hall. I cannot remember what was served, only that it seemed heavenly to eat a real meal after all those months of watery soup. Almost immediately, of course, my stomach began to protest against all that rich fare, but it was a small price to pay for the pleasure of overeating.

After coffee I sank down in an easy chair, facing a screen. A movie had been announced during dinner. Vera sat down next to me, and we started talking, each trying to compress our personal universes into the half hour before the film would start.

"Where did you grow up?" I asked. "How did you come here?"

Vera's voice was urgent and intense. "I am from Moscow. My father is a surgeon general in the Red Army. I fought in the army, in a tank. It was crippled during an attack. We managed to get out and were taken prisoner. I was sent to a camp in Poland, then to one in Germany. That was a lucky thing, because we were freed by the Americans. Since then I've been working as an interpreter."

The drama in what she said about being lucky escaped me at the time, though it became all too clear later on. Instead I laughed, not because I doubted her story, but because the thought of this little creature sitting next to me attacking the German lines in a tank seemed so incongruous. Immediately I regretted laughing. Her dark eyes flashed their angry warning.

"You don't believe a woman can fight against men, do you?" she said. "Well, Russian women can!" With some scorn she added: "You people in the west don't have any idea what it was like. It was awful, our war in Russia. And it was awful to be taken prisoner." Only then did I seriously try to imagine what she had gone through, and I knew it must have been sheer hell, unlike anything I had experienced. I told her, and she threw me a warm glance, just before the lights dimmed and the screen lit up.

I leaned back in my chair and was filled with wonder. How was this possible? Three nights ago I was still in my stinking cell in that pesthole of a prison, scratching my lice bites. And now, here I was, deloused, showered, in a fresh Army uniform, copiously fed, sitting in an easy chair next to a delightful Russian girl, watching an American movie, and bothered by no more than the discomfort of heartburn, the embarrassment of the gurgles and squeals in my rebellious stomach, and the cramps caused by my violent attempts to prevent gas from escaping into this salon of easy luxury. It was all so much, so fast, and so wonderful, and it was all true.

After breakfast the next day, Captain Smith told me I would not stay in Wetzlar very long. In a few days I would be going somewhere else to help set up a new camp. Meanwhile, to make myself useful, he suggested I go along with Vera for the day. I didn't ask for more. It turned out Vera was not just an interpreter; she seemed to be some sort of unofficial assistant to UNRRA headquarters in Wetzlar. And right now her assignment, and therefore my assignment, was to go through all the barracks and confiscate knives and alcohol. The Russians, apparently, tended to go pretty wild. They produced methyl alcohol from wood and drank it. A few had died from it, or gone blind, others had gone berserk and started fighting each other, till the brawl made such a racket that the MP's in the camp had to come out. In bad fights the knives flashed, and there had been some killings. After that the order had gone out: turn in all the knives, and no more alcohol. That was the order, but nothing much had changed. That was where Vera and I came in.

Methodically, we went through the Russian part of the camp, from barrack to barrack. In many, packing crates had been piled up to make walls and create rooms, some of which actually looked cozy, with crates for seats and tables and one or two colorful cloths that made the rooms spring to life and suggested the hand of a woman. For, although mostly male, the camp's population did include women, some of whom lived with a man. There were even some children. There was a constant coming and going, a constant talking and good-natured calling out to friends or acquaintances, and often there was singing to the strings of a balalaika. The singing would stop when they saw Vera and me come in, everybody would break out into wide smiles, heads nodded, and we were invited in and made to sit down on hastily cleared crates. Then the balalaika would start up again, a male voice sang a melancholy line and other voices answered him, until, in my enchantment, I forgot all about our mission. I had, in any case, no illusion about the efficacy of our inspection, for I had been a camp inmate long enough to know that word spreads like wildfire, so that by now everybody knew what we were up to. But Vera persisted, and after enough balalaika she would put up her hand and say, in Russian, that we were here to confiscate all their knives and alcohol.

The reaction ranged from feigned amazement to deep concern to be of help. "Alcohol?", Vera translated for my benefit. "Did you hear, Serge Vassilovitch? They want to know if we have alcohol. Have you seen anybody drink by any chance." "No, not here," said Serge Vassilovitch, walking over to where we were. "But I have heard someone had some last week two barracks over. You know," he added disapprovingly, "that really is bad, getting drunk and getting into fights when it's already something of an anarchy here, don't you think?" Everyone nodded in sympathy with our mission. "Okay then, how about knives?" "Ah, knives, yes, certainly, knives! Nastasya Filippovna, go get the knives." And Nastasya Filippovna disappeared behind a makeshift curtain and returned with two blunt dinner knives. "Is this what you are looking for?" No, it wasn't, just drop it. And we'd go on.

Other than that, we didn't have much to do. Part of the day we just sat on the lawn in front of our barrack, sunbathing and talking with the clerical or kitchen staff or to some of the junior military personnel attached to UNRRA, or just kicking a ball around with some of the camp inmates. Fresh air, sudden peace, freedom to move or doze off, all that and the early spring sun combined to produce a state in which exhilaration alternated with lazy bliss. The limits of my thoughts and feelings were the wall around the camp, and neither past nor future intruded. Lying there in the sun, a voice penetrated my euphoria. I opened my eyes and saw the other Dutch interpreter lying shirtless in the grass near me. He was talking to a Polish girl, who was resting her head on his chest. And suddenly I was wide awake. I watched her turn over slowly, look at him briefly, and bend her head over his body, her long dark hair flowing across it. She started nibbling at him, without haste, almost reverently, now and then tickling his nipples. She was in a world of her own, in which nothing stirred, and every little love-bite seemed an act of utmost importance. Was my countryman's heart pounding as wildly as mine? Something near-forgotten started shifting inside me. In disarray, a memory of Sylvia competed with the image of Vera. I had been attracted to Vera from the start, but now I was conscious of wanting her. Then someone called, and it was over.

But it was not desire alone that could make her occupy my thoughts. She had told me what she knew would await her back in her country, and I could not put it out of my mind.

"But how can that be?" I exclaimed. "Why would they send you and millions of others to camps in Siberia? You fought the Germans, and it wasn't your fault your tank got knocked out and you were taken prisoner! What were you supposed to have done?"

But her voice went on, with relentless lucidity and dark fear. "You don't understand my country. It was total war at Stalingrad. We had been given formal orders to fight until death. No excuses would count. No excuses will count—as far as the Party is concerned, we are traitors, that's all. And that's not even the worst in Stalin's mind. He is scared to death to have all those people come back who have been in the West and who can no longer be told how miserable the working man is outside the Soviet Union. In spite of the war, they've been able to see for themselves, and that makes them all dangerous. Look," she added, "they're all excited right now about going back to Mother

Russia. But they won't even get to see their families. We're all off to Siberia, you can count on that." And Vera closed her eyes on her fear. I was stunned, for she made me believe her, although no one in the West could then imagine such a thing could happen, and it was not until the publication of The Gulag Archipelago that the world learned what Vera then knew. I began to understand why the Americans in our camp winked when they talked about her, why she had the reputation of "sleeping around" and of being ready to marry anyone from the West who was willing. Ready? Desperate was more like it, I thought. Why wouldn't she offer herself to the first taker? Anything to escape a forcible transport back to Russia, where she could hope for nothing better than years of prison life, of cold and hunger and humiliation, perhaps rape, if not death.

From then on my growing desire for Vera, was mixed with a growing tenderness.

Towards the end of my first week in Wetzlar Captain Smith called me in and told me I was going to help set up a new camp in the town of Giessen, not far away, where five to ten thousand people were expected to arrive in the next six or seven days. Early the next morning I was on my way.

47

The contingent that left for Giessen consisted of a British colonel, a British Army nurse who was more or less a nutrition expert, a Polish captain, and three DP's—"displaced persons", as we were generally referred to: two workers to help with the physical labor, and myself as interpreter, though before long my job became that of general trouble shooter.

None of us had been to Giessen before, but we were told there were military barracks just outside town, and somewhere there was a food depot of the German Army. It had been not much over a month since the area had been occupied by the Allies. In what condition would we find the camp? How much food was left in the depot? It was anybody's guess—all we knew was that we had to hurry to get the camp going and set up a kitchen.

The barracks were not hard to find. From the outside they didn't look too bad, but on the inside they were a mess, a chaos of tables, chairs and bunks stacked randomly, it was hard to guess for what reason. There was work to be done, but at least the necessary furniture was there. There were even blankets, and pots, pans, plates and silverware in the main camp kitchen. The army people took over a barrack near the gate for office and living quarters, and the rest of us found one that was divided into small apartments, which gave each of us a degree of privacy. Leaving the heavy work to my fellow DP's, I took off with the dietitian, whose name was Gladys, to go into town by Jeep and find out where the depot was. Gladys was a handsome women around thirty years old, whose body filled her uniform to perfection, and whose mind was filled with calories. Calories was all she could talk. She had already decided how many each of the expected inmates would get before we even knew how much food we were going to find. The magic number seemed to be 1500, which at that time didn't mean much to me. At the mayor's office we got directions to the depot, which was located in a large bunker built into a hill. She was overjoyed when at last we found it and managed to get in: it contained millions of calories, hundreds of millions, in the disguise of vegetables, meats, sardines, and what not, in endless rows of neatly stacked cans. While I made a rough count of the numbers, Gladys set to work calculating the numbers of calories in each kind, and by the end of the afternoon she had a pretty good inventory. Satisfied, we locked the place up and returned to camp.

In remarkably little time we had the barracks and kitchen ready for occupancy, and soon the transports began to arrive. At first they carried mostly Polish DP's. I asked if there were any cooks among them. There were, and thereby the Poles took over the kitchen. For a few days everything ran smoothly, but then the Russians started to come in. Although we kept their living quarters apart from those of the Poles, trouble could not be avoided. There was palpable hatred between the two groups, and in no time there were fights, some of them bloody. On a whim, the Poles in the kitchen would decide to send all the Russians to the end of the soup-line or refuse to feed them at all. It then fell to me to go to over and tell them I'd give the kitchen over to the Russians if they didn't straighten out. It seemed like an awful lot of authority so soon (no more than two weeks) after prison life. Sometimes I felt as if I was single-handedly running that community of five to ten thousand people—running it by default because the British colonel, who was nominally in charge of the camp, never seemed to be around, and the nurse was too busy calculating, and the Polish captain left after a few days, to be replaced by a Russian lieutenant who had been given authority only over the Russian DP's. The lieutenant would come over to my place to talk things over. He only seemed to want to speak with me, or perhaps the colonel had frozen him out. To me he seemed straightforward in his not unjustified complaints and, although he was somewhat dour a fellow, he managed to unbend a little with me, and I with him. We called each other by our first names. "Robert," he would say in only slightly accented English, "Robert, we have a problem again." I was probably the only Westerner he trusted not to look down on the Russians. The problem with the Poles eventually (very soon, as a matter of fact) disappeared, since they were the first to be transported back to their country, while at the same time the camp was flooded with new Russian DP's. It was now their turn to run the kitchen, and my turn to protect the remaining Poles and ask the Russian lieutenant to read the riot act to his countrymen, which he did. Years later I realized what the lieutenant's real role had been in that camp. He was to see to it that all Russians were shipped back to the Soviet Union in conformance with Stalin's demand at the Yalta Conference—no defections permitted.

I worked hard, but felt useful helping to run the camp smoothly. One of my jobs was to go several times a week with Gladys to the food bunker to help her. The other two staff members came along to help load, but waited outside in the truck, smoking and gabbing. Alone with Gladys inside the bunker for up to an hour! Alas, what carnal thoughts she had were confined to canned meat, and only the calories she loved so dearly could warm her heart. One day, the British colonel called me in to say she had abruptly left us, "reassigned", he said. It seemed that morning a handsome American colonel had come in on some sort of mission, or perhaps because he had heard of Gladys. He had taken one look at her, and proposed to take her on as his personal aide. Gladys had said yes, and in little time he had whisked her off to better pastures. Since I knew something of Gladys' mind set, I had no cause to be envious of the American.

The colonel said Gladys had left a note for me in her room, so I strolled over to read it. It was an amazing document, full of tables of cabalistic calculations. "Dear Robert!" she had written. "I am sorry I had to leave in such a hurry. Duty calls, you know! I would have liked to explain all this in person, the DP's daily nutrition allowance and all that. Be ever so sweet, and familiarise yourself with these tables. They are SO important! But I just KNOW you can do it. Much love, and au revoir, as they say. Gladys. PS: You really ARE sweet, you know!" Sure Gladys, I got the message. I think it was right there that I decided there was enough food in the bunker for the likely duration of the camp, and to just ignore the calories. From then on we simply loaded the truck with as many boxes of cans as usual, and then added some for safety and to up the diet a little, for the camp inmates still looked pretty hungry to me.

It was often difficult to keep the truck from being raided when it arrived in camp and had to be unloaded. On one occasion I saw, out of the corner of my eye, an old Russian take off with a whole box of canned food and disappear between two barracks. I ran after him—he was gone, but a door stood partly open. Inside, an elderly man was sitting on something covered with a burlap sack, softly crooning with his eyes half-closed. The scene breathed peace and innocence, but the sack, of course, covered the crate I was looking for. I took it away. Save, perhaps, for the twinge of amusement that was mixed in with my officiousness, how close I was then to the mentality of the prison guard! When, on my way through camp, men asked me for a cigarette, I had learned to shake my head in answer—at first with the embarrassed excuse to myself that there would be no end if I started in on that, but soon with indifference. Now and then, only, did it occur to me to remember the bully I'd been in Grade School, and how rapidly I had been corrupted in my brief career as "office secretary" in Porz, and then I would feel a tweak of conscience. By comparison to these Russian DP's, the camp staff was so well off! We were well fed, had all the cigarettes we wanted to, and could even get drunk on whiskey if we felt like it—one weekend we did, and, to my humiliation, it made me sick as a dog. These poor devils had next to nothing, and, if Vera was to be believed, had even less ahead of them.

I felt I needed a breather, to take off for a while, and went to see the British colonel to suggest he give me leave for the weekend and allow me to hitch a ride in one of the Jeeps or trucks that went to the Wetzlar camp almost every day. The colonel didn't mind. Admittedly, I had an ulterior motive. In Gladys' room my eye had fallen on an open closet. She had left something behind, probably because it was too small for her: a very feminine-looking pair of pink pyjamas. It was not difficult at all to see them on Vera's body, so I had taken them to my room, wrapped them up, and sent them to her. Since then, I had been having heady visions of Vera in pink panamas, and I was getting anxious to find out if she liked them and would model them for me, and if she would look as great in them as in my fantasy.

On both accounts, my expectations were exceeded by far. She flung her arms around me and thanked me with a flurry of kisses. "Let's go for a walk," she said, and hand in hand we walked out the camp gate and into the sunny fields beyond, where we fell down out of sight. "Well?" she asked, and with that I bent over and kissed her neck and then sank into the flower of her mouth, and as the world fell away, so did the memory of the last eighteen months, and I felt reborn.

A century later Vera pulled away and looked at me with mocking eyes. "Crazy boy," she said, "come, crazy boy, let's go back. You might as well move into my room, don't you think? I share it with another girl right now, but tomorrow I'll get her to take one of her own."

We walked back. My head was swimming, but way down something was gnawing at me, an uncertainty about myself. This girl had experience with men, and was very much in charge. Would I be able to live up to her expectations? It had been so long since I had made love with Sylvia. But by chance or instinct Vera did exactly the right thing. Matter of factly, back in her room, she said: "Let's go take a shower," and we went to the communal bathroom, empty at this time. We showered side by side. It was an easy way to get to know her body and drop some of my awkwardness, and it was a natural prelude to love making. I still felt far from being the perfect lover, but when I held her silently afterward I was glad she seemed appeased, temporarily released from the black spectre that haunted her thoughts. That night she slept huddled against me in her narrow bed, and listening to her breathing I felt protective of her, at peace with myself. Vera's girl friend came in later in the evening. Undisturbed by my presence, she lay down on the other bed in the room, and soon we were all three asleep.

After that weekend I felt less involved in the camp in Giessen. It was now more or less running itself—DP's from all parts of Europe kept arriving daily, while others left for home. As for me, I intended to spend as much time in Wetzlar as I could. Somewhere around this time V-E day occurred—the end of the war in Europe. For five years I had awaited that day, hoped for it, longed for it, and now that it had come I was barely aware of it. It was also about that time that I saw a car drive into our camp and a lanky, dark-haired, jovial American in khaki clothes get out. I walked over, supposing he wanted to see the colonel. "Hi," he said, "I'm Bill McGregor. I'm with the CIC here in Giessen." He laughed. "I guess that means beans to you, doesn't it? Counter-Intelligence Corps is what it means. We're supposed to track down Nazis. There are eighteen of us in the Giessen office." He paused. "You look like you're the interpreter here. Right? You're Dutch, aren't you? We've heard about you." He floored me. How did they know about me, how had he picked me out right away? "Ah," he laughed again, "professional secret! Knowing is our business. How would you like to come over for dinner, let's say Sunday noon? We've got the best cooks in town. Okay? I'll come pick you up." He got back in his car, and I had barely time to say "okay" before he roared off. The whole thing had taken three minutes. Apparently, he had come to see me, not the colonel! But why? Not just to invite me to dinner. Why?

Sunday came, and McGregor drove up to the camp gate just before noon. He stuck his head out the window and shouted: "Glad you could make it. Get in." On squeaking tires the car made a U-turn and took off for town at breakneck speed, McGregor turning the wheel with casual abandon. He was fast winning me over.

48

The CIC had taken over a hotel in the center of town, lock, stock and barrel, including the chief cook and the pastry chef. There was a relaxed atmosphere about the place, perhaps because the agents were considered civilians attached to the Army and therefore not part of the military hierarchy, except for the agent-in-charge, who was a first lieutenant and the only one to wear a regular uniform with an officer's insignia. They were all there, eighteen of them, and after introductions had been made I was ushered into the dining room. A long table had been set with white linen, silver ware, and crystal wine glasses. I had seen nothing like it since the time my parents gave fancy dinner parties before the war, parties from which the kids were excluded. But here I was the guest of honor! I still didn't know why, and wasn't going to know till I had eaten my way through a sumptuous four course dinner and I had been dazzled by three glasses of superlative Riesling, and the pastry chef had brought in a giant cake—a profiterole, my favorite. At that point McGregor winked at me and said: "Not bad, eh? You could be eating like this every day", and I began to get an inkling. Afterward, we repaired to the salon, where cognac was served. To great hilariousness, an agent called Jim Shea related how the day before he had had a run-in with an angry colonel in town, who demanded to know how the CIC had been able to commandeer so many private cars, when regular officers had to ride in Jeeps, and how many did the Corps have, anyway? "Well, now, let's see, colonel," Shea had said casually, "I guess I don't know just how many we've got—fifteen, maybe, give or take a few. But I could be wrong. I don't think we ever got around to counting them." The colonel had exploded, but from the general laughter I gathered the CIC was invulnerable, and the agents all knew it. I began to like this place better all the time. Only the lieutenant in charge wasn't laughing, for he was military, of course. Instead, he turned to me, suddenly all business, and broached the subject I had begun to anticipate.

"What would you think of changing?" he asked. "I mean, work for us for a while. We have a big job here—weed out the real Nazis in this area, party functionaries, and especially war criminals. When we hear of one, we go out to get him. Others are brought in. They all have to be interrogated. After that, we either let them go or send them to prison for trial. We badly need an interpreter—can't use Germans, of course. You would be very useful to us, and you could help bring those bastards to justice. And give 'em back a little of what they gave you. What do you say?"

I really didn't know what to tell him. It seemed disloyal to leave the camp. On the other hand, I had started to feel a little stuck there lately. And now the lieutenant added something that made me prick up my ears. "We have an adjunct office in Wetzlar," he said. "At times we might ask you to go out there for a week or so to help them out—or to another of our regional offices."

Wetzlar, he had said! That did it. I felt sure a week in Wetzlar could be turned into a week of living with Vera. And a week in Giessen would mean a week of terrific food and divine pastry. Between Vera and profiterole, UNRRA was no contest. The camp really didn't need me any longer, I told myself.

"I would like to do it," I said. "But I want to make sure the colonel at the camp finds someone to take over my job. I'll let you know by Wednesday, and if it's okay, I could perhaps start working here on Monday next week." The lieutenant said that was fine with him, and that McGregor would come around on Wednesday to see me. Would I like him to put in a word with the colonel, too? I said that wasn't necessary.

The colonel's reaction, the next day, was as I had thought: he couldn't care less. "I say, my boy," he commented, sipping his daily Scotch, "do as you like. I wager we can get along without you." It was a dubious compliment, but I now felt free to go.

When McGregor showed up on Wednesday and I gave him my answer, he slapped me on the back. "Good going!" he said. "Shall I come back to pick you up Sunday night?" Actually, I told him, I would sort of like to spend the next few days in Wetzlar. "I left some of my things there," I added hypocritically. "No problem," he said. "Get your stuff ready—it so happens I have to go there today myself. Then, on Sunday, our Wetzlar boys will come for you at the camp there, and you can spend a couple of days working with them until I come back to take you to Giessen. Okay?" Was it ever okay! Within half an hour I had gathered up my few belongings and said goodbye to my co-workers, the colonel and the Russian lieutenant. "I don't like it that you are leaving," he said stiffly, as if he smelled an international conspiracy. It was the closest thing I got to recognition from the Giessen staff.

At Wetzlar, that evening, I got a different reaction. "So," said captain Smith, "you prefer taking your revenge on the Nazis to helping your fellow men get back to their families." I wasn't prepared for that, and suddenly felt ashamed—perhaps less of the implied reproach than of disappointing the captain. I liked and respected him. "Well, too bad," he went on, making it worse, "I was going to ask you to become my assistant here in Wetzlar." Now he had given me a real reason to lament my decision! Still, I didn't feel I could pull out of my commitment to the CIC. All I could do was stammer my regret. I left the captain feeling terrible. When I told Vera how I had shot myself in the foot, she shrugged it off. "You'll be here more often anyway," she said, "and besides, you'll be working for people with more influence than those at UNRRA." It didn't dawn on me then why she said that.

The rest of that week was better: lots of sleep, lots of sun, lots of Vera. She was as intense and self-willed as ever, but more and more often she would escape into a moody anxiety beneath, where I could not follow her. God, I thought, what a crazy existence this is. Here I am, without a care in the world, going where the wind blows, and I can afford to live from day to day because I know there's a safe life out there as soon as I decide to go back to it. But for her, living from day to day is the only way to dispel the knowledge of approaching terror. It may have been towards the end of that week that I began to think I should marry her, but it was a thought too vague still, and at the same time too momentous to be acted upon right away. On Sunday night a CIC Jeep drove into camp, and with a heavy heart I said goodbye to Vera. Two days later I was back in Giessen.

49

Now, at last, I had a room of my own, on the top floor of the hotel. I had been living the communal life for so long that I had forgotten what it was like to occupy a space all by myself. Not that I spent much time in it, but I knew it was there, and just that was a good feeling. The need for an interpreter was sporadic only, so I had a fair amount of free time on my hands, during which I could roam the streets. I discovered a pleasant city, home of a university, hardly touched by the war. It had lots of trees and there was a swimming pool just out of town. Just being in a city again did me good. But I had to roam and swim by myself, for I wore U.S. Army clothes, and there was a rule against fraternization, impressed upon me by the lieutenant. In any case, I was not overly fond of the Germans just then, especially now that some of the horrors of the concentration camps were starting to come out, nor did I assume the Germans were overly fond of the occupant.

For a short time I was friends with a G.I. stationed in Giessen, a pleasant fellow with whom I had struck up a conversation in the street. "How can you be Dutch and wear G.I. clothes?" he had asked. "I thought we had been fighting the Dutch." He was from Pennsylvania. It took him a while to grasp the difference between "Dutch" and "Deutsch". He would come up to my room after dinner, and we had drinks, smoked, and talked. Twice he forgot the time. "Christ, it's past curfew!" he exclaimed. "I was supposed to be back twenty minutes ago." It was risky, he said, to go back to the barracks now, for the area was all lit up and the MP's would be out. The first time he almost got caught, he told me later, so when it happened again he asked if he couldn't spend the night in my room and go back early the next morning. I had an extra couch in my room and saw no reason to say no. We were both slightly drunk that evening. I went to the bathroom, and when I came back he had stuffed two small pillows under his shirt and tried to make up to me. I had a hard time getting him away from me, but at last he fell asleep on the couch. He woke up early, terribly embarrassed. "That happens to me sometimes when I'm drunk," he mumbled, his eyes avoiding mine. "Don't worry about it," I tried to reassure him, but uncomfortable myself. Would he feel better if I told him it was not the first time I had been approached by a man? I thought better of it. He never came back, and I made no effort to look him up.

On the work level, most of the CIC's activity turned out to be largely routine. The official policy was to arrest all members of the Gestapo and the SS and all Nazi office holders from the rank of Ortsgruppenführer on up. The Ortsgruppenführer often turned out to be a small town grocer or a farmer who, but for the war, might have spent his life as an unremarkable pater familias, and had been more or less shanghaied into taking the job or seen it as a way to give himself importance, his main crime being that he, along with millions of other Germans, had been hypnotized by Hitler's voice, had believed everything he said, and had looked the other way when Jews were rounded up and beaten, or perhaps even looked upon it with approval. Others looked to me like dyed-in-the wool Nazis. Unsurprisingly, no one had ever heard of concentration camps, and there were times I couldn't help breaking out of my role as interpreter and ask them how they thought I found out about Buchenwald back in Holland two years ago. I got only blank stares. It was hard to know if they were lying now or had simply refused to look or listen then. Not mankind's finest, but there were thousands like them, and it was obvious they couldn't all be locked up for very long. It was also impossible to find members of the SS, or any German male for that matter, who had fought against the western Allies. "Nein, nein," they protested, "am Ostfront, nur am Ostfront." It was the Russians, they said, trying to make common cause, the Russians who were our enemies, "nicht die Amerikaner." Jim Shea, one of the agents who seemed to be doing most of the interrogating, always broke out in a horse laugh when they said that. You had to wonder why it had taken the Allies almost a year to go from Normandy to Berlin.

I came to like Shea a lot. He had more depth than most of the others, and also the best sense of humor. He had taken to me, too, and showed an interest in my well-being. One day he took me aside and said: "You know, there's nothing in American law that says a foreigner can't be a member of the Armed Forces. I bet we could fix it up for you through the Military Governor in Frankfort." "But why would I do that?" I asked. "Well," he said, "for one thing, you'd get paid. It's not much, but why should you keep working for free? More important, you would become eligible for the Veteran's Bill." He explained what that meant: after six months or so I would be able to study for free at an American university. He assumed, of course, that no one would turn down a chance to go to the Promised Land, and the thought did appeal to me, but I didn't share Shea's optimism that this was for real, and in any case was not ready for the idea of switching universities. In the end I preferred the freedom I had. "But some day I'll come see you in California," I promised. Two years later I did. By that time the Veteran's Administration was paying for Shea's long stay in a sanatorium for tuberculosis, and I was near-broke and wishing I had the VA to pay for my second year at the University of Michigan.

Another agent I liked and often translated for was Bill Taylor, a Texan from Houston, as tall as Texans were supposed to be. Unlike Shea, he was a silent type, more the way I imagined Westerners to be. Because he was a man of few words, we didn't exchange many ideas, and so I am still not sure why I took to him, except that I had never encountered such a combination of gentleness and strength Actually, I got along well with nearly the whole group. Their free-wheeling style went well with my own enjoyment of the freedom I had. The only one I positively disliked was an agent called Mike, an overweight, morose man with cold fish-eyes, who also drank like a fish. In the bar after dinner he would drink astonishing amounts of whiskey, and it was best to stay out of his way. Once, he managed to corner me and start in on his favorite subject: what a lousy place Europe was, and how each time the Americans had to come in to straighten things single-handedly. He added a scurrilous remark about the cowardice of the Dutch Queen, who had abandoned her people and fled to London. By now he had my hackles up. I felt like irritating him by saying something really outrageous. Twirling my own glass of whiskey, I feigned boredom and told him: "But you know very well you people would never have won the war without the help of the Dutch resistance." "What did you say?" asked Mike. I stuck the needle in again. Slowly, Mike moved his hand over to his holster and pulled out his pistol. He pointed it at me. "Now say it again," he said. He hadn't clicked the gun yet, so I repeated it. Then he did click it. "Now don't move, and let's see if you can say it just once more." I didn't really think he would shoot, but on the other hand, he was half-drunk, and I figured I had not survived the enemy to be done in by an inebriate Ally. Opting for a compromise, I got off the bar stool and walked off without comment, though not without unease. No, decidedly, Mike was one I did not much care for.

After a week or ten days, the lieutenant called me in. "I hate to let you go," he said, "but they need help for a while in one of our other offices." (Wetzlar, I thought: Vera, here I come!). "Kassel," said the lieutenant. "Taylor and McGregor are leaving this morning. Do you mind going with them?" Well, yes, actually I did, though I didn't say it. I was hazy about how far Kassel was. It had to be a long way off from Vera. But how could I tell the chief I had been getting more eager by the day for another shower? "For how long?" I asked.

"Two weeks," the lieutenant replied. An eternity! I resigned myself—Kassel it was. "Okay," I said, and went upstairs to pack my duffel bag and scribble a note to Vera, which I gave to someone who was driving over to Wetzlar that day. By noon we were off in a Jeep, McGregor at the wheel, driving in his inimitable style. I did not feel as light-hearted as he that day.

50

It was Kassel that gave me a full grasp, at last, of the disaster Germany had brought upon itself. The city's face was one of leprous wastage, a lifeless realm of ruin and wreckage, of piles of brick and slabs of concrete, punctuated by gaping holes and, here and there, the blind remains of gutted dwellings and commercial buildings, their walls charred by fire. For Kassel had been not only destroyed by explosive bombs, but in the final months of the war had known the apocalypse of fire-bombing. The most amazing sight was that the streets not only had been cleared, but had streetcars running in them, as in any proper, well-ordered city—overcrowded streetcars, that stopped at intersections without discernible habitats in sight, to let off people who seemed to know where they were going, who picked their way through the acres of debris and disappeared into whatever it was they called home—basements, I assumed. Only the residential quarters at the city's outskirts were relatively untouched, or at least the one in which the CIC had taken over a large villa for its personnel, and in which Taylor, McGregor and I were now comfortably installed. Winding lanes were shaded by high trees and lined by expensive homes. You could almost believe the war had never happened. There was a wooded park nearby, and, within walking distance, set on top of a hill, a wide-winged palace out of the days of the German empire. A broad, well-kept lawn swept all the way down the hill, allowing a view of the palace from the ravaged city below—a reminder of better days. There was no one to stop a man in U.S. uniform, so I went there on weekends to lie in the grass and sun myself.

In the center of town a few large buildings were still intact, one of which housed the local CIC office. This one was a lot busier than the Giessen office, so I had less free time to sneak out and walk around, but there was nothing to see downtown anyway. The interrogations were tougher, too, for the Nazis that were brought in were not all small fry, and each was pressured to finger others. That way I heard, one day, that there was a Dutchman in town who had worked for the Gestapo. McGregor looked at me. "Do you want to go get him?" he asked. "I sure would," I said, remembering the one who had hit me in Amsterdam and told me I would be shot. "Okay, let's go," said McGregor.

We found him in a dilapidated apartment building, where he lived with his wife and two small children. "I was wondering how long it would take you to come for me," he said calmly, all ready to go. The kids cried as we took him away, and I didn't feel too great. The following morning someone at the CIC office told me there was a woman out in the hall who had asked to see me. It was the man's wife. She looked distraught. "Help me, please," she begged. "I have no money for food or to pay the rent, and I don't even have ration coupons, because we're not German. There's no one to help us. What can I do, what can I do?" She wrung her hands. Her face was streaked with tears. "I'll ask," I said, and after a while came back with the address of a German municipal office where she should go for help. She shook her head slowly, looked at me again, but saw no hope there. She turned around and left the building. I tried to rationalize it that evening. After all, she had chosen the German side, so were not the Germans responsible for her now? And had she ever worried about the people her husband had helped send to prison or death, or about their families? War was war, I told myself. Yes, yes, but what if she had suffered under it? What did I know about her? What choice had she had? Most of all, what choice had those two crying kids had—it was not their fault their dad had worked for the Gestapo. Captain Smith's question came back to me: whether I preferred taking my revenge on the Nazis, or do some good in these postwar days, and the more I rationalized, the less I liked myself. I managed to put that little episode into the back of my head the next day, but there it stayed. And to this day I hate to think back to it.

A week went by. During my after dinner walks along the meandering lanes of our pretty neighborhood I had begun to notice a girl who also seemed to like going out in the evening. She had probably noticed me, too, for there were few people out at that hour. On Sunday afternoon I saw her again and said Guten Tag. To my surprise she stopped and answered me with Grüssgott. An Austrian! She had long auburn hair and slow eyes as sultry as the summer air, eyes that confused me and drew me in. There was no rule against fraternizing with Austrians. We talked for a while, and then with pounding heart, I crossed my Rubicon. "Would you like to go for a walk in the woods?" I asked. In a low voice she said: "Yes, let us go there."

Holy heaven, alone in the woods with her, with all that rich long hair to caress, those smouldering eyes to sink into, and all the delights that were sure to follow! A thought struck me. "We must not be seen together," I said. "There are a lot of military living here, and they won't believe you're not German. Why don't you walk ahead of me, and I'll follow you from a distance." The girl nodded, turned around and started out in the direction of the woods. Behind her, I did my best to imitate a casual stroll, keeping her silhouette in sight. One more block to go—she was already at the edge of the woods.

And then my heart sank. Halfway down the block a captain was talking with two soldiers. There was nothing to do but go on. Passing them, I gave an awkward salute, and then I heard the voice behind me: "Hey, soldier, come back here." I came back. "What's your rank and serial number?" I said I had none. In the distance I saw the girl turn to look around, then disappear between the trees. "Okay, wise guy, let's go for a ride." I tried to explain my unorthodox situation, but the captain remained unbelieving. In a Jeep he took me to the MP's. A phone call to the CIC straightened things out and McGregor came to pick me up. When I explained what had happened he nearly collapsed with laughter. Back in the villa, of course, he told everyone. They all thought it was hilarious. But I never saw that girl again.

51

Late one afternoon the chief of the Kassel CIC called me into his office. He had two MP's with him, an officer and an enlisted man. "We are loaning you out for a couple of days," he announced. "They need an interpreter to go with them." In little time we were on the road out of town. The two men were silent. They did not explain their mission, and when I asked about it the officer said: "You'll soon find out." It sounded mysterious. I had no idea where we were going. Night fell, and still we drove on. Dark clouds scudded across the sky, heavy drops began to fall, in the distance there were flashes of lightning. The whole atmosphere seemed foreboding. Towards ten o'clock the lights of a town appeared in the distance. To the left of the road was a hill. Now the officer broke the silence, telling the driver: "Up there is where it happened." He pointed up the hill. All I could see were the lights of a few houses. What was it that had happened?

At last we drove into town and in a while the Jeep stopped in front of a hospital. I followed the two men inside towards the reception desk. "Ask them if we can talk with the girl who was brought in last night," said the officer. "Tell them it won't take long." The nurse called a doctor, who took us to a room upstairs. "Please, be brief," said the doctor. "She is still nearly hysterical." In the single bed was a girl perhaps seventeen years old, her head bandaged, her blackened eyes two slits in a swollen, frightened face. The doctor explained who we were, and then the officer began to talk, in a voice suddenly gentle. "Please, explain to her that we are not here to harm her, but that we must know just what happened," he said. "Tell her to take it as easy as she can, to go slowly. Tell her I understand how hard this is on her."

I translated. The girl started to sob; it took her a minute before she became coherent. Haltingly, she told the story of a nightmare. Her home was in town, but she had gone to spend the weekend with her aunt, who lived in one of the isolated houses I had seen half an hour earlier on that forbidding hill. Late last night there had been a pounding on the door, but when they asked who was there, there had been no answer. They heard someone walk around the house and try to force the shutters to one of the bedrooms. In panic, the two women had fled for the dining room and tried to push a cupboard against the door, but it was heavy, a man had succeeded in entering, and they were too late.

The officer interrupted. "What kind of a man, what did he look like?" he asked. "Ein Schwarzer," the girl said. "Was he in uniform?" Yes, he wore khaki clothes. "Tall, short?" Tall, the girl said, but couldn't tell how tall. In a nightmare you probably can't tell, either, I thought—the terror of phantoms is not in their size. "Was he light black or dark?" was the next question. The girl looked puzzled. It was a distinction she had not grown up with. "Never mind, ask her to go on, please," said the officer. The girl closed her eyes and wept silently. Then she went on to the end I was afraid to bear.

The dining room table was between the women and the intruder. He had chased them around. The girl had escaped into the kitchen. The man had caught her aunt and stabbed her to death, then kicked the kitchen door open, dragged the girl out, beaten her down and raped her. Then he had left. She had heard a car drive away at high speed. After a while she had got up and managed to stumble over to a neighbor's house.

The officer nodded, meaning that was all he needed. Gently, he touched the girl's hand. "I am sorry," he said, and no more, because there was nothing else to say. He turned around and left.

The next morning he told the driver to take us up the hill to the aunt's house. A neighbor saw the American Jeep and came walking up the road to speak to us. In fairly good English he explained it was to his house the girl had fled. He handed a slip of paper to the officer. "An Army truck drove up earlier this morning," he said. "It slowed down in front of the aunt's house, turned around, and drove past it again. Then it speeded up and went back down the hill." He had memorized part of the license number and written it down. The officer looked at it. "U.S. Army," he said to the driver. "It's classic: the criminal returns to the scene of the crime." He folded the paper and thanked the neighbor. "I think we've got him," was all he added on the way into town. That afternoon we drove back to Kassel.

Now I had something to reflect on during my evening walks. After years of German violence and impatient waiting for the shining liberators across the sea, I had come to think of nations as good or evil, and the G.I.'s, naturally, were the good people. How naive, I thought now—obviously violence was all around, waiting for an opportune time to strike out. And what time more opportune than wartime? So what was the difference between nations? It could only be that brutality was licensed in some and not in others, or at least more so in some than in others. I suppose several things were germinating inside me: an understanding of the relativity of good and evil, a hatred of war far removed from my excitement in May of 1940, and an elementary appreciation of government by law that heightened my growing sense of affinity with America. At least, the violence to which I had been so close that sinister night was not being tolerated, I told myself. Crime was not licensed. The murderer, a U.S. soldier, would be tracked down by his own Army, and there would be a legal trial.

Later, I heard that a G.I. had been arrested, tried, and convicted. I was told also that there was a good chance he would be shot. And that taught me another lesson: that the law itself can be brutal.

More and more those thoughts led me back to Vera—Vera, who expected nothing but brutality from her government. How could I not act to save her, when all I needed to do was marry her? It would be an impossible marriage, I knew. Though my want of her became more urgent by the day, I had a dim awareness of the distinction between that and loving her, loving as I had loved Sylvia. And I certainly had no illusions about her being in love with me, or that her faithfulness would outlive her gratitude for long. But what did it matter? By marrying her I could do two things at the same time: save her skin and, for a while at least, keep her for me. The high road and the low road led to the same decision. I talked about it with the tall Texan, Bill Taylor. He was appalled. "With a Russian wife you'll never be able to come to the United States," he said. Like Shea, he assumed going to America was mankind's highest aspiration. "Besides, what will your parents think?" he added in a fatherly way. "Yes, but what about her?" I answered. Taylor didn't believe a word of what Vera had told me. But I remembered the darkness in her eyes and her silences of fear. At least, I believed that she believed. "You said you have to go back to Wetzlar for the weekend," I said. "I'd like to go along—who knows, her time may be up soon." "Okay, Robert," sighed gentle Bill Taylor. "Okay, if you've really made up your mind."

We left on Saturday evening and drove all that starry night in an Army Jeep, and all that night Taylor kept trying to talk me out of it. We arrived in the camp just after sunrise. Without waiting for breakfast, I headed for the barrack where Vera had her apartment, ready for her joy and eager for my reward. I knocked. The door that opened was next to Vera's. It was her girlfriend. "Where is Vera?" I asked. "She was put on a transport yesterday afternoon," said the girlfriend. "Back to Russia. Twice this week Captain Smith got her off the list. But she finally had to go."

Too late, oh God, was it possible? Too late by a day! Stunned, I walked back down the stairs and into the morning sunlight. Vera on her way to the future she dreaded! Right now, she would be in a train, rolling east, and if her forebodings were right, she would already be a prisoner and her journey would go on for thousands of miles until she arrived at a camp somewhere in Siberia, her living hell for years to come—if she was even to live—for she had spoken of death, too. And I could have changed it all so easily if I had been decisive. She would be out here in the sun with me now, we would have been happy for a while, until she left me, but what matter if she did, she would have had a life. Why had it taken this disaster before I could tell myself I really cared for her? Because I had believed her, why had I been so dumb, why had I waited. Too late, too late, she was gone. All day I walked around the camp and could think of nothing else, nor the following day on the way back to Kassel, sitting next to Taylor in silence and remorse. After that I began to tell myself that, perhaps, Taylor was right—not that Vera had invented her story, but that her nightmare was only that—yes, that must be it, she was really on her way to Moscow and she would soon be back with her family. Her family: of course, her father was a general, so even if others were sent to Siberia, the general would certainly be able to save his daughter! Those thoughts quieted me down at last. Still, how often in the years to come did an image of proud Vera in a subarctic prison camp not come back to me, as in a faded photo found in a forgotten drawer. But in time she slipped into the deeper recesses of my memory.

Then, thirty years later, the clarity of Vera's instinct was confirmed when Soljenitsyne, in The Gulag Archipelago, revealed to the West the full horror and humiliation of the purgatory to which Stalin had sent his soldiers who had had the misfortune to be captured by the Germans, and whom he feared in his contorted mind. And so I found that old photo again, and I know I will never lose it now.

52

My days in Kassel were coming to an end. A week after my return, agent Taylor and I set out for Limburg, a small town on the river Lahn. It was a pretty town, but something happened there that disturbed me. Taylor had to interrogate several Nazis who were kept in the local jail. The interrogation room was in the jail itself and reminded me unpleasantly of the one in the prison of Amsterdam where I had been interrogated by the Gestapo: bare walls, a single table, two chairs, nothing else. The most important prisoner was a high-ranking SS officer, a man thirty-five or forty years old. He was brought in by a stocky, tough-looking sergeant. Taylor started in on his questions. He mentioned the names of SS-men the prisoner must have known. Where were they now, he asked. The officer remained silent, and Taylor repeated his question. Silence again. Suddenly the sergeant walked up to him, hauled off with his fist, and gave him a hammer blow in the face. "Talk, you son of a bitch," he said, "or we'll make you." I was too shocked to translate that, and didn't need to. The prisoner's face was bleeding and I wondered if his jaw was broken. But he hardly flinched, and remained silent. Taylor looked as if he had a bad taste in his mouth and seemed to notice I felt sick to my stomach. I wanted him to tell the sergeant off, but he only gave an impatient gesture to waive him away from the German. I had no illusions about what the sergeant would do to his prisoner when he took him back to his cell. After we were done with the interrogation I walked down to the river. I sat down and asked myself (Captain Smith again) if this was really what I wanted to be doing, playing the role of conqueror—worse, no more than a little assistant to the conqueror, a bit actor without even the conqueror's choice to be magnanimous: the kind of person I had learned to detest in the past five years.

It was the beginning of the end of my CIC career. Although it went on for another few weeks, I no longer had much stomach for it. In any case, by now we were in July, and my thoughts more and more began to turn towards Holland.

I felt at last ready to go back, find my family, my friends, the university . . . and Sylvia. Though about Sylvia my thinking was still confused. I knew our relationship had to come to an end before long, change into something I could not readily imagine. If I had returned with Vera (and how close it had come to that) the ending would have been abrupt and for her perhaps cruel. Or had she in her mind finished it already? She had always been clear-headed about that. Perhaps our long separation had created the easiest and most natural end. But I, was I looking forward only to seeing her again, or to more than that? I knew the answer: more than that.

Back in Giessen, I talked with Shea about going home. "Not right away, necessarily," I said, "but let's say in early August. That will give me the chance to spend a little time with my family and find a room in Amsterdam before classes start around the middle of September." Shea nodded. "We'll miss you here," he said, "but you should go back." To go home—but how? After walking around for three months in an American uniform and working for the Counter-Intelligence Corps, I found it beneath my dignity to fade back into the dullness of the DP-camp I had once helped to run, and arrive back home in a pack, without any of the glory I had pictured. "Let me think about it a little," said Shea. "Maybe we can find a better way to get you there."

A few days later a Gestapo man was brought in, and during the interrogation it came out he had hidden a motorcycle, a 500 cc BMW. Shea winked at me. "Remind him it is Allied property now," he told me, "and that it's in his interest to tell us where it's being kept." After some prodding the man said it was out on a farm and gave us the address. "There's your way home," said Shea after he was gone. "You have earned that motorbike after two months of free service." Then he noticed I looked embarrassed "I've never learned to ride one," I admitted, "or drive a car or anything like that." But he waved away my doubts. "It's nothing," he said. "You'll learn in no time."

Fine—but no one seemed in a hurry to go out to the farm with me, and I was more afraid by the day that the motorcycle would disappear before we got there. Shea was busy, McGregor was busy, Taylor was busy, although fewer Nazis were arrested and I had more time off than before. Free time, but lonely time. The rule against fraternization with German citizens had been relaxed and ordinary G.I.'s were now picking up girls left and right, but it was still in effect for CIC personnel, and I assumed it still applied to me. In any case the German girls fawning over the conqueror reminded me too much of the Dutch ones during the war who had gone out with our conqueror. But one morning I met one who was obviously different, a well-dressed young woman who had come into the office to obtain some information. I found out what it was she needed to know and tried to talk with her for a while. Suddenly she blushed and said: "I have to leave, or else people will say I talked with an American."

Then she blushed more deeply, and added: "I am sorry, I should not have said that." But what had escaped her was something I could relate to, for I had too often felt the same way about talking with a German. She was shying away, but proudly, I felt, like a race horse, and I was charmed. Here was a German I would not mind fraternizing with. I told her I was not American, but Dutch. She threw me a sidelong glance and fled. What was hiding behind that look? By chance, I saw her again a few days later, hurrying along the street. I caught up with her and asked if she felt like meeting me at the swimming pool. At first she did not answer, then, quickly, without looking at me, she nodded. "In an hour?" I suggested. She nodded again.

Great! At the swimming pool no one would know I worked for the CIC, and we could lie next to each other and get to know each other. An hour later I saw her walking past the hotel in the direction of the swimming pool. When I got there it was crowded. I spent over an hour looking for her. She wasn't there. Had she panicked again or fooled me from the start? I will never find out but either way it mixed my disappointment with admiration.

53

Meanwhile, the lieutenant was looking around for someone to replace me after my departure, and he heard there were two Dutch girls in the DP-camp who spoke fluent German and English. Shea pulled me aside one evening to tell me about them. "They will come in tomorrow morning," he said. "They need to be cleared before we can take them on." (Had I ever been cleared, I wondered—I didn't think so.) "I would like you to interview them," Shea added. "Just ask them the standard questions."

Two look-alike beauties walked in the next day. They were twin sisters, about my age or slightly older. Something about them looked different from the average displaced person. How had they kept such healthy complexions, where had they got the good clothes they wore? My suspicions aroused, I asked them what had brought them to Germany—had they been in a concentration camp or a prison? No, they said, they had spent almost all of the war years in Holland, but they had a German grandmother, and towards the end their parents had decided it would be safer if they went to live with her. The story seemed fishy to me. "Where is your grandmother, and where did you live in Holland?" Their grandmother, they said, lived out on a farm somewhere to the east, and they were from The Hague. The Hague! I pricked up my ears. From the way they spoke they had to be from a relatively high-class family, and the probability was high that my cousins would know of them, especially Prul. "What was your address?" I was right, they were from one of the better neighborhoods. I felt sure they were lying, that they had been girlfriends of Germans with enough clout to take them back to Germany, probably high-ranking Nazis.

I told Shea about my suspicions. He pulled a face. "I guess we'll have to check out the grandmother," he said, "and when you get back to Holland try to find out about them and write me. But I doubt it will make much difference—they're needed, and they're good-looking." Shea was a realist, not a cynic, but I was still naive enough to believe I could make justice prevail.

I would ferret out their past and, if it was as I thought, prevent them from making a smooth transition from Nazidom to the Counter-Intelligence Corps of the United States of America.

Less than a week later that belief in justice received a severe jolt in Frankfurt. Shea had to go there for some reason and told me to come along to see the Military Governor. "You'll need some sort of letter from him to get you through all the checkpoints between here and Holland," he said. I realized he was right: all I had was a small card given to all displaced persons, but it was likely that my DP-card would only get me on an UNRRA transport back home, and would do nothing to smooth my way for the glorious return I had in mind. So I joined Shea and went to Frankfurt.

When the Military Governor had heard me out, he nodded sympathetically and said "Sure, I'll write whatever it is you need, but first you and Shea can do something for me. There's a Hungarian woman here who needs to be cleared to work for the Army. And I mean cleared! One of our generals needs her." When the woman came in, I appreciated why the general needed her. I needed her myself. She had high-heeled shoes and a fur cape, which she wore with indescribable elegance, revealing the bare minimum of a gorgeous body, and she had a way of crossing her legs that was immensely exciting—way out of my class, I knew. She was so sure of herself that she made little effort to hide that she had until recently been the mistress of a German general. I began to understand why the job of clearing her had been given to Shea, from the CIC-office at the safe distance of Giessen, rather than one of the agents from the main CIC-office down the street. The Military Governor was not about to create problems for either the general or himself. The woman was duly cleared and within minutes shimmied out of the building, presumably toward the general's bed. Fortunately, I had my righteous indignation to hide my envy. The reward for my cooperation was a fine letter stating I had performed inestimable services for the CIC, that the motorcycle I was riding was confiscated Allied property given to me in lieu of wages by order of the Military Governor, and that this letter was to serve as a title of legitimate ownership. With that we left.

But I still did not have my motorcycle! I spoke of my frustration to a Dutch lieutenant attached to the CIC who was spending a couple of days in our hotel in Giessen, and he offered to go out with me and get it. I thought it over, but was not sure he would have the gall that might be needed to confiscate it without any proper authority. And so I stalled some more.

We were approaching mid-August, my mental deadline for my departure. It was probably obvious from my face that I was getting edgy, and at last it was McGregor who said: "Okay, let's go out tomorrow and pick up that cycle." Early the following day he took a small pick-up into which, winking at me, he stowed a canvas cover. "We had better not make this too obvious," he explained. "What we are doing is not exactly Army regulations." I wondered if that was the reason they had waited so long. In any case, if nerve was needed to carry this off, I was going out with the right person. We left in high spirits, McGregor singing a tune from "Oklahoma!" in his loud baritone voice: "Oh, what a beautiful morning…" Have you seen Diana Durbin—in a film, I mean?" he asked. "Sweet little thing!" I had never seen Diana Durbin or heard her sing, but knew half the U.S. Army was in love with her. Ahead of us a German was approaching us on a bicycle, struggling against the wind. McGregor made a beeline for him and at the last moment the terrorized man steered his bike onto the low shoulder and fell off it. McGregor roared with laughter, veered back to the right side of the road and looked back. "A Heinie in the ditch!" he shouted. I laughed, too, but uneasily.

Well before noon we had found the farm where the BMW was supposed to be. "Nein," said the farmer's wife, she knew nothing about a motor ycle. My heart sank, but McGregor didn't believe her and turned on the screws by telling her that hiding Allied property could get her into jail. She caved in soon and said the motorcycle was in the garage of a service station in the nearby village. And that was were we found it, all shiny, practically new, with plenty of promise of speed and power. I felt instantly in love with it. The mechanic looked sour and asked if this was an official military requisition, but McGregor brushed him aside and told him to help put the motorcycle into the truck. Once out of town he stopped to cover it with the piece of canvas, after which we drove back to Giessen feeling like the cat that swallowed the canary.

I spent the next day learning to ride it, and that was when I noticed there was a fuel indicator, with "empty" on one side. I hadn't thought about that problem before. A rough calculation made it obvious I would never get from Giessen to Eindhoven on a single tankful of gas. "How am I going to get gas on the way?" I asked McGregor in consternation. "Well," he said, looking at a map, "after you leave the American occupation zone you'll be passing through a corner of the French one, but mostly you'll be in the British zone, and that's where you'll need gas. You can try your luck and see if the Limeys are willing to give you gas on the strength of that letter you're carrying, but I wouldn't bet on it—it's a different ball game in the other zones." I felt the glory of my reentry into Eindhoven slip between my fingers. "So what do I do if they say no?" I wailed. "What you do, he said, "is get some iron wire and attach a Jerry can to the frame of your bike. With those five extra gallons you should be able to make it home." I worked at it for an hour that evening, weaving a crude basket for the Jerry can to fit into, and as best I could attaching it next to the right rear wheel. Then I put the few belongings I had into an old suitcase I had liberated from the house of a Nazi we had arrested, and fastened it to the baggage rack with rope. My beautiful BMW had lost much of its sleek allure carrying that unsightly burden, and the back was so overloaded that a little bit of extra pressure from my hand was enough to tip the front wheel off the ground. Never mind, I thought, it's only temporary. With that I said farewell to my CIC friends and went to bed early, all exited about the adventure of the next day.

54

By six in the morning I was on the road. It was a splendid day. I was riding through farmland. On the green meadows drops of dew glistened like diamonds in the early sunlight and cows raised their heads and lowed as I flew by. I felt exhilarated by the speed, experimented with leaning into curves, loved the rush of the fresh morning air on my face and the smells of the country in my nostrils. My BMW purred along quietly as if it shared my joy, as if it were part of me.

But after an hour or so, I became aware of a strange rattle in the rear of my bike, and brought it to a stop. My wire contraption holding the heavy, gas-filled Jerry can was coming undone and the end of the wire was hitting the spokes of the rear wheel. I was lucky it had not already become entangled in them and sent me head over heels, gas can and all. It was too dangerous to go on like this—I would have to take my chances with the British. I unwound the iron wire and left the Jerry can standing in front of a farm, smiling at the thought of the farmer's amazement when he found it.

Before long I was on the Autobahn, heading north, riding in the wake of U.S. Army trucks at well over a hundred kilometers per hour. This was child's play! How casually at that age you play with your life when you have so much to lose. Here and there an overpass was out, and I followed the trucks, down a detour, and back up a steep incline to return to the main road. Here and there, too, there were check points and I produced my famous letter. Each time it was examined with curiosity, but each time it worked. Soon I entered the French zone and expected I might have more trouble, but the French soldiers simply waved me on. It was not until I was well into the British zone, in the vicinity of Bonn, that it dawned on me my route would take me right past Siegburg. Why not stop off at the prison and see if my watch was still there? I could at the same time try to find gas somehow. Now I saw the Zellwolle factory on my left, where a few months earlier I had been afraid for my life, and a little beyond was the Siegburg exit.

Although I had never really learned the lay-out of the town, I homed in on the prison as if by instinct. There it was, cold, somber, forbidding. But to my surprise I was received with open arms. As soon as I announced I had been a prisoner there, I was taken to the office of the British colonel in charge. He asked me to sit down in an easy chair, and offered me a cigarette and a glass of sherry. "I say, things must look a bit different to you from this side of the fence," he said, with apparent comprehension for the thoughts and feelings that flooded me. "This place is full of Nazis now—their turn this time, though I wager we are rather less hard on them than they were on you. Most of them we shall have to let go; some may stay a little longer." He sipped his sherry. "But there is one," he went on, "just one I would like to see behind bars for a long time. And that is where you can help us."

"The prison warden?" I asked. "Well, yes, alright," the colonel conceded, "he ought to be in the same boat. But he may have saved his skin the day before the assault on Siegburg. He knew the game was up and locked the gates against the SS, who tried to come in and finish off the inmates." Another sip. "But there is another one," he added, "someone with total contempt for all prisoners, and responsible for the death of hundreds of them." An image floated into my subconsciousness: that of a bald-headed old man in a white coat with a look of disdain on his face.

"The prison doctor," I said. The colonel gave a faint smile. "Fine," he said, "I'm glad you came up with it yourself. We know a lot about this man already. He had been condemned for murder at the end of World War I, but the sentence was not carried out and we can't get him for that now because of the statute of limitations. But tell me, have you had occasion to see him?" Then I told the colonel about my diphtheria, about Henk, my half-paralyzed cellmate, whom I had had to prop up as we stood at attention in the freezing hall, dressed only in our bed shirts, waiting with two or three dozen other inmates, the sick, the weak, the emaciated and the dying, waiting for hours for what we had been told was our medical check-up, until at last the German doctor deigned to walk past us, carefully avoiding to look at us.

"Were the sick given any medication?" the colonel asked. "To my knowledge, none," I replied. "Not when I had diphtheria, anyway." He nodded. "We found a pharmacy stocked with medicines in the sick ward. You see, in the Nazi hierarchy this man ranked above the warden and overruled him when he tried to take even the most elementary measures against the typhus epidemic and treat the sick. Having you people die off was a good thing to his mind, a deliberate policy, you might say. For that reason we want him tried as a war criminal. We are preparing the case against him."

I was all in favor of that. "But how can I help?" I asked. "Ah," said the colonel, "our problem is that his victims, or those who have seen what he did, are either dead or no longer around, scattered all over Europe. The inmates were kept here in quarantine for a month, but all we have now is second-hand accounts of what they told the soldiers who first occupied this area. None of those are left, either. Or rather," he corrected himself, "there was no one until you showed up. You are the only one who could face that doctor in court as a witness."

That took me aback. "Do you mean I'd have to stick around until his trial?" I asked. "When would that be?" The colonel sighed. "I'm afraid it could still be weeks away," he replied. Weeks! I would have liked to avenge Henk and all the others, but did my desire run as deep as that? The colonel had read my face. "Well," he said, "I can hardly blame you for wanting to go home. But perhaps you could do something else today that might help us. Would you be willing to go with me to see the doctor now and repeat in front of him what you told me? Afterwards, you could sign a deposition which we would present in court." To that I eagerly agreed.

As we left the office I explained why I had come back to begin with: my watch. "Why, of course," said the colonel. "Let us go to the files and take a look." And he led me to a room filled with filing cabinets. In no time he had pulled out a sleeve with my name on it. I am not sure if I really expected my watch to be in it, but it was! I wound it and it started right up. And there, too, were all the documents on me. How could I have doubted it, I thought, it is all so German, so gründlich—after all, it had been my good luck to be sent not to an annihilation camp, but a regular prison, in which files were kept on every inmate. Files are not to be destroyed: they represent a minimal sense of accountability that says there should, in principle, be individuals to match them and that may actually have given us a small measure of protection absent in the terrible camps in the east, where, I imagined, files were kept not on people, but on numbers. "Would you like to take it with you," the colonel asked? I saw no reason. For all I know it may still be there.

I had expected the doctor to be called out of his prison cell, but to my surprise he was just under house-arrest. So we drove to his home, the colonel, an officer with a legal function, and I. Sitting in the man's living room it was hard to believe that the shriveled old man across from me could have inspired such fear at one time. Still, he had not lost his arrogance and flatly denied what I told the two officers in front of him. Back in the prison office I wrote out a statement, signed it and gave my address in Eindhoven. I never heard about it since and doubt it ever came as far as a trial for crimes of war.

It was getting on in the afternoon and I wanted to get going. But I still needed to fill up my gas tank. The colonel wrote out a note for me and told me to present it to the Military Governor in town. "He will come off a little stiff," he said, "but he is not a bad type. He will probably give you some coupons in the end." Stiff he was. Seated at his desk he read the note as well as the letter from his counterpart in Frankfurt, then looked at me and asked: "And what might it be that brings you to this office?" To get gas for my motorbike, I explained. "I beg your pardon?" "Gas," I repeated. He raised his eyebrows. "Gas? Whatever for, my good man?" Was he dense, or was he playing a game with me? "For my motorcycle, sir, so I can go home," I repeated, trying to keep irritation from creeping into my voice. "Aowl" exclaimed the Governor. "My dear man, is it petrol you might be wanting? Don't let me guess it. Don't let me guess it." And I understood he had understood from the start, but wanted me to say "petrol", not "gas", like the Americans. Yes sir, indeed, petrol was my need. And petrol I got. Within thirty minutes I was leaving Siegburg, following the Autobahn, heading north again, hard by Porz, skirting Cologne and Dusseldorf, then turning west towards Munchen-Gladbach, the Dutch border, and Roermond, the first town in Holland.

"Home tonight," I told myself, and that thought filled me with emotion.

55

In the vicinity of Dusseldorf it started to rain—a slight drizzle only, but as I had no raincoat it did not take long before I was soaking wet. I also got a quick warning that it is easy to slip when it's wet, and was fortunate I got it not on the highway at a hundred kilometers per hour, but while I was traversing a town, going uphill on cobblestone pavement. It could have been a nasty fall, even so, but I only had a scrape on my arm and another one on my dignity, for I felt that someone wearing a G.I. uniform ought not to fall off his motorcycle in front of German onlookers. A woman was about to rush over, but I waved her off majestically. On towards the border, but at lower speed. It was dusk, and raining hard by now, when, at last, a sign loomed up announcing the Dutch border. Within minutes I stopped at the boom across the road. I had been a little apprehensive about this last check point in Germany, but everything had gone so well that I was no longer very worried. I should have been.

To the left of the road stood a long, one-story building. A door was opened and a man in British uniform, a sergeant, it turned out, told me to come in. He was not about to go out in the rain himself. I showed him my DP-card and told him I was returning home after a year in prison in Germany and several months with the U.S. Counter-Intelligence Corps. He listened without much interest, and said: "That's a story the Dutch immigration people here will want to check out. But where did you get that motorcycle?" I produced my letter. He read it and shook his head. "You can cross the border if they let you," he said, "but that motorcycle stays here." I was thunderstruck and asked him the reason. "No reason," he said laconically, "it just stays here." Trying to argue my case I started to shiver, whether from anger, nervousness, or simply because I was wet to the skin. But the sergeant got up, opened the door and told me to go to the office next door. How was I going to find a way out of this sudden disaster? How? For the moment I had to do as he said.

Next door was Immigration—three men in uniform who listened sympathetically as I explained again what I'd been doing in Germany. "Would you state your name again, please?" one of them asked. He walked over to a table on which lay a big, fat book. "Just a formality," he added, turning the pages. Suddenly he stopped. He turned around, glared at me and motioned me over. "Read this," he ordered, his tone a lot less friendly. He had his finger on a line, and I read: "Robert Scholten—SS."

"What is this?" I exclaimed. "What is this book? Where does that information come from? It's all wrong!" "This is our black book," the other said. "It's a register of all known Dutch Nazis and collaborators. A lot of them fled to Germany towards the end and are now trying to sneak back in." Looking up I met only cold eyes. "But I'm telling you it's a mistake!" I shouted in desperation. "That's got to be a different Scholten. After all, it's a fairly common name." My name in the black book as an SS-man—what a come-down from the hero's reception I had envisioned. I almost felt as if I had something to be ashamed of.

The official in charge spoke up. "Sure, Scholten is a fairly common name, but how many Robert Scholtens are there, and how many of those would be coming out of Germany?" It was not hard to see his point. "Then call my family," I said. "Or if you don't trust them, call the man who was head of the Resistance in Eindhoven, Mr. Elkerbout." I did not yet know that Mr. Elkerbout had been caught and shot.

"Well," said the chief, "as it happens there is an easier way to find out. If you have been in the SS, you are carrying a tattoo under your arm, three points in a triangle. So take off your shirt." I did, and the three crowded around me to look. "Nothing," said one of them, "he's alright." I heaved a sigh of relief—thank heaven my namesake had not been a mere collaborator, member of the Dutch Nazi Party or an assistant of the Gestapo.

And now I did get the welcome I felt I deserved. A fire was lit in a small wood-stove to dry out my clothes and, because I was still shivering, they put me in a chair in front of it to dry me out as well. After my teeth stopped chattering I could answer their questions: where had I been, what had it been like, how had I been arrested? But then I came back to my current problem: my beautiful BMW. "Why am I not allowed to take it across the border?" I asked. The chief spoke up again. "Unfortunately," he said, "we have no say over that. If that sergeant wants to take it away from you, we cannot stop him. And I'm sure he would like to—he has done that sort of thing before, and then he sells what he takes." He mused for a moment. "Listen," he went on, "I'd like to help you. We don't like that man any more than you do, and besides, you deserve that motorbike for your time in prison. Listen carefully. Go tell the sergeant you have decided to go back into Germany on your motorcycle. He can't stop you from doing that. As you turn around, you'll be going uphill. When you get to the top of the hill, turn around again and come back this way, but free-wheeling, your engine turned off. Your lights, too, by the way. Halfway back down the hill you'll see a dirt path going off into the woods to your right. Follow that path. We'll be waiting for you and guide you across the border." I thought that was mighty nice of him and thanked him.

The sergeant showed no reaction at all when I told him I had decided to return to Germany to try and sell my bike. There had been no let-up in the rain. The road led up a hill, as I had been told. Following my instructions I turned off the lights and the engine at the top of the hill, turned around and, with my heart in my throat, coasted slowly back towards the border, peering ahead to spot the opening between the trees where the dirt path would lead off into the woods. There it was—perfect! I smiled as I made my turn to the right. So much for you, mister sergeant!

56

Or rather, so much for me. In the dark I had not noticed two figures beneath the trees at the entrance to the path. But now I did. From the back of a motorcycle a soldier was pointing a Tommy gun at me. In front of him sat the sergeant. He had seen through the whole game. I put the brakes on and stopped.

"Alright," said the sergeant dryly, "you wanted to go back to Germany? Back you go! And we'll follow you to make sure you do. Don't try any funny business, either."

It was near midnight, and the rain was now coming down in buckets. The two men behind me had waterproof clothing from top to toe. I only had my shirt and trousers. On we rode. As if I had eyes in the back of my head, I could see that Tommy gun still pointing at me. How far were they going to take me? After a long time the road seemed to be entering a town—Munchen-Gladbach, I thought. Only then did my escort turn around and leave me. I continued on, without a clue what to do next, through empty streets and across deserted squares, back and forth in the rain through the center of town till at last I spotted some lights and saw a row of barracks and a sign that said UNRRA. I had stumbled upon a DP-camp!

A light was still burning in what looked to be the office. The door was opened by a kind-looking man who turned out to be a Dutch civilian in charge of the camp. "You're wet," he remarked without exaggeration. "Come on in." I was also dead-tired, and was grateful it did not take him long to say: "We can talk tomorrow. Let's go find a towel and some bedding. I'll show you where you can sleep." Soon I was dry again and lay between clean sheets. It was not home, but it almost felt like it. The emotions of the day kept me awake for a while yet. That bastard of a sergeant! But then I felt some satisfaction creeping in. With no thanks to the sergeant I was safe and dry, I had kept my BMW out of his clutches, and tomorrow, I felt sure, I would find a way to get it across the border.

"I don't think there's much of a problem," said the camp chief at breakfast. "There are Dutch occupation troops stationed in town. Every day Army trucks go back and forth to Holland with soldiers on leave. Ask the captain in charge. He's a friend of mine—an easy-going man. I think he'd be willing to have his men hide your BMW in one of the trucks and take it to Roermond. Then you go there yourself in two days on a regular UNRRA transport."

Within the hour I was ready to find the Dutch Army. "Let me add something before you leave," said the camp chief. "The captain will perhaps offer to hide you in the truck together with your motorbike, but I hope you won't do that, because by now you are registered in this camp, and I have to account for you." I promised.

Everything went exactly as he had foreseen. The British sergeant seemed to be disliked by everyone, and the captain enjoyed the idea of putting one over on him. "Bring your motorbike here by two in the afternoon," he said. "My men will hide it under a tarp, and we'll give you an address in Roermond where they will take it. It will be there tonight. For that matter," he added, "there's no reason you couldn't come along yourself. They'll hide you under the tarp, too." Now I was sorely tempted. I could be home that night if I took him up on it! I told the captain about my promise. "Do as you like," he said, and went to talk with one of his men. He came back with a slip of paper with a name and address on it. I left walking on clouds, as happy about getting the better of that sergeant as about saving my BMW.

The camp chief seemed relieved to see me. "I'm glad it worked," he said. "And now there's something I would like you to do for me." He spoke of his concern about two Jewish girls in town. "They are German," he said. "their parents are dead, but they have a relative in Holland, and they are waiting for permission from The Hague to go there. But it takes a while. Meanwhile they are living in town on some money their family has sent them, but they live alone, though they're only fourteen and fifteen years old. I don't like what I hear about their relation with an Army officer, for food or money, or whatever. I would like to know if it's true. It is really a German civilian affair, but I feel some responsibility here and I'll do something if need be. So I would appreciate it if you would go to their place and talk with them—find out what is going on."

I found the girls that afternoon. It was hard to believe they were as young as the camp chief had said; they looked more like eighteen and nineteen to me. Yes, they had a little money, they said, to pay for the apartment. "How about food?" I asked, and from their veiled answer I gathered that someone brought them food for favors, someone who had the key to their apartment and of whom they seemed slightly afraid. But I could not shake a feeling that it was not all coercion. Were they willing partners themselves? "I think you should move to a different place," I said, "and you could take your meals at the UNRRA camp from now on." "Can you get us an apartment that's nicer than this one?" asked the older of the two, as if that were her main concern. Was she manipulating the situation? "Perhaps," I said, "but more important for you would be to have a place to which only you have the key." They looked so delighted that I felt half-guilty about my suspicions: maybe they were innocent victims after all.

Back at the camp, the chief nodded when I told him of my conflicting impressions. "It is a murky case," he agreed, "but I think they should move. I'll see if I can pull some strings." He had pulled them within twenty-four hours, and the next evening I helped the girls move into the ground floor of a house surrounded by a pleasant garden. They were happy with their new surroundings and, convinced it was all due to me, so abundant in their gratitude that they made me feel like their new sugar daddy. But I had no desire to plumb the depths of my depravity and, to the salvation of my soul, could not get beyond seeing them as the children they still were, in spite of the early sexual maturity they had been forced into.

That afternoon a Dutch DP asked me to be his interpreter, because he had to see the camp doctor, who was French. The poor man itched all over his body. "C'est la gale," the doctor pronounced. "La gale?" I did not have the faintest notion what that meant—but then something struck me: 'galbulten'," a Dutch word for itchy lumps that in medieval times were thought to be caused by gall. Gale, gall? Of course! and he was itching! "You have 'galbulten'," I informed the sufferer. Then the doctor started telling him what to do: fumigate all his clothes, blankets, pillow cases and bed sheets, cut his hair very short, wash his hair thoroughly with a Lysol shampoo and apply an ointment he gave him all over his skin for three days. I translated and the patient left the room.

I turned to the doctor, "That seems like a complicated way to get rid of la gale," I said. Looking puzzled, he asked: "Do you know of another way?" "Well, I've never done it like that," I said, proud of my superior medical know-how "Oh, you have had 'la gale' yourself?" the doctor asked. "Sure," I said. "almost every year. His eyes opened wide: "EVERY YEAR?" "Sure enough, and my brother, too, usually in the spring and sometimes even my father had it. It used to drive me crazy." The doctor shook his head in disbelief. "So, what did you do about it?" "Nothing, really", I said, "it just went away by itself". He shook his head again, and on that note we parted.

Three days later, back in Holland, my body started to itch all over, so I went to see the family doctor. He told me I had to fumigate my clothes bed sheets, pillow cases and blankets, cut my hair short, shower and wash my hair thoroughly with a Lysol shampoo and apply an ointment, he gave me, all over my skin for three days. "But, what is it?" I asked him. "Don't worry," he said, "it's just scabies you must have picked up in Germany." And to this day I wonder how often that French doctor has told his countrymen about those Dutchmen with their reputation for cleanliness, who had scabies every year and did nothing about it. He was never to know the young man and his brother were allergic to strawberries and suffered annually not from "la gale", but from the hives.

57

The next day, seated in the rear of an Army truck together with several others from the camp, I felt as if the distance to the border had shrunk considerably since that long rainy night three days before. In what seemed like no time we were on the slope down to the border. There was the dirt road on the right where I had known defeat, and a minute later we came to a stop at the boom across the road. Out of his office came my foe, the British sergeant. He threw a cursory look into the truck, but did not seem to recognize me. One of the Dutch immigration officers did, however, and I took special pleasure in telling him how my BMW had been smuggled in. "Good for you," he said with a wink. Then we drove on into Holland.

What a mixture of thoughts and emotions! Much more than time separated me from the day I had been in a cattle car rolling eastward across the border—I had seen so much, heard and felt so much, and grown into manhood. I was back in my country, but it was the place of my adolescence, and right now I felt almost estranged from it, a little as if trying on last year's suit and not being sure it would still fit you. Yet, cohabiting with that in my heart was a keen and moving sense of homecoming. On a shallower level was another feeling, that of disappointment at entering Holland in an UNRRA truck as a run-of-the-mill DP (I, who had practically run a DP-camp once!) instead of as a G.I., even though a fake G.I., on a Gestapo motorcycle. But I took heart in the knowledge that the situation would soon be remedied.

I got off in Roermond, and asked the first person I saw for directions to the address I had on my slip of paper. Carrying my battered suitcase, I found it without much trouble and rang the bell. A pimple-faced youth about sixteen years old opened the door. I told him I had come to pick up the BMW that had been placed at his house two days before. The kid blushed a deep red and stammered something I didn't hear, or didn't understand, or didn't want to understand. "What did you say?" I asked. "Well," he said, "I just rode it around for a few minutes the night before last, and then the police stopped me, and because I didn't have the papers they took it away."

Took it away? What was he saying? "TOOK IT AWAY?" I shouted. "What are you saying? Who did? Where did they take it?" Why, oh why had I left the key in it? I raged, at myself, at the kid. "How could you do a dumb thing like that, ride it without permission, without any papers, without plates, without a driver's license, either, I bet!" He was trying to tell me something, and I stopped long enough to listen. "But you can get it back," he said. "The marechaussee have it, and all we need to do is go there so you can show your papers—that's what they said." It got worse all the time! I might have been able to bluff the municipal police, but this was the State Police he was talking about, and they would be tough. I had counted on not being stopped on the highway, that the police would assume I was an American soldier, but now they would know I was just a plain Dutchman in disguise. "You don't understand," I snarled. "I don't have any papers either, not the right ones, anyway, no title, no registration—not even an ID-card to show who I am. You really did me in, kid, you did me in fine!" What could I do? Nothing, except go to the State Police office and see if my Frankfurt letter would work. The boy led the way.

And there it stood, my proud possession, my shiny 500cc! Never had it looked more beautiful. The officer in charge listened not unsympathetically to my explanations and read the Military Governor's letter. But then he shook his head. "It's not that I don't believe you," he said, "but the report is already on the way to The Hague, and we have to get authorization from the Ministry of the Interior before we can release the motorcycle. In any case," he added, "even if we could release it, you would need registration plates and a driver's license before you could ride it away, plus a special road permit, and those permits are given out only for military or essential commercial purposes—private citizens are not yet allowed to drive cars or ride motorcycles." I could see the situation was hopeless. The sergeant had triumphed over his foe: I had lost my BMW for good this time. It was a hard pill to swallow. And now a new thought occurred to me.

"How am I supposed to get to Eindhoven?" I asked the policeman. "I haven't got a cent in my pocket to pay for the train." He agreed that was a problem. "Try hitch-hiking," he suggested. "It's the only way." I threw a last glance at my sleek beauty, picked up my suitcase, and left the office. Outside I vented my last anger at the pimple-faced youth. "Thanks again, kid, thanks a million!" With that I turned to walk out of town.

Standing there alongside the road next to my suitcase, thumbing for a ride, I felt downright silly. What a come-down! And I had to thumb for quite a while, for traffic was sporadic. The sun was already on the way down when a trailer truck carrying a load of steel pipe slowed down and came to a stop to pick me up. I was in luck: the truck was from Eindhoven. The other hitch-hiker the driver had already picked up slid over to make room for me and we started off. It was slow going, but the talk was lively, and little by little I stopped mourning my misfortune of the day and grew excited again about coming home. It was nearly 7 o'clock when I began to recognize where we were: familiar woods, side roads I knew—and suddenly it dawned on me we would pass within a couple of hundred meters of Sylvia's home. Why not go and surprise her—just stay a minute and then borrow a bicycle to ride home? Following my impulse I asked the trucker to stop and let me off. It was an impulse I regretted later, when I sensed it had hurt my father to know that I went first to see not my family, but friends of the family.

Sylvia's house was close now, just around the curve in the country road. So familiar—and yet, when it came into view, something seemed to have changed. Then I realized: it was the bright lights falling through the windows of the living room into the front yard. Of course, the war was over: no more nighttime black-outs! It would take a while to get used to peace time in Holland.

With thumping heart I walked up to the front door and rang the bell. Would it be Sylvia who answered the door? It was, and the instant I saw her I felt again the flow of the deep current she had set in motion five years earlier. She looked lovely. For a second she appeared confused. Then, "Rob!", she exclaimed, and again, turning her head towards the living room: "It's Rob!" I had a terrible urge to take her in my arms, but there was no time even for words, for the rest of the family was already behind her, welcoming me with shouts and hurrahs. Pulled into the living room, besieged by a torrent of questions, it was hard to be coherent, hard to look at anyone besides Sylvia. I thought she looked pale and anxious, but I did not yet know why.

Before I knew, the minute I was going to stay had turned into half an hour. "I must call home," I said, and went to the hall phone. After three rings (always three rings, I remembered) I heard my father's voice answering with our number, as was his custom: "Thirty six-twelve." I was too moved to speak right away. The voice came straight out of my childhood, with the ceremonious intonation that fit so well with its owner's straight-backed bearing, both voice and bearing belying a love of family just short of sentimental. "Hello, thirty six-twelve here," my father repeated. I found my own voice. "Hello dad," I said. Now there was silence on the other side. Then he said: "Is that you, Rob? Where are you? Are you here at last? Are you alright? Are you coming home?" "Aright, dad," I said. "And I'll be home in less than an hour." He was still bewildered—where was I? I explained. "A truck took me this far," I said. It was the truth, but not the whole truth. My father gave up trying to understand. "Come quickly, son," he said. "Your mother and your sisters are here, and we can hardly wait." My sisters, he said—but where was Pieter? Jack, I supposed, was living in town somewhere, but why had he not mentioned our older brother? Had his condition worsened? I decided not to ask now, afraid of the answer. "Okay, dad," I said, "I'll be right there." And with that hung up.

On the borrowed bicycle I sprinted home, back to the patrician house that, above its front door, carried the name of "De Haven" on a sign my father had painted years ago in the flourishing letters that were his style. Now, as I entered the side yard, I thought it appropriate to return beneath that sign of Haven instead of by the back yard as we all used to. Leaning the bike against the great chestnut tree that shaded the kitchen, I walked back to the front door and rang the bell. And the bright ring of that bell suddenly made it all seem real: I was back in port.

PART III

HOLLAND: BACK HOME AND AWAY

58

Behind the door I heard a rushing of steps and the high giggle my stepmother always gave when she was delighted. Then the door opened, and there was my father, with tears in his eyes. "Welcome home, Rob," he said, somewhat ceremoniously (he was that way), but from the depth of his heart. Behind him, my stepmother giggled again, then gave me a long, hard hug. Over her shoulder I spotted Marjolijn. "Come on, man, give us a chance, too, for a change," she said in her best Brabant accent. We all laughed out loud while I embraced her and Lydia. Then I inspected them at arm's length, and, in my own Brabant voice, said: "Tarnation! Ye have both turned into handsome maids while I wasn't looking." How good it felt to laugh together, to walk through the hall into the dining room and from there into the living room and find all the furniture where it was supposed to be. But as soon as we sat down I had to pose the question that had to be on all our minds, though I knew it would change the joyful mood and cause pain, especially to my father, for, whatever the answer, it would not be a happy one. "Where is Pieter?" I asked. For a moment no one spoke. Then, slowly, my father spoke: "Pieter's condition became so serious that he had to be put into a sanatorium. He is as comfortable there as it possible for him to be, but his mind and body will keep getting worse. There is no hope."

I suppose I had expected as much, but still, I was stunned by the news, especially because the sanatorium turned out to be in the center of the country. That part of Holland, north of the great rivers, had not been liberated until the very end of the war, and even now transportation would certainly be difficult there. I had to assume Pieter had not seen anyone of his family for many months. I made a mental note that I would find a way to go there and see him as soon as possible. I would find out later that Pieter had been receiving visits, not from any of us, but from two ladies, one of whom was the mysterious Aunt Bé. For a long time it had been unclear to me what relationship Aunt Bé had to us, or if we just called her "aunt" because she was an old friend of the family. She would always arrive at our house on Pieter's birthday, carrying presents for him. Later I came to understand what Pieter himself never knew: that she was his aunt only, and that the presents were from her sister, whom my father had divorced for reasons of adultery when Pieter was only two. And much later still I learned at last the full truth never known to Pieter: "Aunt Bé" was his mother.

"And how about you?" I asked my parents. "How have you been? And how was it to be liberated?" I knew Eindhoven had been taken by parachutists of the 101st U.S. Airborne Division—one of the first Dutch towns to be liberated, eight months before the central and northern parts of Holland. The question I really wanted to ask was about the state of my father's health, but I knew I would never get a direct report on that, health being the taboo subject it was in our house. My mother spoke up. "The liberation went so fast, we hardly noticed it," she said. "But you can't imagine what happened then!" She waited, and took a deep breath. "You know those people in our neighborhood, how they hate us because we live in a big house and are not Catholic—well, they went to the authorities and denounced us as collaborators, and then they came to arrest us." Her voice was full of hurt, and I felt for her, though what she told me did not come as a great surprise. "Those people" were the ones it pleased my father to call "the plebeians" and both my parents to treat with a benevolent condescension that could not have failed to spark rage in the hearts of some of them. In the confused days following the liberation they were bound to take their chance to get even, especially since my parents had handed them a ready-made accusation on a silver platter: the frequent visits of Herr Liese, the affable Nazi Treuhändler, or wartime manager, of the Philips factories to whom my father had shown such unquestioning friendship. It had even made me mad, so why not "those people?" Much as I hated to think of my parents in that situation, I could not in all honesty drum up much righteous indignation.

"So what happened?" I asked. By now my mother had tears in her eyes. "They made us do street repair work right in the center of town—unload cobblestones from a truck in front of the crowd, and they jeered at us! Can you imagine? Your poor father! We were not allowed to talk to anyone." People's justice. I remembered prisoners meeting it out amongst themselves, and how I had despised it.

"How long did they keep you there?" I asked, not daring to look at my father. My mother's voice rose in anger and disdain. "Well," she said, "they didn't get away with it for very long. So many important people know us, someone was bound to recognize us and interfere. Police inspector Deis himself came by in the afternoon. When he saw us, he was horrified and ordered us freed immediately, and he had the police take us home." Now, triumph showed through her anger, but when I finally glanced at my dad I could see only embarrassment and wounded dignity in his face.

"It's not pretty—settling scores, I mean," I said, just to say something, and decided it was time to change the conversation.

"And how is Jack?" I asked next, but that also turned out to be a painful subject, for the family feud had apparently been picked up where it had been left when Jack went into hiding. He was back in town, but there still was virtually no contact. "He did not want to come and see us," said my father. "It was his choice." But I knew why, and felt irritated at my parents. What would it take for them to learn? With an effort I threw off the pall it threatened to cast over my homecoming, and we ended up talking till late in the night.

I went to see Jack and his family the next day, and heard what had happened since the day he had left to go into hiding in Zeeland, at his wife's parents' home, waiting for the forged papers I had promised him and that never came. For a year and a half he had stayed in the attic, while Brigette and two-year old Rob lived below. Little Rob had been instructed not to mention his father to anyone, and he never did. When the British Army invaded Zeeland and bombed the sea dikes, causing widespread flooding, they had been forced to flee, Jack going his own way on a bicycle. Inevitably, he had been stopped by a soldier, who could have turned him in as a spy, since he carried no papers. But the man had said: "Aw, I am Austrian, why should I care? This war is over anyway. Just go off." There had been stories like that all during the war about Austrian soldiers, some of whom had been among the thousands of children who, at the end of the First World War, when their country was in shambles, had been received in Dutch families for months, to escape the famine and misery back home. Perhaps the soldier that stopped Jack had been one of them. In any case, for Jack it had been a narrow escape.

I found my former school mates from High School, and in the weeks that followed we had almost nightly parties. Everyone had a wartime story to tell, some amusing, others harrowing, still others sad. Some had not come back—the children of Jewish families, first of all, but other, too: a timid friend who had never engaged in anything and was picked up for no reason at all, and another one, who had spent the war years safe in America, but was killed by anti-aircraft shrapnel a few days after the family's return to Eindhoven. One family that returned was that of my friend Bob. He had been my bosom buddy in Grade School, but I hadn't seen him since then, because his dad had been appointed head of Philips' Argentine operations in Buenos Aires. I had never paid much attention to his sister, whom I remembered as a skinny kid with an odd black beret, but I sure noticed her now! She had become a tall beauty, indefinably Argentinean, I thought, with smouldering dark eyes and carrying exotic hats instead of her perennial beret. Now the shoe was on the other foot, for this wild mare from the pampas, who could have thrown me to the ground if she had wanted to, hardly noticed me, and I didn't try to join the circle of admirers that surrounded her all day. Prudence, loyalty, love and lust all drove me back to Sylvia.

It took days of impatient longing before I could see her alone, but as soon as I took her into my arms I was aware of a resistance that had not been there before. It took me by surprise. "What is it?" I asked uneasily. She drew away and looked at me, searching my face. "Do you really think . . .", she began, and stopped. "Think what?" I exclaimed. She took a deep breath and went on. "I have thought a lot about this moment," she said. "I have looked forward to it so much, but I have also dreaded it. I mean, it has been so long, so much has happened. It has been exquisite between us. Maybe it could be again, but if it is not, it will diminish a beautiful memory. And if it is, it will be very hard for me when the time comes, when you go on with your life where I can't follow you." She took another deep breath. "For more than a year I have tried to ease into the thought of this. I think . . ." Her voice trailed off again, then she concluded quickly: "I think it would be best if we decided to be friends—not "just" friends (I hate that expression), no, close friends, no more—the best." By now she had tears in her eyes.

Oh God, for the wisdom in that woman, her strength and her vulnerability, for her beauty and the depth of her love! Naturally it would have been best. Not for me, no, I could just go on accepting the delight that was Sylvia until the day I would fly the coop and leave her behind. Not for me, but for her. With an ounce more of understanding, a particle more of concern for her, I could have protected her from the pain that day would bring her, and from the loneliness in those that would follow. But I didn't. And so, we made love, and it was as before. Or so it seemed to me, but it really wasn't, of course, for Sylvia had been right: it could never quite be the same again. For our love had begun at the same time as the war, had blossomed during the war, and in an important way was identified with it. The war had encapsulated it, protected it almost, and allowed it to grow into a glowing intimacy that was out of time and without season, undisturbed by thoughts of an ending. Now it had become open-ended, and its glow had become the glow of autumn, and that awareness was with us, but most of all with Sylvia. For she, more than I, knew you can't go home again.

59

We were well into September. I was getting itchy to go up to Amsterdam to see my friends there and, most of all, find a place to live. On the way I wanted to see Pieter. I started out by train, but knew I could only go as far as Utrecht. I would have to hitch rides the rest of the way.

Three soldiers and a young Dutchman shared my compartment. They were talking about the last year of the war. Someone said General Montgomery was the real military genius. I couldn't let that go by unchallenged. Full of my pro-American sense of superiority I assured my travel companions that Patton was much the greater general and that he and his Army could have ended the war six months earlier if he had not been hobbled by Montgomery. There was no comment. The soldiers looked out the window. Only then did I notice they looked emaciated. The Dutchman broke the silence. "You know," he said in Dutch, "these men here are British paratroopers. They went through hell in the Battle of Arnhem. They were lucky. Most of their buddies got killed, but they were only shot up. They survived in a PW-camp and are finally on their way home. Perhaps," he added, "you'll want to apologize to them now." I felt myself blushing to the roots of my hair. Why did I have to be such a blow-hard? What a bad aftertaste I had given them of the terrible duty they had performed. I stammered something of an excuse and an awkward thank you for what they had done. Fortunately, we were close to Utrecht, and I was glad to get off the train.

A truck took me to the place of Pieter's sanatorium, where a nurse told me to follow her. Walking through the halls she filled me in on his condition. He was permanently bedridden, she said, and had several convulsions a day. "Don't be too surprised if he doesn't recognize you," she warned, "his memory is pretty much gone. Now and then it comes back a little, and then he knows at least where he is." How long was this likely to go on, I asked.

"There's no telling," she said. "Months, years, who knows? He is such a terribly sweet person," she added. "Too good for this world. We love him." Her words both pained and consoled: at his life's end Pieter would be surrounded by love, but it would not come from his family. Would he know that, would he feel it?

The nurse led me to a large room with many beds. At the end lay Pieter. He was asleep. I sat down on a chair next to him and, as I watched him, I started remembering. Sweet, the nurse had called him—yes, and infinitely patient, too. From the start he had borne his terrible affliction without a murmur of rebellion. Uncomplaining, he had suffered through two day-long brain operations, and had submitted to long, massive X-ray bombardments of his head that had perhaps destroyed his brain, his fine intellect, more surely than the tumor. The bulging of his left eye, hidden behind a dark glass, the gradual paralysis of his legs, the frustration of failure in school and the loss of a future and of his friends when he had to drop out, he had accepted it and remained gentle through it all. Was there an afterlife, I wondered, or a reincarnation in which such souls are rewarded? The unfairness of his fate made me want to believe it.

Pieter slept on peacefully. What did I feel now, looking at him? Love? Admiration? For the first time, did I feel pity? He had never asked for it and, although my father was consumed by it, it had not occurred to either Jack or me to make him that poisoned gift. To us, he was just Pieter, our brother, as my uncle Wim had just been my uncle Wim. Their afflictions were part of them and so could not come between us.

Now my thoughts went back to the last summer vacation the three of us, Jack, Pieter, and I, were able to spend together, before Pieter's legs became too weak for long days on a bike. It was the year 1937, and I was fourteen. We had been given one hundred and twenty guilders to go on a four-week journey to Luxembourg, through the Ardennes Mountains. Pieter kept a detailed journal, complete with photos and reports on the daily luxury of a chocolate bar which we allowed ourselves. We had that journal for years, but it disappeared after the war, when my parents moved to Hilversum and all the house contained was sold to the next occupant, lock, stock, and barrel, for less than two thousand guilders. How Jack and I have regretted losing it!

But I have my memories . . .

"Bonjour, Messieurs!" The cheerful voice greeting us every morning was that of the baker's wife in Gedinne, a village in the mountains of southern Belgium. We had pitched our tent on a meadow along the river Lesse, some

8 miles away, and had decided to stay there for a while, not just because it was a beautiful, secluded spot, but because we were exhausted from pedalling our loaded bicycles up the steep slopes of the Ardennes and, most of all, because Jack had been injured.

It had happened on a Sunday, which was a good thing, because on that day there were people around to help us. They came up from Dinant to picnic by the river. When they wanted to go for a swim, they would go inside their cars to change discreetly into their bathing suits. A young couple asked us if they could change in our tent. Sitting on a log nearby, I turned my head away as the pretty wife slipped off her clothes, but my wandering eyes caught the quick glimpse of a breast. It took my breath away. Had she noticed?

"Come on, let's go swim!" I heard Jack say. "Okay, let's swim," I agreed, still full of excitement and guilt. Pieter went back to the tent, to sweep it out, fold our sleeping bags, put away food and clothes. It was in his nature to be meticulous, but this was also a hang-over from his days as a Boy Scout. In fact, the leader of a group of English Boy Scouts camped in the nearby hills had been so impressed with the model look of our tent that he had made everyone of his charges come over to look. Whenever we encountered that group marching down the road, we answered their salutes, Pieter smartly, Jack and I (never having been Boy Scouts) awkwardly.

We were standing on the river bank, ready to dive in. "I'll go first," said Jack, and jumped, and right away the water turned I red. "Don't jump!" he warned, as soon as he came up. His head had hit a rock. He waded back to shore and lay down in the grass, pale as a sheet. It scared the daylight out of me—what should I do? But others had seen what happened and came running over. A man kneeled down and inspected Jack's wound. It was still bleeding, and he complained of dizziness and a headache. The man turned to his wife—it was the couple that had used our tent. "He may have a concussion," he said. "We had better take him to the hospital." They helped Jack up and installed him in the back of their car. Before leaving, the woman turned to Pieter and me. "Don't worry," she said, "we'll look after him. You can visit him tomorrow in the hospital in Dinant. They'll give you our address there. Come see us, too." And with that they were gone. The whole thing had taken less than ten minutes.

Left alone with Pieter for the next couple of days, I drew closer to him than I had ever been, or could ever be again. Together we rode to Gedinne for bread and chocolate, together we swam in the Lesse, and together we pedalled the long road to Dinant. Jack was sitting up already, his head still bandaged, but otherwise none the worse for wear, although he had to stay under observation for a couple of days. Afterward, Pieter and I went to see our Good Samaritans. It turned out they were French. He was the manager of the local gas company.

His wife served us coffee with brandy in it—my first alcoholic drink ever. Her French sounded like a song. I was rapidly falling in love with her and felt we shared the bond of my guilty secret.

When Jack was released from the hospital he was told to take it easy for a while, which was all the excuse we needed to stay in our camping spot and call it quits on Luxembourg. We had two golden weeks there. In retrospect it seemed amazing how well we three brothers got on with each other. If we had spats at times, they must have been minor, and I don't remember any. We didn't let our parents know what had happened. Eventually, they learned about it from the Philips representative in Liege, who was our contact point in Belgium in case of emergency, and who, in the Liege newspaper came upon a small news item saying that "un boyscout hollandais" had hurt his head on a rock while plunging into the Lesse and was being treated in the Dinant hospital. By the time he contacted the hospital to find out if that "boy scout" was one of us, Jack had already left, and no one could tell him where we were. By the end of our third week in Belgium we started to run low on cash and had to head back north, picking up dinners at the homes of the French couple in Dinant and the Philips man in Liège. All in all, our forty guilders each had lasted us twenty-five days—twenty-five of the best days of my childhood, days of promise and innocence, I thought now, before the threat of war and the precipitous decline in Pieter's health . . .

—

Pieter stirred in his bed. I drew up close. Now he awoke and saw me, but without comprehension. "Pieter," I said, "Pieter, it's me." Still he looked, and at last a glimmer of understanding began to show in his one uncovered eye. Slowly, unforgettably, a smile carrying all the sweetness and pain of love and remembrance spread across his face, and: "Gee, Rob," he said. We held hands and stayed like that without speaking, until they came to feed him. He had slipped away again. I got up softly and slowly walked away, turning at the door for a last look. I never saw him again. In 1947, in the Wyoming summer camp of the University of Michigan, I received a letter from my father saying Pieter had died. I sat down against a rock and thought for a long time.

60

Amsterdam! At last I was back in my adopted city. Barely out on the square in front of the railroad station, I felt again the heartbeat that, in some indefinable way, seemed to cause time to accelerate and events to take on color, and I knew the city's pull on me was as strong as when I first came to live there.

In the streetcar on the way to the Geology Institute I wondered if I would find all of my fellow students. I thought in particular of Ab Cohen and Victor de Munck, both of whom had disappeared halfway through the war. Ab was the gutsy Jewish fellow, who had gone into hiding after knocking out our Nazi doorman. Could he have survived? Where? How?

As it happened Ab was one of the first I saw when I entered the building. It turned out he had been rounded up and sent to one of the terrible camps in the east. He had had no contact with anyone on the outside for more than two years, and came back to learn that all of his own family and that of his wife had perished. No one could tell him the fate of his wife, but she had to be dead, too. Waking one day past the apartment where they had lived three years earlier, he saw the curtains were pulled and decided to ring the doorbell. It was she who opened.

Victor had two stories to tell: his own and that of Meck, his girlfriend, with whom he had wandered across two borders only to be arrested just when they were to cross over into Switzerland. While she was sent to the camp for Jews at Drancy, he ended up in one near Jena, in eastern Germany. That camp was eventually freed by the Russians, who simply opened the gates. With a friend, Vic commandeered a flatcar and a horse from a nearby farm and set out for the nearby Leitz factories, where they loaded up with optical equipment worth countless thousands of dollars. Then they set out for Holland. They almost made it to the Allied occupation zone, but at the last moment were stopped by the Russians and sent back to Jena. They spent several more weeks there before they were allowed to leave. In Amsterdam, Victor found not only Meck, back from France, but a Russian girl carrying a baby he had fathered on her in the Jena camp. It took a hefty sum of money to get her to leave, baby in arms.

These were among the more dramatic stories I listened to on that and the next few days. I also went to see Kees and Boetie, my former room-mates and co-conspirators. "God, am I glad to see you!" Kees exclaimed. "We've been plenty worried about you." Freewheeling Boetie was now a happily married man and a father to boot, looking like any proud pater familias. It surprised me only until I met his bride and fell under the charm of her sparkling beauty.

I was eager to talk—now, at last, I would find out what had happened on the day of my arrest, almost two years ago. How soon had they found out about it? Had I saved them by outwitting the Gestapo that day? Not at all, as it turned out. Kees explained. "We had our contacts in the Amsterdam police. Within the hour we knew you had been caught, and so we scrammed. But we kept an eye our place for a day or two, until we were sure it was not under surveillance. Then we moved in to empty it."

Boetie began to laugh at the memory. It seems they had wedged a bicycle across the high staircase leading directly from the street to our top floor apartment. If they should hear it removed, they could be out the window and try to escape via the roof. While they were working feverishly stuffing things into suitcases, they heard the bike fall down the stairs. "We were out on the roof in a second," Boetie laughed. "Out on the roof, and there we lay. I was afraid the SS could hear my heart pounding through the tiles. But nothing happened, and so we went back in. It turned out the bike had fallen down on its own. Together, they removed everything relating to the resistance, but forgot about the radio we kept wedged beneath the seat of an easy chair. The Gestapo found it, and I remembered that illegal possession of a radio had been part of my formal indictment.

Both Boetie and Kees were now active in organizing the University's first Student Parliament and in weeding out wartime collaborators. That term used to denote Nazis and Nazi sympathizers, but was now being stretched far beyond its original meaning to include all students who had signed the loyalty oath back in 1943 and the professors who had advocated signing it—in short, all those whose backbone was judged to have been insufficiently strong. A panel was set up to examine each case, and recommendations for suspension were forwarded to the university administration. When they were not followed, student strikes were threatened, and in one or two cases it actually came to that. In the heady post-war days all that seemed just and proper; it was easy to wear a white hat. In retrospect, I feel more dubious about the pseudo-legal climate in which all this was carried out. We may have learned all too much from the enemy. The Student Parliament (to which I was soon appointed) now smacks to me of the Paris Commune. I hate in particular to remember that Walter and I gave the name of one of our fellow students to the panel, which called him in and promptly suspended him. Boetie's case was more difficult: his father-in-law was Professor Wibaut, who had been Rector Magnificus of the University during the war. As President of the Parliament, Boetie had to work to get sanctions imposed on him, too. A strike was voted, and eventually Wibaut was for a time suspended from teaching. Also suspended for six months was my own Professor Brouwer, for the sin of having proposed a field excursion to Germany in 1941 in front of our German Professor of Paleontology, Hans Gerth. Actually, Gerth was a most mild-mannered man, and I doubt anyone felt greatly threatened. Although Brouwer had dropped the plan after the merest hint of opposition, that did not save him.

But all of that was still in the future. For me, the present meant finding a place to live. That proved not to be easy. In the last year of the war many empty houses (Jewish homes) had been gutted for firewood, and there was now an acute shortage of living quarters. At the end of my second day of searching I went to call on my aunt Clara, who had moved from The Hague to Amsterdam with her four daughters. They were now living in an apartment on a street in the southeastern part of the city, called the "Musschenbroekstraat". The street was short, but for me it was to become long on memories of happy days and hilarious events.

Seeing my aunt and four cousins again felt like another homecoming. They had done much worrying about me, though, what with my aunt's imprisonment for hiding Jewish property and the execution of her ex-husband in reprisal for the killing of a Nazi, they had had their own share of wartime drama. I mentioned I was hunting for a room. Right away, my aunt said: "We have one here, a small one, but you're welcome to move in. You could eat hear, too." I did not hesitate long. A small room was all I could afford anyway, and this one was only a ten minute walk from the Geology Institute. Most of all, I was fond of all five of them, and the idea of living with that beautiful, spirited all-female cast appealed to me. I expected they would make my life turn up another notch, and they did not disappoint me. But that, too, was still in the future.

All my missions accomplished, I returned to Eindhoven to pack what few clothes and books I still had. Within the week I was back, ready to pick up my life as a student—a doctoral student, this time.

61

At that time, and for all I know to this date, education in Holland followed a path almost opposite to that in America. American High School students lead a fairly easy life, without many tough demands, and in consequence learn comparatively little. In college, they have so much catching up to do that they have to be loaded with course work. In Graduate School the pace usually increases further, competition being what it is, and the student is given his Ph.D. only when he is ready to drop from exhaustion. In Holland, by contrast, High School was hard work just to stay afloat and not be forced to duplicate a year, as many eventually had to. You absorbed subject matter like a blotter: three foreign languages, literature, math through calculus, organic and inorganic chemistry, years of physics and biology, history and geography, plus economics or Latin and Greek if you chose to, it was all poured in by the barrel-full. When you arrived at the University, the first two years could still be pretty tough, but then the pace began to relax. Coasting began with the title of "Candidate", and by the time you did nothing any longer you were handed your doctor's diploma. That last stage could be stretched out considerably. In the years I was at the Institute a grandson of the famous physicist van der Waal (he of the "van der Waal's forces") was well beyond his tenth year and still coasting. After the war he did finally finish. As I had managed to get my degree of "Candidate" shortly before the University was closed in 1943, I had just arrived at the coasting stage.

I say all this to account for the fact that I've so much less memory of my scholarly activity in this first post-war year at Amsterdam than of my first two and a half years there, or, for that matter, of my first year at the University of Michigan, where I arrived at the point where the American system goes into high gear. Specifically, while I have little memory of going to the Institute in the morning, I can still savor my anticipation of returning from it in the afternoon. There was a reason for that, but to explain that I have to give a little background.

Amsterdam, that year, was a "rest and relaxation" center for Allied armed forces on leave. They were all over town: tall, good-looking, well-fed Canadian soldiers and American G.I.'s and officers carrying jaunty caps and Eisenhower jackets, friendly folks on the whole, ready to offer chocolate bars and cigarettes to deserving aborigines. The most deserving, of course, were girls between 18 and 25—my age. And the girls, they had stars in their eyes and dreamed of romance and marriage and a house on a California beach. Who could blame the soldiers for feeding those flames? It seemed there were no married men among our Allies, or even men with girl friends back home steady enough to present an obstacle to a permanent liaison with a Dutch girl. "Just wait—as soon as I get back I'll arrange for you to come over and we'll get married." How could we hope to compete, poor, pale, hungry young Dutchmen in our threadbare, outmoded civvies, carrying no cigarettes or candy? No nylon stockings, either, and those were the ultimate come-on. They were just arriving on the market, but still almost impossible to buy. Women camped out in the street overnight when the first ones were advertised for sale, and they were soon sold on the black market for hundreds of guilders a pair. A pack of American cigarettes could be had for a hundred guilders. Why, then, should a girl refuse to accept all that for free from a handsome, generous man in a sexy uniform, a liberator to boot, who asked nothing more than to please her?

The need for facilitating such meetings was soon recognized, and Prul, the eldest and most enterprising of my cousins, quickly became one of the facilitators. In downtown Amsterdam a club was organized for service men on leave—or rather, two clubs, one for commissioned officers and one for the lower ranks. Girls from "good" families who, before the war would not have dreamed of doing such a thing, my cousins included, would go there in the late afternoon or evening and wait to be introduced by the hostess to a lonesome military man looking for a date. At the officers' club, the hostess, of course (or at least one of the hostesses) was Prul. It would begin with drinks at the club, and after that the girls were on their own. Given the mores of the time, they would not, in most cases, have allowed action to go much beyond the kissing-and-petting stage, no doubt to the disappointment of their dates. Inevitably, however, there were partners who failed to understand they were dealing with high-class girls and tried to go beyond the mores. One time, my sweet cousin Sonja came home black and blue. She had not been told that G.I.'s don't ordinarily purchase etchings, and when her escort asked her to come up and see the ones he had just acquired, assuring her of his honorable intentions by saying his driver would come along, she agreed, touched by his solicitude and impressed by the level of his culture. Once in the room, needless to say, the "driver" turned around and left, and her date locked the door behind him. Since there were no etchings, Sonja began to smell a rat and wanted out, but he threw her on the bed, and it was only after savage scratching and biting and yelling for help that he abandoned his dark designs and let her go.

Among the service men who frequented the club (British and Canadians, mostly), many were actually stationed in Holland, and of those quite a few liked the idea of a more or less steady sweetheart in town. Those were the ones who might start hinting at marriage, or actually come right out and propose. In love or not, genuine or feigning in their intentions, they would often gain entry into the girls' homes. And so it was with my cousins, and with my aunt, too. Each, for a while, had her Canadian or American boyfriend, and my aunt was hooked on a British major.

Which takes me back to what caused me to smile on my daily walk back from the Geology Institute. For I knew what was awaiting me. The large living room would be mostly dark, but in the center would be an easy chair and a coffee table loaded with chocolate bars and packs of cigarettes: my payola for keeping quiet. Munching away on a Hershey bar and puffing on a Lucky Strike, I would sit down and read the newspaper, ignoring the low moans coming from couches in various corners of the room, where aunt Clara might be in a clinch with her major, or Prul with her Canadian swain. I was proud of my cousins' and my aunt's beauty, and they gave me good reasons to be grateful as well.

Life was never boring with those five—more like a three-ring circus. One day, Prul came home in disrepair, her panties torn. But unlike Sonja's adventure in a hotel room, hers had occurred in the street and involved a story of greater levity. She was still laughing so hard that she had a hard time telling it. It seemed she had been riding home in a streetcar, barely hanging on while standing on the steps. In those days of few taxis and no private cars the trolleys were loaded to the gills at all hours of the day. As hers gathered speed, a man ran behind it trying to catch up and, almost there, in a last, desperate lunge, reached forward to grab onto something and found it beneath Prul's skirt. He was left behind on the pavement holding a shred of her underwear in his hand. A gray-haired gentleman next to her said: "Lady, your husband will never believe this. If you want, I'll go with you to explain what happened." Holding up what remained of her pink panties, Prul collapsed on the couch in hopeless laughter.

As I had expected, Prul was able to tell me about the two Dutch girls I had interviewed for CIC clearance the day before I left Giessen. They were from Germany but had family in The Hague, they had said. "Those two?" Prul asked scornfully. "They were known all over The Hague. They were mistresses of Nazi officers and probably informers, too, and they followed their men to Germany when the hand writing was on the wall." The news didn't surprise me. I wrote to CIC agent Shea and eventually got a letter back from him saying he wasn't surprised either, but that the two were now working for the Military Governor in Frankfurt, and that little could be done about it.

That fall, I had several other reminders of my time in Germany. One day the doorbell rang and I was the one who opened up. A man smiled at me. I smiled back, and then did a double-take. "Henk!!" There he was, my paralyzed cell mate of Siegburg, long assumed dead. "You're alive!" I shouted. "You're well again! What in the world happened? Come on in." Henk came in. He seemed in perfect health, a strapping man as different as night from day from the one they had carried out of my cell over a year ago. He told his story, and an amazing one it was. It seemed that there had been people at Philips who tried as best they could to keep track of Dutch prisoners in Germany, and that at times they managed to get one out. Somehow, they had heard about Henk and his illness (through that kind priest? I wondered), and had succeeded in convincing the prison authorities that Henk's illness was contagious and presented a danger to everyone. A truck was sent to Siegburg with signs warning "Contagious Disease—Stay Away" plastered all over, so that it was waved on at all check points. The evening of the day they took him away, weeping and begging for help, he was back with his family in Amsterdam, and there he recovered completely, just as Dr. Helberlein had said he would—only neither of us had believed him. "The only after-effect," Henk said, "is that I used to be a tenor, and now I am a bass." We laughed and felt good. It was like another victory.

I also heard from the Comte de Coucy in Paris and from Jean Juliot, the de-railer of trains in Normandy. Jean's message came on a postcard. "J'ai retrouvé ma famille et mon boulot," he wrote, "et tout va bien, sauf que j'ai eu un petit accident avec ma locomotive. Elle a déraillée, et je t'écris dans une chambre de l'hôpital." How could you not love a man like that? Unable to shake his wartime habit, he had derailed his train and was in the hospital! De Coucy wrote to invite me to Paris, and I made a firm promise to myself that I would take him up on it as soon as visits to France were again permitted.

As to my aunt's and cousins' matrimonial prospects, little, of course, came of them in the end. Only Sonja ultimately married a Canadian, a pilot in the Air Force. Aunt Clara's major turned out to be married already. Others had a change of heart once they were back home and, if they were kind, sent thank-you letters, or else were never heard of again. Prul, however, did end up with a Canadian hopeful who turned out to be true to his word and heart, but his hopes were dashed in the clash of cultures. Soon, he said when he left for home, she could come over—just as soon as he had settled in and got himself a job. On the strength of that she got a visa. Then came his letter: all was set, he had found work as a garage mechanic. A garage mechanic? For the daughter of the man who had been president of the Holland-England Line?

He had looked great in uniform, but out there he would be in overalls! It was unthinkable. In sorrow—for she had seemed genuinely fond of him and her heart was soft—Prul wrote him the letter that would break his. Then, since she had a visa already, she flew to Toronto anyway, just to see what would happen. And sure enough, in little time she found the man to whom she would remain married for the rest of her life—a Dutchman, of all people in Canada! But I am running ahead of the story.

62

In late fall it was announced that a group of American scholars would visit the city to give a series of lectures at the University of Amsterdam. They were professors at the Army universities that has been set up in Biarritz and one or two other places, where G.I.'s on leave could enroll for short courses. They had been invited to discuss wartime research developments in their fields. Because I was still vaguely a part of the Student Parliament, Boetie, its President, asked me to join the visitors in their bus and take them to the places where they were going to lecture, and where they would be met by the Head of each Institute. Two of them, I was told, were geologists, Professors Allison of the University of Oregon, and Eardley of the University of Michigan. I was apprehensive about that. The two Americans would expect to be received by Brouwer, who had an international reputation. But Brouwer, since his suspension from teaching, had holed up at home and didn't want to see anyone. I was going to have to explain his absence without causing a blot on his name.

On the appointed day I met a bus full of jovial men in uniform. It was my first, and still remote, exposure to American academia, and the informality of it struck me right away. Our first stop was the Geology Institute. On the way over I briefed Allison and Eardley about Brouwer, adding that in my opinion the molehill of his wartime sin had been made into a mountain. Eardley said he understood and would make a point of giving him a call at home. He had a special interest in him because Brouwer had twice spent a year at the University of Michigan in the twenties and thirties. I rather hoped Eardley would forget it, for Brouwer would not be friendly. We got out and, telling the driver I would be back in a minute, went inside, where I was to take them to Professor Westerveld, the number two in command. Professor Westerveld was not in his office, so we went to his lab. He was not there either. What next? I felt panic setting in. After all, I couldn't very well abandon the two there in the hall. We went back downstairs, and I took them to a place where there was a magnificent three-dimensional model of the structure of the Alps. While they admired it, I raced back and resumed my search for Westerveld. Having found him at last, I took him downstairs, introduced him to Allison and Eardley, and chatted with them for a while. Only then did it come to me in a flash: the bus!!! Holy grief, where were the other twenty-two visitors? I ran outside. The bus was gone. I have never dared to inquire what happened, and to this day don't know how they all managed to find their destinations, what with a bus driver who spoke no English.

In the next couple of days I spent a could deal of time shepherding the two American geologists around and got to know them pretty well. Eardley, as he had said, called Brouwer, and Brouwer, as I had feared, brushed him off saying he had never heard of Eardley—an inexcusable lack not only of manners, but of knowledge Brouwer should have possessed. Eardley was puzzled but, being an easy-going man, shrugged it off.

"Well," Eardley smiled as we said goodbye, "it's been a great two days. If you ever go to America, come see me at Michigan. I expect to be back there in January." With that he and Allison left. But that parting comment, spoken sincerely even if it was perhaps not much more than a formula, put a bee in my bonnet and changed the course of my life.

In those months I did not see much of Sylvia. The logistics of a visit of more than a day had become more difficult because of where I lived. Lord knows, my aunt and cousins were not narrow-minded on the subject of sex, yet, I didn't feel I should introduce Sylvia into the apartment, much less my bedroom, and raise the curtain on the beautiful secret we shared. Nor would she have wanted to. I was again home for Christmas, but so was her whole family, so the logistics there were difficult, too.

What was going on inside her? She was as loving and lovable as ever, even in the face of the certain knowledge that, because of some decision I would make, we would go our separate ways, perhaps soon. The initiative that had started our love affair had been hers—now, it would be mine to end it. Once only she could not keep back her tears, and I was overwhelmed with guilt and tenderness, and with the knowledge that nothing I could say or do would alter our course or still her pain even temporarily.

"Remember me," she whispered, "remember us."

63

In January Brouwer's suspension was over and he was back in his office. One of the first things he did was make me his assistant, charged with teaching the laboratory in Structural Geology. He gave me no guidance: I was on my own. In desperation I decided to use a laboratory manual recently published by Brouwer's arch rival at the University of Leiden, Professor de Sitter, later to become one of the world's greats in geology; if Brouwer had known he would have fired me on the spot. I stayed only a hop and a skip ahead of my class, which, because the lab had not been taught for years, consisted of my own classmates and students senior to me, a circumstance that made me more than a little defensive about fielding critical comments. But at least the prof kept his nose out of it and let me learn the art of teaching on my own. That might seem cavalier, but it wasn't. He had long and carefully sized you up as someone worthy of responsibility who could be left to his own devices, and, knowing that, you were inspired with a high level of confidence that spurred you on to your best effort. Uncomfortable as I felt, I preferred his system, and in later years tried to inject some of it into my own way of dealing with my assistants.

The real test, however, came in February, when Brouwer called me in to say we were going to have two long field excursions that year. Before the war he had taken students on excursions abroad every year, but all I had had up till then was a trip to the hills in the southernmost part of Holland. I had often looked with envy and longing at the long row of photographs in one of the halls, photos out of the twenties and thirties showing one or two dozen students and several of the professors in places my heart ached to see—the Swiss Alps, the Appenines, Spain, Indonesia even. I had listened to endless stories about Brouwer being carried back to his hotel room dead drunk, and about the time he got into an argument in a German train over a window he wanted open, when a German kept closing it. "How much does a window like that cost?," he had asked when the conductor came by, and then, having received a ballpark figure, handed over the money and knocked out the window with his geology hammer. It may have been the kind of apocryphal story old-timers like to relate to freshmen, but it was a good one and, given Brouwer's short temper, might as well be true.

Now, at last, it was my turn, and we were going to catch up fast, said Brouwer, with a seven-day trip to the Belgian Ardennes in April and a three week one to Sweden in July. The Swedish trip presented no logistical problems, for Brouwer, smooth, charming and wily as he could be, had managed to talk the Swedish government into inviting us. That meant not only that the entire excursion, except for the flight to Göteborg, was paid for, but that all the arrangements for hotels, meals, and trains were made at the other end. The only thing left for Brouwer's senior assistant to do was to prepare a detailed field trip guide, and for that he had four months.

"As for the Belgian excursion," Brouwer told me, "that will be your responsibility. Figure out where we should go, make the arrangements, and prepare the guidebook." It made my head reel. "How can we do that?" I exclaimed. "You can't even enter Belgium, you can't get Belgian francs, and the place is still devastated from the Battle of the Bulge." (Plus, I added silently, I don't know beans about the geology of the Ardennes—but I knew better than to mention that.) Brouwer made an impatient gesture with his hand. "That, sir, is your problem," he answered, and when Brouwer said "sir," you knew it was better not to go on. So I left, and talked about it with my classmates.

For days no one could think of a way out, or rather of a way in. Even my best friend Walter, who had a knack for finding deft solutions or creating them where there were none, was temporarily stumped. But only temporarily. One morning, just as I was getting despondent, he arrived at the Institute waving a newspaper. "I've got it!" he crowed triumphantly. "Got what?" I asked. "The way to get into Belgium," he said, "the way to get francs, and the way to get lodgings—all of it in one swoop."

He showed me the article that had given him the clue. It said that the organization of Dutch youth hostels was negotiating an agreement with its Belgian counterpart whereby Dutch youths, after paying a fixed amount per day in guilders to the Dutch headquarters, would get permission to enter Belgium and receive an equivalent amount in francs at the border with which to stay and eat in Belgian youth hostels. Belgian kids would have the same privilege in reverse. The problem of monetary exchange was thereby avoided. "So," Walter cried out, "there you have it. All we need to do is join the youth hostel organization, all of us." I looked dubious. "All of us?" I asked. "Brouwer, too? I can't see him doing that." Walter smiled paternally. "He doesn't have a choice," he said, "just tell him that. He'll join."

With some trepidation I went in to see the prof. I had underestimated him. Though he wasn't wild about joining up, he acknowledged it seemed like a good plan. "Do I have to put on short pants for the occasion?" he asked with a wry smile. The enormity of that thought made me smile, too. Geology professors of Brouwer's generation would not be caught dead in the field without a suit and tie and well-polished shoes.

And so, after I had made a few telephone calls to the Dutch youth hostel headquarters to make sure the article was for real, we all joined up. Next, I had to prepare the field guide. That turned out to be fairly easy. All it took was reading up a little on the geology of the Ardennes and leafing through the guides of earlier excursions to that area. My new one was printed up well ahead of time, and now I could tell the hostel organization where we wanted to spend our nights, and when. All seemed set.

64

There was a second project that had begun to occupy my mind at that time, and I discussed that with Walter, too. I reminded him of Eardley's parting words. "Why don't we try and see if we can spend a year in America," I suggested. "We could write to Eardley and ask him if he can help. Maybe they have scholarships we could apply for." Walter was all ears. "After all," I went on, "we can give good reasons. We can say we have to catch up with wartime developments in geology, and that we've been deprived from doing field work in the mountains all during the war. Eardley said the University of Michigan has a summer field camp in Wyoming. We could go there. What do you say?" Walter was not the kind you had to drag into an adventure, but I wondered if he would go for this one, for his situation was no longer the same as mine. He was now a family man, having recently married Emmy, his pretty, vivacious girl friend of many years, in a splendid ceremony in the great church next to the Royal Palace. I expected he wouldn't decide right away. But he did, feeling sure Emmy would be full of enthusiasm. "Great!" he said. "What can we lose? Let's try."

And so we wrote, and to our surprise we received Eardley's answer almost by return mail. It was a cordial letter, in which he said he remembered us well and would like to see us come to Michigan. To help us financially, he had written a letter to the Michigan Graduate School saying he had met us and, though he had little personal knowledge of our abilities, he had been impressed by the intellectual level at the Geology Institute and felt confident in recommending us for a tuition scholarship. We could hardly have asked for more. He asked us to apply to the Graduate School and to request further letters of recommendation from Professors Brouwer and Westerveld. I knew Brouwer would not be very happy about us leaving for a year, and he wasn't, and tried to talk us out of it. But in the end he wrote good letters for both of us, after receiving our promise that we would come back. That was an easy promise to make, since we had no other intention. For good measure we also asked Professor Allison at Oregon to write a letter on our behalf. So far, so good.

But, of course, we needed more substantial financial aid than free tuition. We heard that there was someone at the Ministry of Education in The Hague who could give you ideas about possible sources, or who might even act as a middleman. From Kees we learned that the person to see had been in the student resistance during the war and might be willing to make an extra effort for comrades-in-arms. We called up and made an appointment for the following Monday.

It was to be a remarkable day, though it started out unpromising. I was to bicycle over to Walter and Emmy's apartment which was not far from my aunt's place, around seven in the morning. That would give us plenty of time to catch the train at nine and be at the Ministry for our appointment at eleven. At seven sharp I rang their doorbell. No answer. I rang again, and again, and finally held my finger on the knob for a full minute. Still no answer. I backed off and shouted upward to the second floor. The curtains stayed closed. I rang again. At last I thought I must have misunderstood—he had already left! Like a madman I pedalled across town all the way to the Central Station, checked my bike and ran in. Walter was nowhere to be seen. He's still sleeping, I thought, and ran out again and pedalled furiously back to his place in Amsterdam-South. It was Emmy who opened. "Oh, my God," she said, "we were up late last night and didn't hear the alarm clock. Walter finally heard the doorbell ring and said 'Damn, it's Rob!', but by the time he had opened the door, you had left." I cursed under my breath. "Where is he now?" "He shot some clothes on and left for the station," Emmy answered. He should be about there now." We must have passed each other in the street, I thought, both going like maniacs and neither of us looking. "Goodbye!" I shouted, and made the trip for the third time that morning, sure that I didn't have a chance to make it. But I gave it all I had and must have broken all records. Checking my bike once again, I looked at the clock: two minutes before departure time. Out of breath and soaked in sweat I raced to the platform. There was the train, and there was Walter cool as a cucumber and smoking his pipe, looking urbane as ever. He excused himself. I was too exhausted and too happy at having made the train to start in on any reproaches.

Early fogs are sometimes harbingers of a beautiful day, and so it was with our foggy start of the day, for the rest of it, though bizarre in part, was smooth and successful. By the time the train rolled into The Hague, I had cooled off, and we looked more or less presentable when we arrived at the Ministry. There we had a first interview with our contact. He said he would make some preliminary inquiries that afternoon and asked us to come back at four. With four hours on our hands we walked out into the sun, ate our sandwiches, and discussed how to spend our afternoon "Why don't we go visit the Soviet ambassador?" I suggested. "We could ask him if they would be willing to pay for a geology excursion to Russia." Walter caught fire immediately. "Terrific," he grinned. "If the Swedes can do it, who not the Russians?"

The presence of a Soviet embassy was a new thing in The Netherlands. After the Bolshevik Revolution, Holland had steadfastly refused to recognize the legitimacy of the Soviet government, a position perhaps of high moral principle, but no less peculiar for all that, and no longer tenable when Stalin became an Ally of the Dutch government-in-exile in London. So now, for the first time in a quarter century, we did have diplomatic recognition and, with that, a Soviet embassy. A telephone directory told us it was located in a residential part of the city, away from the center. We set out by streetcar.

It was a pleasant early spring day. As we walked away from the streetcar stop we saw a man walking ahead of us, bent double under a pile of oriental rugs—a Persian or Armenian, we thought. After a while he turned left, the way we had to go. "He's going to see the Russian ambassador, too," Walter laughed. "Poor guy—he must be figuring they just moved in and will need carpets." Improbable things like that tickled his funny bone. The man ahead turned right, then took the second left—he was still on our route. At last he walked through a gate and a garden up to the front door of a large villa. Coming to the gate ourselves, we read the sign: "Embassy of the Soviet Union." "Maybe he's not such a poor guy after all," I said and we followed the rug man.

After a while there were sounds behind the door, keys were turned, latches were pulled, and the door swung open. In front of us stood a hulk of a man, who looked as if he could flatten us with the back of his left hand. Taking in the scene, he motioned to the Persian/Armenian to drop his rugs in the hall; he was apparently expected. Then he turned to us. "Yes?" he asked, without much encouragement. I began to wonder if this had been such a great idea, after all, and took a deep breath to gather the courage to explain our mission. But Walter had already started. "Good afternoon," he said in his most affable voice. "We represent a group of student comrades at the University of Amsterdam who would like to visit the Soviet Union, and we urgently need to speak to the ambassador about organizing an excursion." He had taken a good tack, making it sound as if we were bona fide "comrades." Hulk's eyes narrowed, but, perhaps fearing the ambassador's displeasure if he turned away genuine communists, he stepped aside and let us in, motioning us over to a bench in the hall.

There we sat for over an hour. Secretaries walked by and smiled at us, a big clock ticked away. At last, a woman came out into the hall and asked us to follow her. We entered a large office and were introduced to an impressive looking man in a dark business suit and wearing horn-rimmed glasses. "Mr.

Ambassador," the woman said, "these are the two I told you about." So this was the ambassador! Up to that moment neither of us had really believed in our little joke, which now suddenly took on an earnest character. One thing that surprised me was that the woman had spoken in Dutch. Even more surprising, the ambassador himself began to speak in Dutch—nearly flawless Dutch. I had not really thought about our language of communication, but if I had been asked I would probably have expected French. I was impressed.

Inviting us to sit down, the ambassador returned to the leather chair behind his desk and asked us to state our mission. As soon as he understood he held up his hand and changed direction. "What did you do during the war?" he asked. "And did you sign the loyalty oath?" The man knew everything! We said we hadn't, and I added a few words about having been a prisoner. "Hold on," he said, "I want to see if you are telling the truth." And he picked up a black book apparently carrying the names of all students who had signed the oath. When he didn't find us in it, he nodded, then asked: "Have you two tried to break the dockworkers' strike?" There had indeed been a strike at the harbors of Amsterdam and Rotterdam, largely organized by the Communist Party. Because Holland was still suffering from a lack of just about everything, several hundred Amsterdam students had gone to the docks to help unload the ships. We said we hadn't, and the ambassador checked another list of names. At last he was satisfied and returned to our proposal. "Yes," he said, "it's possible that might work. I gather you hope to be guests of my government, but you would be expected to pay your own way to Berlin and back. After Berlin, we would take over."

I could hardly believe my ears—was our facetious act turning into a real-life adventure? "But tell me," the ambassador went on, "where exactly is it you want to go?" To the mountains, we both replied—the Caucasus, the Urals! At that the ambassador's face darkened. "Ah yes," he said in a tone a good deal less friendly, "the Urals—the heartland of the Soviet armament industry. I can see why you want to go there." I became vaguely aware of Hulk standing somewhere behind me and hastily disavowed our interest in the Urals. Any mountain range would do, I said. "Why not Siberia?" the ambassador asked. Was the joke on us now? I thought I could feel Hulk breathing down my neck.

But Mr. Ambassador gave us a slight smile. Then he got up and said: "Your professor can work that out with the Soviet Academy of Sciences. I'll make some preliminary inquiries. Ask your professor to write me a letter about it, as soon as possible." With that we shook hands, and in no time we were walking back to the streetcar, somewhat overwhelmed by our unexpected success. Unfortunately, Brouwer would have nothing to do with it and never wrote the letter. He had been burned once when he had proposed a field trip to an unpopular country, and could hardly be blamed for shying away from another hot potato.

Back at the Ministry of Education, we were told that an effort would be made to get us the funds we needed through the Institute of International Education in New York, and that, if it all worked out, the Dutch government would try to get us cheap passage on a boat. We were on a high all the way back to Amsterdam where we arrived in time for dinner. In the train we made a pact: either we would both go to America (or rather, all three of us, for Emmy, of course, would come along), or neither of us would go. The next day we wrote to Eardley about our progress, and to the Graduate School at Michigan to apply for a tuition scholarship In that letter we had to show we would be able to support ourselves for a year. We could, we said. We would take part-time jobs and live frugally. We stressed the importance of Emmy coming with us, for she could save us money by darning our socks. That argument, we found out later, caused no small amount of hilarity among the staff of the Graduate School.

All we could do now was wait and hope. Meanwhile, the time had come for our excursion to Belgium.

65

Belgium—yes, but I was thinking about Paris, too. There had been rumors that you would soon be able to travel to France on a Dutch passport. If that came through in time, I could take the train to Paris at the end of our excursion. I wrote to the count to say I would try to make it and would call him from Brussels. Paris! I hardly dared to believe it.

The excursion started on a Monday. I had told the bus company to have the driver pick me up at my aunt's place at eight in the morning. My fellow students would be waiting at the Institute, and from there we would drive by Brouwer's house and be on our way. At ten to eight that morning the doorbell rang: a telegram for me, from Belgium! From Belgium? I sensed disaster, and when I read it, I was in panic.

Agreement not yet signed STOP Postpone arrival till further notice STOP.

The message was from the secretary of the Belgian youth hostel organization in Brussels. Good grief, how could this be? What now? I was speechless. Outside a horn was honking: the bus, damn, the bus! And then, as sudden as it had come, despair was gone and I could think again. Why, might not that telegram just as well have arrived two minutes after my departure instead of ten minutes before? Of course it might! I tore it up in little pieces and went downstairs to meet the bus.

Before long the bus rolled south toward the Belgian border. I had told no one about the telegram, but not because I wasn't worried. The closer we got, the more I tensed up, not so much about entering Belgium, as about what would follow. What in the world would we do if the Secretary refused to come across with the money? I was taking a high risk, and I knew it.

As soon as we were across the border I made the driver stop at a cafe, where I put in a collect call to the official in Brussels whose telegram I had torn up a few hours earlier. Fortunately, he was in. "Here we are!" I said in the most cheerful, carefree voice I could muster. "Don't tell me you are in Belgium!" the Secretary exclaimed. "Didn't you get my telegram telling you not to come?" My voice, I hoped, expressed amazement. "A telegram? No sir, that must have arrived after we left. But now we are here, sir, and we need our Belgian francs." The Secretary was a decent man. He sputtered a little more, but in the end he accepted the fait accompli. "Just go to the hostel in Liège. I told them your trip had been cancelled, but I'll call them again to scrap the cancellation. I'll wire you the money there." I hoped he didn't hear my sigh of relief, thanked him, and hung up. Victory! It was only then that I told Brouwer, who gave me a thin smile of approval.

The excursion came off without further hitches. Though it was still cold, a sparkling sun lit up the somber beauty of the Ardennes. In the towns and villages, many of which I remembered so well from my camping trip with Bieter and Jack in 1937, we must have been the first post-war tourists, and we were well received. Because of the widespread destruction there were few hotels and restaurants, and even Brouwer began to realize that the youth hostel solution had been a god-sent, although he drew the line at calling our hosts by the customary name of "father" In the countryside some of the hostels were no more than the loft of a farm barn, but they offered the advantage of food that was good and plentiful by the standards of those days.

That trip gave me my first exposure in the field to complex problems involving the internal rock structure of a mountain range. Although Brouwer's spell-binding lectures had certainly prepared the ground, I think it must have been on the day we visited a famous feature called the Fenêtre de Theux (the "Window of Theux") that my life-long love was born of the field of tectonics, which deals with the deformation of rocks and the architecture and evolution of mountains. The Fenêtre was a place where you could see ancient rocks resting on much younger ones—an abnormal relationship explicable only by postulating that the contact between them was a great horizontal fault surface along which, during the Paleozoic Era, the old rocks had been pushed. forward from far away, inch by inch over millions of years, until they had reached the place where you could now see them. Standing by the critical outcrop along the side of a road, two giants in the field of tectonics, professor Fourmarier of Liège and our own professor Brouwer, both impeccably dressed, debated the problems and implications of the Fenêtre. Fourmarier had been introduced to us that morning by Brouwer (in French) as "a legend in his lifetime", which was true enough, but a surprising tribute coming from Brouwer, who was nothing if not jealous. Brouwer also recalled how they had first met in the early twenties in some distant land. Fourmarier, a spry charmer of a man, groaned in mock despair: "Pas si vieux, mon cher collègue, pas si vieux!" Ah, I knew again why I had chosen to become a geologist—to learn about the living earth, yes, but also to see the world, meet people from all over, and (I now added) to acquire the sophistication these two possessed, who had been everywhere.

The last two days we stayed in Dinant, where, nine years ago, the young French wife of the manager of the gas factory had given me coffee with cognac in it. The hostel "father" was a sour man, who insisted on locking the place up at ten. To go to bed at that hour was unthinkable, but what could we do? At that point one of us found a ladder. We put it up against the window sill of our sleeping quarters on the second floor and, content at having outfoxed our host, spent the evening going from bar to bar, talking with the natives. I inquired about the French couple. Several remembered them well, but the two no longer lived in Belgium. Towards one in the morning I walked back with my friend Victor, both slightly unsteady. Just before we got to the hostel a girl past us, hurrying along the empty street. "Well, hello there," Victor said, and started following her. But she entered a door, and was about to close it when he placed his foot across the sill. "Come on, Victor!" I shouted. "You'll get us all into trouble," but to my astonishment they did strike up a conversation. I walked on and climbed up the ladder, sensing I had a lot to learn about the opposite sex. It was true that in his free-wheeling way with women Victor was at least twenty years ahead of his time.

Later that night I was awakened by a loud clattering of breaking glass. Hurrying over to the window I saw Victor standing by the wall. The ladder had slipped and he had fallen through the top of a glass-covered box used for raising vegetables. "Are you hurt?" I asked in a loud whisper. "No," came his voice from below, "but hold on to that ladder, would you?" I did, and after a while his face appeared above the window sill. "You're crazy," I said, and he didn't deny it, but gave me his winning smile. Next morning, the "father" was furious and wanted to call Brussels and bring in the police. It took all of Brouwer's legendary tact and some of our remaining money to calm him down.

Our trip ended in Brussels, where I left it to Brouwer to thank the authorities while I high-tailed it over to the Dutch consulate. Had the travel restrictions to France been lifted for people from Holland? Not yet, I was told, but rumor had it that they might be at midnight. No one knew for sure. I had to decide: take the chance, or go back to Holland with the bus. It was not a hard decision to make. I called de Coucy and told him I would try to make it and, if all went well, hoped to arrive in the morning. Our bus set out without me, and I boarded the night train to Paris. I seemed to be the only Dutchman. Shortly after midnight the train stopped at the border and was boarded by French customs and immigration. I showed my passport and tried to appear casual. The effort was unnecessary: they leafed through it quickly without even looking at me, stamped it, and moved on. I exulted in silence: Paris, here I come.

66

Soft days of spring, Paris, and a young man on a lark—can there be a headier cocktail? From the moment I stepped out of the Gare du Nord I felt enveloped, drawn in by the city as at one time I had been drawn in by my newly adopted home of Amsterdam. Only, this was the Big Time, this was the World, not the capital of my dear little "frog country", as the Dutch themselves call their homeland. Paris, as it looked then, would by today's standards seem positively sedate. Motor traffic was mostly confined to buses and taxis. But it did not look sedate to me then, but struck me rather as wonderfully chaotic, a quality I immediately identified as Gallic individualism and which I appreciated after five years of Germanic discipline.

De Coucy was at work and had asked another former inmate of Porz to meet me at the train. We sat down in a cafe, out on the terrace, of course, and ordered coffee and my first croissant since before the war. It was also my first acquaintance with "le café filtre," and ever since that morning I have been fond of it—not because it is all that good, but because it is so very, well, French, and right away convinces you that you are back in France. Sipping our filtre, we talked about Porz, walked around a little, had a long lunch, and in mid-afternoon took the Metro to Neuilly, where the count lived in a large upper floor apartment overlooking the Avenue de la Grande Armée. It was an emotional reunion. I was truly fond of that man and knew my feelings were reciprocated. Again, much of the talk was about Porz, and we exchanged notes about former inmates we had seen or from whom we had heard. Soon came the question I knew he was going to ask, because I knew how much it bothered him: "Et Baas-Becking, tu l'as vu?" I had not seen him, but we had exchanged letters. He had gone back to Indonesia to be director of the famous botanical gardens at Bandung, and had written to say he hoped I could come some day. De Coucy shook his head. "Pauvre type," he said, "il a du craquer." Faced with Baas-Becking's eccentric behavior he preferred to think his mind had cracked under the strain. But I knew that, as close a friend as Baas-Becking had once been, de Coucy was so different in temperament that he would never understand what had gone on inside that man. It was like Descartes against Savonarola, a rationalist next to a burning soul.

The next morning the count gave me a map of Paris, a map of the Métro, a Michelin guide of Paris, and some pocket money (there was as yet no free exchange of currency), and I started out for Montmartre. Climbing the steps, I turned around to take in the exhilarating panorama of Paris and felt proud that I could identify the landmarks that seemed familiar to me just from what I had read and the pictures I had seen: the Notre Dame, the Tour Eiffel, the Pantheon, the Invalides. At the top of the stairs I marveled at the sugar cake architecture of the Sacré Coeur and fell in love with the Place de Tertre, which was still genuinely picturesque then. "If I were a student here," I said to de Coucy that evening, "that's where I'd live." For some reason he considered that a capital joke, worth telling to friends who came over to meet me.

On the third day I gave a call to a young Frenchman I had met in Amsterdam. It was my cousin Liselot who had brought him into my aunt's house, where he had charmed the family. He was the Marquis de St. Pierre, then a journalist and later a novelist of moderate renown in France. He had been impressed by Lieselot's artistic talents, including her flair for fashion design, and encouraged her to come to Paris to live. Eventually, she did, and she spent several years there as a painter. The Marquis lived in the rue du Faubourg St. Honoré, which did not mean much to me until de Coucy explained that it was a pretty fancy address. When I rang his number, a male voice (the butler's, as it turned out) asked me if I wanted to speak with Monsieur le Baron or Monsieur le Marquis. Speaking from the home of Monsieur le Comte, I was impressed. The Marquis came on the line and invited me to lunch at his house. Two hours later I entered the patrician cobble-stoned courtyard leading up to a massive door, checked the number, and rang the bell. The butler opened the door and I followed him through spacious halls and salons until we came to a large dining room at one end of which a table had been set for two next to a window overlooking the Place de la Concorde. The Marquis arrived, and we sat down to a lunch the likes of which I had never tasted. I recall most distinctly the "filet de saumon."

Each day I roamed the city, going to all the places millions of tourists had gone before me, and millions would go later. I loved the Eiffel Tower, disliked Napoleon's tomb, lost track of time along the Seine, felt my spirits soar in the Sainte Chapelle and beneath the high dome of the Pantheon, where Foucault had proved the rotation of the earth, and felt all along I was living a dream. At the end of the fifth day, the end of my stay, I knew I had made Paris mine and swore I would come back soon, never guessing that "soon" would turn into five years. Nor could I have guessed, when I said goodbye to de Coucy, that I would never see that truly aristocratic friend again.

67

On the way back to Holland I had to change trains in Antwerp. At the information counter an English couple was making a desperate effort to get through to an attendant who spoke no English. "Can I help?" I asked. "Oh, yes!" the woman exclaimed, turning around eagerly. "We are trying to find out how we go from here to Eindhoven," the man said. "That's in Holland," he added for good measure, and looked slightly embarrassed when I told him I knew, inasmuch as I lived there. "You have to change trains in Breda," I said. "I am going to Eindhoven myself, so if you like we can travel together." Obviously relieved, they introduced themselves. He was an architect, a soft-spoken man with a gentle smile, who was also a painter. Like many men of few words, he had married a woman who could talk for two, and did, in an intense sort of way. It was she who, in the train to Breda, told me the purpose of their visit to my home town. Her husband's brother, she said, had been a pilot in the RAF and had been shot down near Maastricht in the summer of 1941. They had found out he had been buried in a cemetery at Eindhoven. At that, I sat up straight. "That summer," I told them, "I was in Maastricht. I was spending a week with a friend (it was Victor de Munck), who was doing field work in the area. And I remember lying in bed in a small hotel on my last night there, and hearing the roar of an engine overhead, and then an explosion, and I knew an Allied plane had been shot down." For a moment there was silence. The husband seemed lost in thought. There was no proof, of course, that the crash I had heard was that of his brother's plane, but I think all three of us assumed that the unlikely coincidence was nevertheless likely. Should I have kept quiet, not have touched that painful nerve? But the husband gave me an affectionate smile. "That makes me even happier to have met you," he said, and then we talked about other things.

In Eindhoven I steered them to a small hotel on the central market square and went home. I should have known my mother better, though, for as soon as she found out about the English couple, she told me to go back to the hotel and invite them to stay at our house. The next day they did, and for several days after that we were together. I helped them find the cemetery, where we soon found the grave. Then I started walking away to leave them alone. But the woman held my arm. "We would like you to stay," she said, and I understood I was a link to the brother's last moments. Deeply moved, I turned back. They had bought flowers and, ever so softly, he laid them on the gravestone. We stood there in silence for many long minutes, lost in our own private thoughts, but aware that they touched at the point of the dead pilot. At last the brother turned toward me. "I want to thank you again," he said simply. As I replied, I was afraid of sounding false, but he gave me a warm smile of recognition. "I am grateful for what he has done," I said, "and so are all the people of Holland." And then we walked away.

When I came back to Amsterdam, Walter looked as if he had won the lottery. "It's in the bag," he said with a wide grin. "You mean about Michigan?" I asked. "What else?" he said. "We have our tuition scholarship from the University, we each have a $600 scholarship from something called the Netherlands-America Foundation in New York, plus a letter from the Institute of International Education in New York, which we are supposed to show to the American Consul in Amsterdam, so we'll get a visa." It seemed too good to be true. "Terrific!" I shouted. "Now, how are we going to pay for the boat trip? Did they do anything about that in The Hague?" I was worried about it, for I really had no idea where to find money for the fare. "You bet," said Walter. "We are going there on an oil tanker from Rotterdam, some time in August, and it will cost us all of a hundred and sixty guilders." At the exchange rate of that time that amounted to about forty dollars. "Terrific!" I shouted again. "But I didn't know they shipped oil from New York city." "They don't," Walter replied, "and we're not landing in New York—we're landing in Texas." Texas? Holy cow, that seemed like a long way from New York, or from Michigan, for that matter. "We'll have to take the train up, then," I speculated. "Yes, or the bus," Walter replied.

It took me several days to believe I was really going to America. What a wild thought! It had started out as an almost casual idea—could it really be happening now? But once the reality had settled itself into my brain nothing could displace it, and I started feverishly learning about America. I took an atlas and memorized the forty-eight states and where they were, plus as many of the capitals and major cities as I could squeeze in. All three of us (Walter, Emmy, and I) read the encyclopedic book "Inside USA" by John Gunther, which provided such interesting tidbits as the fact that the second greatest concentration of prostitutes could be found in Butte, Montana (I don't remember which place took the number one spot). Eager to learn still more about that far-off country, we went to see a professor who had spent the war years there. "Let me give you an example," he said. "In America, if your watch stops running, you don't have it repaired, like here. You throw it out and buy a new one." That statement, although somewhat hyperbolic, perhaps, was probably as good a metaphor for the New World as any he could have given us in a nutshell. About that time, too, Brouwer called me in to say the Swedish government was offering a one-year scholarship to a geology student from Amsterdam, and I could have it if I wanted it. I didn't give it a thought. America, America! The scholarship went to a far more deserving older student, who had started field work for his dissertation in Swedish Lapland and spoke Swedish fluently. He stayed there for more than ten years and became a professor at Uppsala University.

The letter from the Institute of International Education stated we had to give proof of proficiency in English before we could get a visa, and that we could make arrangements for a test at the U.S. Consulate. Alternatively, a certifying letter from a professor of English at the University of Amsterdam would be acceptable. We decided on the Consul and went to see him. He read the letter and looked puzzled. "We have never given tests like that," he said, "and I don't know we have the authority." He puzzled some more, then walked out of the room and returned with a fat book under his arm, which he placed on a table. "I'll tell you what," he said. "This book has all the rules and regulations for consular officers. I'll leave you alone with it for an hour. If you can make sense of it, your English is better than mine. Find me a clause that gives me the authority, and I'll write out some sort of a certificate."

It was a hopeless task, and we soon gave up on it. "Too bad," said the Consul, "but not surprising. Try to find someone at the University." We started to get up, but he went on. "Something else," he said. "Before I can give you a visa, I am supposed to find out if you'll be able to support yourselves once you are there. How about it?" There, at least, there was no problem, we proudly told him, for did we not each have a six hundred dollar scholarship from the Netherlands-America Foundation? "Six hundred dollars, eh?" said the Consul. "Sounds okay to me. With that much a month you ought to be able to make it. Anyway," he added, "a student visa allows you to get a part-time job in case you need some extra cash." We suppressed our smiles and left. It seemed hilarious the Consul thought we might be able to scrape by for a month on our stipend for the year.

An elderly professor of English was kind enough to give us a proficiency examination. He seemed pleased by our performance, while emphasizing that his own students were expected to do better than we. Who cared? We had our certificate, and shortly thereafter our visa. About that time, too, a letter came from The Hague telling us that we would sail on the oil tanker "Barendrecht" leaving Rotterdam on the tenth of August. All the pieces were starting to fall into place.

Still, I was a little worried about the money angle. How much would a dollar buy? What would it cost to go from Texas to New York and from there to Michigan? And how much, the following summer, for our trip to the Rockies, the main justification of our scheme? I was thinking about all that when I came home late one afternoon. "There's a letter for you," my aunt announced. It was from the Ministry of the Interior. Of course, I thought, the only way you can get bureaucrats to answer you is by throwing mud at them. Ever since the preceding summer I had been sending missives to government offices in The Hague and to the state police in Roermond in a desperate attempt to reclaim my confiscated motorcycle. It was like dropping pebbles into a pond without causing a ripple. But I kept it up. Finally, in June, though I had by then written it off, I sent a last letter to Roermond, a nasty one, worded to imply, without actually saying so, that I was up to their tricks and knew they were dragging the affair out on purpose while probably using my motorcycle, or were perhaps hoping to sell it and pocket the money. I mailed my letter with mixed bitterness and satisfaction. So now they must have felt stung, and this must be the answer from the top—some sort of obfuscation, no doubt. I opened it up. In a single paragraph it informed me I could retrieve my BMW in Roermond upon presentation of the letter.

"Hurray!" I shouted. I could hardly believe my eyes. "What happened?" my aunt asked, and I explained. Once again, my feelings were mixed—now they were of elation over my victory and shame over that last note to the state police. But shame was the lesser of the two. BMW spelled money, and the end of my worries. I knew I already had a buyer, whom I had lined up in the unlikely event I would ever get my treasure back. He was the brother of a classmate to whom I had once mentioned the existence of my motorcycle. I gave him the letter from the Ministry and another one authorizing him to pick it up in my place. And suddenly I held in my hands a check for one thousand guilders!

With that windfall I could start to relax. Now I could look forward to the great event that was still to occur before our departure for the New World: the long-awaited excursion to Sweden in the month of July, now only a few weeks away.

68

Nothing could have quite prepared us for the cornucopia that was Sweden in those postwar days. One had simply forgotten what it was like to live in a consumer society, where people looked well-fed and well-dressed and drove around in cars and ate bananas and smoked American cigarettes as if that were the most common thing in the world. This really was a different world, and it felt strange at first. Suddenly you felt a little awkward, like a country yokel come to the big city, aware of your threadbare clothing and of the measly amount of money in your wallet. "Look at that," said Ab Cohen, gazing through the window of a tobacco store in Göteborg, his voice hushed in awe. "Look at that: Tareytons! My brand, six years ago." He bought a pack, lit one up, and closed his eyes. It was as if the war itself was going up in smoke.

We had that day arrived from Amsterdam. A representative from the Swedish government had met us at the airport, bid us welcome, handed over a packet of money to Brouwer (who gave it to his chief assistant, Kees Egeler, for safe-keeping), and introduced us to the congenial young man who was to be our interpreter for three weeks, a student of English literature at the University of Stockholm. There was time left for a touristy boat trip around the harbor, where the houses looked like nothing so much as along the canals in Amsterdam.

Walking through town that evening, you became aware of another material delight: Swedish womanhood. It was not just that the girls looked glorious, but that we seemed to create an electric effect on them. Where back home, in the contest for the fairest of the Dutch girls, you were up against strapping, crisply uniformed, candy-bearing soldiers from foreign lands, here in Sweden the tables were turned. For here, the girls had been looking for six long years at tall, beefy young Swedes who had been nowhere and who suddenly looked like bores compared to our scraggly group of ravenous, penniless Dutchmen with the mystique of imagined suffering on their brows. To tell the truth, the advantage we drew from that would seem pale today, but it did add spice to our trip.

In all, there were about twenty of us, plus professors Brouwer and Westerveld (in suit and tie) and the new wives they had recently married. Both women were charming, and you couldn't help wondering how they had got themselves teamed up with such unaccommodating types. Later, as it turned out, they would wonder, too. For three weeks we traversed the length of Sweden by train, from the lake district in the south all the way to Lapland above the arctic circle. We had all been issued bicycles, with which we toured each area for several days before putting them on the train to the next stop. We felt good, slept well, ate well, learned a lot, and laughed a lot.

One of the non-geological things I learned was to dislike goat-cheese, a constant component of our every breakfast, lunch, and dinner. Unjustly, no doubt, it was the goat cheese I accused of upsetting my bowels. By the fourth day, I was crouching in agony behind a bush near the shore of Lake Vanern, whose sparkling azure color I was at that moment unable to appreciate. I was searching desperately for anything that looked like paper when, praise heaven, I finally found some in my back pocket. Much relieved, I rejoined our group and listened to Brouwer expounding on whatever geological phenomenon we had stopped for. And then, all at once, my heart was gripped with fear. My hand went back into my pocket, though I had no hope—for I knew the paper I had used was my train ticket for the following day. It was too mortifying to tell even to Walter. No, somehow I had to deal with this alone. In the train the next day, when I saw the conductor coming my way, collecting tickets, I gathered all my courage, jumped up with what I hoped would be a convincing expression of excruciating pain and, ignoring his astonished look, rushed past him to lock myself up in the toilet. After half an hour I dared to peek out—the coast was clear, and my dignity safe.

We got off in Norberg, a pleasant little town in the iron district of central Sweden, where we stayed for close to a week. It remains in my memory chiefly for three remarkable moments. The first came during our visit to one of the great underground mines. They were impressively maintained, with wide, well-lit galleries and the most modern machinery. You could almost call them clean. The mining engineer who took us around was justifiably proud. To impress upon us just how new everything was, he took us over to an enormous winch and pointed to the big steel plate that showed the name of its maker and the date of manufacture: "Krupp, 1943." All this equipment, he said, they had received in exchange for iron ore shipped to Germany during the war. And suddenly we were all aware of the emotional gulf that separated Sweden from most of the rest of Europe, a gulf so wide that this kind engineer had no inkling of our sensitivity on the subject of aid to the enemy. But I thought I saw our young Swedish interpreter wince, and later talked to him about it. "Of course," he said, "we all know, but we don't want to think about it. And it's not just the iron ore, for that matter. In 1940 it was no secret that the 'Red Cross' trains we allowed through on the way up to Narvik carried German troops and military supplies to the front line. We don't talk about that, either".

After that conversation I began to wonder if Brouwer had perhaps heard about it, too, and if we weren't on this free trip because he had exploited the guilt feelings his Swedish colleagues might be harboring by suggesting their government might be interested in making some amends. A Machiavellian move like that would certainly have been quite his style. In fact, he gave us a dazzling display of his hustling ability the very next day. Towards noon we had run into one of the company managers, and Brouwer had asked him if he knew of a cafeteria or a not-too-expensive restaurant where we could have lunch. The manager had said he saw no reason why we couldn't eat at the company canteen. At the canteen the system was that you went through the line, got your check, and paid when leaving. While we were eating, Brouwer saw the manager come in and, with the grace he was capable of summoning, invited him to sit at our table. With equal grace the manager accepted, and then Brouwer sprung his trap. He got up and made a little speech in which he thanked the manager for not only arranging our visit to the mine, but for offering us this fine lunch. From the man's face it was clear he was as flabbergasted as we, but what could he do but cough up? When it came to gall, it was difficult to outdo Brouwer.

The third memorable event occurred at the end of our stay in Norberg, while we were standing on the railroad platform waiting for the train that would take us far to the north. In a way we regretted leaving, for we had taken the town by storm, much to the disgust of the frozen-out young male population. Suddenly, just as the train hove in sight, there was a loud concert of bicycle bells, and around a curve in the road came a score of Norberg lasses, ringing and waving. They had come to see us off. I was standing next to Kees Egeler, who was standing next to Mrs. Brouwer. At the sight of so much feminine pulchritude, Kees lost his head. "Quick!" he shouted to the rest of us. "The train leaves in five minutes, and we still have to fuck them all!"

And with that he ran off. "Well," I heard Mrs.Brouwer say, "I'll have to wash my ears out." But I saw she had a hard time controlling her laughter. Meanwhile, the train had rolled in, and the sad truth was that there was barely time for fond farewells before we had to board it. We were all hanging out the windows, pressing female hands, when suddenly Kees shouted again, but this time in real panic. "What is it?" I asked, looking around. But Kees was already back on the platform, blindly running back and forth. "The briefcase!" he yelled. "The briefcase—it's gone!" I froze. That briefcase contained all our travel documents and all the Swedish money we had for the rest of our excursion.

Kees had not let it out of his sight since Göteborg. Who could have taken it? What should we do? The train would leave any moment now. Kees was frantic. Then I noticed Walter. He was walking over to the door and stepped out onto the quay. What was he doing? I saw him stoop, then straighten up again. "Is this what you are looking for?" he asked calmly, between two puffs on his pipe. Kees stopped dead in his tracks. "Where in the world . . ." he began. "It was sitting here all along," said Walter. And then I remembered Kees had been carrying it until the moment the girls arrived. In his over excitement he must have put it down before running off.

The station chief blew his whistle. Kees and Walter got back into the train without a second to spare, and we started out for the far north. "I nearly had a heart attack," sighed Kees. Walter just smiled.

69

The train took us all the way to the pretty little town of Abisko. I had been there before, together with Jack, on a quick day-trip from Narvik in 1939. This time, having come up through the vast no-man's land to the south, it looked even more like the end of the world than it had at the time. Who would have believed I would be back here one day?

There was one small hotel, and it was too small for our group. Arrangements had been made for four of us to be stationed in a private home, and I volunteered to be one of the four. The home turned out to be that of the local parson, a kind man with an effacing wife and two daughters who could not have been more different: the younger one, about seventeen, acutely conscious of her sexuality and obviously ready to fly the coop at the first opportunity, while her sister, two years older, was reticent, dreamy, deeper, and unaware of her silent beauty. We saw them mostly at breakfast and after dinner, which we ate at the hotel.

Lapland was as beautiful as I remembered, as warm in this month of July, and as full of mosquitoes. A bus took us to far-off places and from there we hiked to far-off mountains over grass-covered slopes where the reindeer were grazing. In charge, during the last few days, was Professor Westerveld, for Brouwer had in the meantime literally knocked himself out of the running in a manner characteristic of aging professors of geology, who are prone to develop the need to show they are still as tough as their students, who themselves take an unconcealed delight in proving they are not. Several of us had done that to Brouwer once before, in 1942, while walking back to the railroad station at the end of an excursion in the south of Holland. Straining to stay abreast, he had gasped: "Why don't we sit down and wait for the others?"—but we had pretended not to hear and left him in the dust. The same thing, of course, would later be done to me. Here in Lapland, Brouwer was ahead on his bicycle, going like a house afire, with a graduate student called de Boer at his rear wheel, when his bicycle slipped our from under him in the curve of the gravel

273

road. I saw his head slamming on the ground, and him skidding into a dry ditch. He was out cold, and when I got to him I was frightened by the sudden pallor of his sunken cheeks and the loud snorting that came out of his open mouth. Somewhere, a telephone was found, and an ambulance came to take him to a hospital. He had a heavy concussion, which kept him in Sweden for three more weeks, and we went on without him.

Some of the dash was gone now, for, though Westerveld was a most worthy man and not unpopular, no one would have thought him dashing. We would at times laugh at him in a way unthinkable if it had been Brouwer. Down in the iron mine near Norberg we had all had to climb up a long ladder. De Boer (the same one), who was ahead of me, poked the person above him in the rear with his rock hammer, saying: "Come on, slowpoke, get your ass moving." In that particular place it was half-dark, and de Boer had not seen that it was Westerveld's august behind he had abused. I nearly fell off my rung laughing, and relayed the message down-ladder, causing great hilarity. Westerveld preferred dignity to revenge and did not insist on knowing the identity of the hammer's proprietor. And now, in Lap country, we were all standing by a stream, looking for a place to jump across. We jumped, but when it was Westerveld's turn, he hesitated, took a little run, stopped, looked flurried, and turned upstream, where he decided to wade. Wade he did, slowly and gravely, in his city suit, first up to his ankles, then his knees, and at last up to his waist. By then we were all rolling around in the grass, cruelly ignoring our professor's plight and mental suffering.

Back at the parson's house I tried to talk a little with the older daughter, whose name was Helga. Though at first she blushed deeply, she did not turn me away. "Do you spend the whole year here?" I asked. "Oh, no," she said, "I go to a school in Böbö. I am here in the summer." Böbö, I found out, was in the north of Norway, about a hundred miles from Narvik. I wondered what secret hopes were held by this solitary girl in this solitary country. She, too, I sensed, dreamed of breaking out. I told her I was going to America, and knew that to her I must seem cosmopolitan, representing that whole far-away world she longed for. What was there for a young woman to look forward to here? Marriage to one of a handful of young man in town, children, duty, everything that was predictable. Was I imagining it, or had romantic Helga begun to fasten on me her day-dreams, in which, perhaps, I had arrived providentially to whisk her away? No, I thought, there was no mistaking the way her eyes lit up when we spoke.

On our last morning, while walking towards the breakfast room, I heard someone play the organ and walked in to listen. It was Helga, playing Handel's Largo: "Ombra mai fu . . . Cara ed amabile soave più!" Suddenly I felt deeply moved, and sad about leaving. "That was beautiful," I said when she had finished. She turned around, and I saw she had tears in her eyes. "Do you know it?", she asked. "Do you like music, too?" Why did that word "too" touch me so? I felt it as a last, desperate attempt to establish a bond between us, and that feeling stayed with me throughout breakfast, during which she remained silent while I talked with the parson. "Come on," I told myself, "you are beginning to romanticize all this yourself." But in my heart I knew better, and felt vaguely guilty.

And then, suddenly, we were saying goodbye. We were late and knew the rest of our group would already be waiting in the bus and that Westerveld would probably be furious. So, our farewell had to be quick, which was just as well. Before long we were rolling east. But something in me had changed a little, and I found it hard to put the thought of Helga out of my mind.

Towards dark we arrived at a train station from where a bus took us on a long ride to the newly developed mining community of Kristinaberg, near the northern end of the Baltic Sea. Not only the mine (an enormous open cut), but everything else there seemed to be company-owned: the bus, the houses, the big, brand-new hotel, the restaurant, even the personnel. Being from Eindhoven myself, which might as well be called Philipstown, I had learned to dislike company towns (the idea of ever working for Philips had been enough to make me shudder even in High School), but now it was pleasant to come into one as an outsider, for once—the pampered company guest.

The promise of a good time ahead started right upon our arrival in the parking lot. Looking up, we could see blond Swedish maids laughing and waving at us from what seemed like every one of the hotel's windows. The reason they were especially glad to see us was that they were bored stiff, the hotel apparently being empty much of the time. We waved back and filed into a waiting room, where we sank into leather chairs and were offered smokes as if we were Wall Street bankers. I cannot say we behaved like Wall Street bankers, but rather like impoverished country cousins crashing a party. I feel embarrassed to this day at the memory of my fellow students grabbing handfuls of cigars and cigarettes out of wooden boxes and stuffing them into their pockets. Late in the evening, after a sumptuous meal and much free-flowing wine, we invited the girls up to our floor and partied till the early morning hours. At one point someone asked: "Where is Victor?" Victor de Munck had been hitting it off with a very pretty girl, but the two had disappeared. We decided to track them down and, after much roaming around, found them in the basement kitchen, where, Victor told us later, he had pinned her down on the meat block. Victor liked to tell fantastic stories like that just for the laughs of it, but this one may have been true, for the following morning he showed me a mad love letter the girl had written him (in English). We were all jealous, but to tell the truth, no one else had Victor's particular combination of daring and innocence, added to a primal masculinity, that made him irresistible to the female sex.

On the morning of our departure the hotel manager asked Kees Egeler, as the chief assistant, to write something appropriate in the guest book. Kees was uncharacteristically short on imagination perhaps because of the early hour, and handed the pen to me, as the second assistant. "Here, you do it," he said. "Compose a little poem about what we did in Kristinaberg." He should not have said it that way, for the symbolism was too obvious to ignore. In a flash of inspiration I wrote (in Dutch, to be sure) a doggerel of a poem expressing our appreciation for the hospitality shown us, and ending with something like: At Kristinaberg we ate our fill, and then we climbed its Venushill. I handed it back to Kees. As he read it, his eyes opened wide. "Jesus," he said, "we had better get out of here in a hurry, before they find someone who can read Dutch. Make sure Westerveld doesn't see it." Then he handed the guest book back to the manager, who thanked us with smiles, bows and hand shakes. And thereupon we left.

After one day at the University of Uppsala, we got to Stockholm, where we stayed for a couple of days just for sightseeing. In a restaurant I struck up a conversation with Karen, a young woman of striking beauty, with copper red hair and green eyes. Her fiancee was on a consulting trip in Abyssinia, so she was temporarily free and had time to take me to museums and show me around town. And then, suddenly, our Swedish excursion came to an end and we found ourselves in the night train back to Göteborg. I shared my train compartment with several French girls who had spent a few weeks in Sweden, and we exchanged impressions. Like us, they had had a great time, yet we were all ready to leave, and for the same reason: the wartime experience somehow estranged us from these neutral people, and after a while we had begun to feel ill at ease. Happily, that shared feeling drew the French and the Dutch together, figuratively at first, and more literally by the time we approached Göteborg. This excursion was turning out to be a novel and instructive experience from more than a scientific perspective.

"Just wait," said Kees Egeler, "just wait till you get to America". "You're going to come back exhausted." I smiled, knowing he was putting himself into my shoes, but knowing also he possessed a brand of eroticism more casual than was in my nature or than I aspired to.

70

It was now less than two weeks before our sailing date, and I wanted to spend those last days at home in Eindhoven. I sensed my father was a little sad to see me go, much as he was also proud of me, and I tried to cheer him up by saying it was, after all, just for a year. He smiled wanly. Did he have a premonition that it was to be four years before we would see each other again, and then only for a few weeks—that I was now really flying the coop for good, that I would make my home in America?

Perhaps I had such a premonition myself. But even without it I knew that an era of my life was coming to an end. Stretched out in a folding chair under the big apple tree in our back yard, my excitement over the future on the horizon was mixed with some nostalgia over the past I was leaving behind, of which, to a large degree, the gracious old house I was looking at was somehow symbolic—the house in which most of my growing up had occurred, and where I had by and large been happy. For ten years I had shared two rooms there with my two brothers: a snug daytime room on the street side, and a Spartan bedroom I could see from where I was now lying, in which, at my mother's instructions, a carpenter had built three identical high cots, painted a bright orange, with shelved cabinets below the thin mattresses for our shirts, socks and underwear. Unheated as it was in the winter, ice flowers would form on the windows overnight, so that you had to breathe on them first if you wanted to look out to see the snow-covered trees in our back yard.

I had only to close my eyes to remember, to hear again the sounds of my childhood and the voices of those who had peopled that house. There was the deep sound of the gong in the hall, suspended from a wooden arch held up on either side in the open mouths of two fiercely carved Balinese dragons. Year in, year out, that gong was solemnly struck at five minutes before every meal. In the morning whoever of the boys was "on duty" that week had to get up and dress at seven to strike it at twenty past as a signal for all others to rise, again at twenty-five past, and finally at seven-thirty, when all would come to breakfast. Other sounds: the voices we would listen to in bed, of guests below, seated at one of my mother's or grandmother's famous Indonesian "rijsttafels", especially the booming voice of Mr. Maarschalk, a portly man who, my mother liked to tell us, would turn his eyes skyward in gastronomic rapture while mopping his bald pate with a large handkerchief, his florid face turned even redder by the hot "sambal", curries, and countless other spiced dishes. Other voices: those coming from the old livery stable on New Year's Eve, where that afternoon we had been allowed in to admire the walls on which my father had for weeks spent his artistic talents in the painting of colorful, imaginative sceneries, and where a long table was now set up on trestles, covered with a snow-white sheet, elegant dishes and our best silver. Those parties were not for us, although my parents had once relented and brought us down at midnight to participate in the greeting of the incoming year, an experiment never repeated on account of the foul temper I displayed in my half-sleep. Still another voice now, in the dark of the back yard the quiet sobs of our djongos, the Indonesian cook my mother had hired a few months earlier in The Hague to be our house man, but whom she had now accused of thievery and summarily dismissed. "Djongos" (the word is derived from the Dutch for "boy") was a man already well into his fifties, but still capable of weeping. And then, out of nowhere, the voices were crowded out by an altogether different sound, one that had amazed me at the time. Then, too, I had been in bed, recuperating from the mumps, and I was listening to my father peeing in the toilet across the upstairs' hall, a sound by itself unremarkable enough, except for what seemed to me its incredibly and admirably long duration: well over a minute, I estimated. I was at that time perhaps overly sensitized to those anatomical parts, which I had to wear in a sling because the malady had affected them. My father had taken to calling me "Balzac".

I knew I was going to miss my family. It had been a close-knit one, bound by an odd combination of love and iron discipline. Would my father's health deteriorate further in my absence, I wondered (and while writing this I am aware my children worry in the same way about me). Pieter's condition was almost unbearable to him, I knew, and the break with Jack was continuing and not good for either of them. My sisters Marjolijn and Lydia had grown into beautiful girls of whose secret dreams I knew little, but in my absence they, too, would perhaps leave home. My parents would then probably have to move out of that great, big house, and that would be hard on them, especially on my more sentimental father.

I thought much about Sylvia also. Too much caught up in my other life, I had not been home much since Christmas and we had not seen each other alone for months. Much as I knew she had prepared herself for that inevitable moment, I had found it difficult even to write her I was going to leave. Once more, I relived the intimacy of our relationship during the time the events of the world had allowed it to flourish in isolation. The shreds of a song came back to me, one often played on the radio in the year after the war, full of nostalgia, to which we had listened together in shared, but already separate pain. It was on the simplest of melodies, each line on a single note, first ascending the scale, then descending—a song of poignant reminiscence of someone lost:

> The funny way you hold your hand,
> Oh, darling, don't you understand . . .

and ending with a sudden octave leap upscale on the last word:

> All off a sudden my heart . . . SINGS!

"That," Sylvia had said, "will always be how I remember you." The thought of that now tightened my heart.

There was not going to be a way to see Sylvia alone even then. Two days before my departure I just went to her house in the evening to say goodbye to the family. She was quiet and looked pale, but as beautiful to me as on that day when we had first run into each other in Amsterdam—in another life, it seemed. And so, because we were not alone, our farewell, in the end, was undramatic, and it was as well that way. Neither of us could have suspected that we would never see each other again.

On the way back a cop stopped me and gave me a ticket for not having a light on my bicycle. I smiled, thinking the arm of the law was not long enough to reach all the way to Michigan to collect the fine. To me, that little event served a different purpose: it broke my heavy train of thought and yanked my mind back to the future.

71

And suddenly it was the morning of the tenth of August, and I was on board the "Barendrecht", together with Walter and Emmy, floating down the wide Meuse River towards the Hook of Holland. There was a fourth passenger, a physics student on his way to do graduate work at Berkeley.

It was a bright, light sunny day. On both banks stretched sparkling meadows of an unbelievable green, such as only Holland's fertile soil and wet climate seem to produce. Cows were lowing in the distance. Here and there faint voices floated over from the water's edge—farewell shouts of wives and children of crew members come to wave their men off. Never had my country looked so intimately and serenely beautiful. Little by little the banks receded and the river began to blend imperceptibly into the North Sea. And then we were in open water, with Holland fading away on the horizon.

Our destination was Port Arthur, Texas. Oil tankers not being built to set transatlantic records, it would be a long voyage; we were scheduled to arrive in somewhat under three weeks. I didn't mind: it was like a marvelous enforced vacation, and excitement alone would keep boredom away. We took long sun baths and for exercise took walks up and down the long deck. We read a lot, and from a map of America I kept stuffing my mind with the names of states and cities, getting pleasure out of funny-sounding or picturesque ones like Massachusetts and Connecticut (hard to get in that second hard c before the t, and not yet aware you shouldn't), Alabama, Des Moines (French for Monks, but how do they pronounce it in English?), Buffalo, and Little Rock. How about Arkansas—what did that "Ar" mean before Kansas? We ate at the captain's table, and ate well—more than our forty dollar fare could possibly cover. As for passenger comfort, it was clear that naval architects had not conceived oil tankers with that thought on the front burner. Walter and Emmy shared the single guest cabin. The physics students and I were put up in the hut that also held the gyroscopic compass. It made one hell of a racket, and there was a constant coming and going of crew members in the night, but I got used to it and learned to sleep through it all.

I was conscious of feeling on top of the world. This, I knew, had to be one of the high points of my life, this feeling of being totally alive day by day, while anticipating a future that was unknown and bound to be wonderful. I loved being out on the high sea again; it brought back memories of my trip to Trondjeim in 1938, and with Jack to Narvik in 1939. When I told the captain about those trips and that I had been allowed steering duty, he said: "If you feel like it, go ahead." From then on I spent a couple of hours a day on the bridge behind the wheel. It wasn't very demanding, for all during the voyage the weather remained splendid, and on some days the sea was as smooth as glass.

On the evening of the sixteenth day the captain called us up to the bridge. He pointed to the western horizon. Faintly, you could see lights flickering in the distance. "Miami," he said.

And that single word finally made it all seem real. Across that horizon a new life would begin. Over there was the New World.

Edwards Brothers Malloy
Oxnard, CA USA
December 27, 2013